Learn French for Adult Beginners

Speak French In 30 Days!

7-Books-in-1

Explore to Win

THIS COLLECTION INCLUDES THE FOLLOWING BOOKS:

<u>Learn French for Adult Beginners Handbook:
Your Guide to Speaking French in 30 Days!</u>

<u>Complete French Workbook for Adult Beginners:
Essential French Words and Phrases You Need to Know</u>

<u>Learn French with Short Stories for Adult Beginners:
Shortcut Your French Fluency! (Fun & Easy Reads)</u>

<u>Learn Intermediate French for Adults Workbook:
Go from French Beginner to Intermediate in 30 Days!</u>

<u>Practice French with Short Stories for Adults:
Shortcut Your French Fluency!(Fun & Easy Reads)</u>

<u>Learn Advanced French for Adults Workbook</u>

<u>Learn French with Short Stories for Adults: Engaging Stories to
Shortcut Your French Fluency! (Fun & Easy Reads)</u>

Disclaimer:

The content in this book is for educational purposes only and does not constitute legal, financial, or medical advice. Readers should consult qualified professionals before acting on any information contained herein. The publisher disclaims liability for any loss incurred as a result of the use of this material.

Table of Contents

BOOK 1

Learn French for Adult Beginners Handbook

Book 1 Description _____ 1

Chapter 1: Basics _____ 2

Chapter 2: Who Are You? _____ 13

Chapter 3: Such a Beautiful Place! _____ 21

Chapter 4: This or That? _____ 29

Chapter 5: It's Just Around the Corner _____ 45

Chapter 6: My Family Is... _____ 51

Chapter 7: Every Morning... _____ 60

Chapter 8: Let's Grab A Bite _____ 68

Chapter 9: Can You Do It? _____ 81

Chapter 10: Other Uses of the Present Indicative _____ 90

Cultural Annex _____ 99

Conclusion _____ 100

BOOK 2

Complete French Workbook for Adult Beginners

Book 2 Description _____ 102

Chapter 1: Numbers _____ 103

Chapter 2: French Conversations _____ 110

Chapter 4: Work and Relationships _____ 120

Cultural Annex _____ 126

Conclusion _____ 127

BOOK 3
Learn French with Short Stories for Adult Beginners

Book 3 Description _____ 129

How to use this book _____ 130

Chapter 1: Les courses – The grocery shopping _____ 131

Chapter 3: Le rendez-vous – The date _____ 139

Chapter 4: Sortir faire du jogging – Going out for a jog _____ 149

BOOK 4
Learn Intermediate French for Adults Workbook:

Book 4 Description _____ 158

Chapter 1: Blast from the past _____ 159

Chapter 2: Describing People, Places, and Things _____ 175

Chapter 3: Present Subjunctive in Use _____ 185

Chapter 4: Anecdotes _____ 195

Chapter 5: Hypotheses _____ 206

Chapter 6: Nothing Personal _____ 218

Chapter 7: That's an Order! _____ 230

Chapter 8: Step into the Future _____ 240

Cultural Annex _____ 251

Conclusion _____ 252

BOOK 5
Practice French with Short Stories for Adults

Book 5 Description _____ 254

Chapter 1: L'anniversaire de Thomas – Thomas' birthday. _____ 255

Chapter 2: Mon enfance – My childhood _____ 263

Chapter 3: Le voyage de Cristina – Cristina's trip _____ 270

Chapter 4: Mes objectifs – My goals _____ 278

Conclusion _____ 285

BOOK 6

Learn Advanced French for Adults Workbook

Book 6 Description _____ 287

Chapter 1: I Am What I Am _____ 288

Chapter 2: Careers _____ 298

Chapter 3: Anecdotes and Gossip_____ 308

Chapter 4: Protecting the Environment_____ 317

Chapter 5: Online and Offline Relationships _____ 326

Cultural Annex _____ 337

Conclusion_____ 338

BOOK 7

Learn French with Short Stories for Adults

Book 7 Description _____ 340

Chapter 1: Les voleurs – The thieves_____ 341

Chapter 2: La compétition – The competition _____ 349

Chapter 3: La nuit – At night _____ 357

Chapter 4: Le dernier rendez-vous – The last date _____ 365

Conclusion_____ 373

$1000+ FREE BONUSES

$297 FREE

**Learn French
Video Course**

$197 FREE

**French Pronunciation
Video Course**

$147 FREE

**Learn French in 30
Minutes Video Guide**

$97 FREE

**French Flash
Pack**

$97 FREE

**Paris Travel Guide +
France Cultural Guides**

$47 FREE

**French Stories
Audiobooks**

$27 FREE

**20 Native French
Conversations Narrated**

$150 FREE

**Premium French
Learning Software**

Scan QR code to claim
your bonuses

— OR —

visit bit.ly/4edZbO7

BOOK 1

Learn French for
Adult Beginners Handbook

Your Guide to Speaking French in 30 Days!

Explore to Win

Book 1 Description

Are you tired of struggling to learn French? Have you tried language courses, but none seem to stick? Do you want to finally leave dull French textbooks behind?

If so, we have the perfect solution.

Learning French doesn't have to be difficult. In fact, it's much easier than you might think.

With this book, you can become a French beginner in just 30 days.

With "Learn French for Adult Beginners Handbook: Your Proven Guide to Speaking French in 30 Days," you'll uncover:

- The most common grammar mistakes in French and how to avoid them.

- A wide range of useful French phrases for everyday situations.

- Secrets to pronouncing French like a native speaker.

- The most essential verbs in French and how to conjugate them.

- All the vocabulary you'll need for your next trip to France.

- and much more!

This is the perfect book to immerse yourself in French. No matter your age or whether you know a little of the language or none at all, this book is designed for everyone. It covers all the essential topics so that, in just 30 days, you will have the skills you need to communicate and hold conversations in French.

Chapter 1: Basics

C'est en essayant encore et encore que le singe apprend à bondir.

- Antoine de Saint-Exupéry

In this chapter, we will focus on a foundational kit to kickstart your French learning journey. The kit includes a guide to the French alphabet, pronunciation, and some essential vocabulary.

The French Letter Sounds

French letter sounds are quite distinct from English, especially when it comes to vowels. While English vowels can vary greatly in sound depending on their placement in a word, French vowels are more consistent, with each one typically having a single, clear pronunciation.

The French Vowel Sounds

In French, there are 6 vowels, though they can have diacritical marks that affect their pronunciation. Let's see these sounds and some examples!:

Vowel	English Sound	Example	Pronunciation	Translation
a	"a" in "father"	ami	ah-mee	friend
e	"e" in "bed"	mer	mehr	sea
i	"ee" in "see"	vie	vee	life
o	"o" in "go"	mot	moh	word
u	No equivalent, close to "ew" in "few"	lune	lyoon	moon
y	"ee" in "see"	style	steel	style

Additional Notes on Diacritical Marks:

1. é: Sounds like "ay" in "say"
   - Example: été (ay-tay) - summer

2. è: Sounds like "e" in "bed"
   - Example: frère (frehr) - brother

3. ê: Similar to "è," but often longer
   - Example: fête (feht) - party

4. ë: Similar to "e" in "bed" but pronounced separately from preceding vowels
   - Example: Noël (noh-ehl) - Christmas

5. â: Similar to "a" in "father," but longer
   - Example: pâte (paht) - paste/dough

6. î: Similar to "i" in "machine"
   - Example: île (eel) - island

7. ô: Similar to "o" in "more"
   - Example: hôtel (oh-tehl) - hotel

8. û: Pronounced like u but slightly longer
   - Example: flûte (floot) - flute

9. ù: The sound remains the same as "u," but it often differentiates between homonyms
   - Example: où (oo) - where

Vowel Combination	Example	Pronunciation	Translation
ai	maïs	meh	but
au	auto	oh-toh	car
ei	peine	pehn	pain
eu	peur	purr	fear
ie	bien	by-ehn	well
oi	moi	mwah	me
ou	fou	foo	crazy
ui	nuit	nwee	night
au	chaud	shoh	hot
eau	eau	oh	water
oeu	coeur	kur	heart
ai	aimé	eh-may	loved
oi	fois	fwah	time (as in occurrence)
oe	soeur	surr	sister

Additional Notes on Pronunciation:

1. ai: Often sounds like "eh" in "bed" but can also be pronounced like "ay" in "say" when followed by a consonant.

   - Example: maison (meh-zon) - house

2. au and eau: Both pronounced "oh," similar to "o" in "go."

- Example: beau (boh) - beautiful

3. eu and oeu: Typically pronounced as "uh" with rounded lips, close to "fur" in English.

   - Example: neuf (nurf) - nine

4. ou: Sounds like "oo" in "food."

   - Example: loup (loo) - wolf

5. oi: Typically pronounced "wah."

   - Example: toit (twah) - roof

The French Consonant Sounds

Consonant	Approximate English Sound	Example	Pronunciation	Translation
b	"b" in "bat"	boire	bwahr	to drink
c	"k" in "cat" (before a, o, u)	café	kah-fay	coffee
c	"s" in "see" (before e, i, y)	cent	sahn	hundred
ch	"sh" in "ship"	chat	shah	cat
d	"d" in "dog"	dent	dahn	tooth
f	"f" in "fish"	fille	feey	girl
g	"g" in "go" (before a, o, u)	gomme	gohm	eraser
g	"zh" like in "measure" (before e, i, y)	gentil	zhahn-tee	kind
h	Silent in most cases	homme	ohm	man

j	"zh" like in "measure"	jour	zhoor	day
k	"k" in "kite"	kiwi	kee-wee	kiwi
l	"l" in "love"	lait	leh	milk
m	"m" in "man"	mère	mehr	mother
n	"n" in "no"	nom	noh	name
p	"p" in "pen"	porte	pohrt	door
q	"k" in "kick"	quand	kahn	when
r	Rolled or guttural "r"	rouge	roozh	red
s	"s" in "see"	sous	soo	under
s	"z" in "zero" (between vowels)	maison	meh-zon	house

Additional Notes on French Consonants:

1. Silent Consonants: In many cases, the final consonants of French words are silent. For example, in "parle" (he/she speaks), the "e" is pronounced but the "l" is silent. However, if the next word begins with a vowel, the final consonant may be pronounced due to liaison.

2. Liaison: When a normally silent final consonant is pronounced because the following word begins with a vowel or a mute "h." For example, "les amis" (the friends) is pronounced "lay-zah-mee."

3. The French "R": The French "r" is typically pronounced at the back of the throat, creating a guttural sound. It's very different from the English "r" and can be challenging for non-native speakers.

4. G and J Sounds: The French "g" and "j" can produce sounds that are distinct from English. The "g" can sound like the "g" in "go" or like "zh" in "measure" depending on the vowel that follows it. The "j" is always pronounced like "zh" in "measure."

5. C and G before E, I, Y: The consonants "c" and "g" change their sound before the vowels "e," "i," and "y." "C" turns into an "s" sound, and "g" turns into a "zh" sound.

Saying 'Hello' and 'Goodbye'

It's time to dive into the various ways to say "hello" and "goodbye" in French. So, let's get started!

Aspect	Details
Greeting	Saying Hello: Bonjour (Hello) – Formal and informal, used throughout the day. Salut (Hi) – Informal, casual greeting. Bonsoir (Good evening) – Used in the evening. Saying Goodbye: Au revoir (Goodbye) – Standard farewell. Salut (Bye) – Informal, same as "hi." À bientôt (See you soon) – Casual, implies you'll meet again soon.
Pronunciation	Hello: Bonjour: Pronounced "bohn-zhoor" with a nasal "on" sound. Salut: Pronounced "sa-loo," with a soft "t" at the end. Bonsoir: Pronounced "bohn-swahr," with the "oi" sounding like "wah." Goodbye: Au revoir: Pronounced "oh ruh-vwahr," where "re" is soft and "voir" has a "vwah" sound. "Au revoir" is the go-to phrase for saying goodbye. "Salut" can be used informally, and "À bientôt" is used when you expect to see the person again soon.

Explanation	Hello: "Bonjour" is the most versatile greeting, suitable for most situations. "Salut" is best among friends, and "Bonsoir" is used in the evening. Goodbye: "Au revoir" is the go-to phrase for saying goodbye. "À bientôt" is used when you expect to see the person again soon.

Some Useful Phrases

Let's explore some helpful phrases that you're likely to find useful no matter where you are in France!

Word or Phrase	Pronunciation	Translation
Merci	mehr-see	Thank you
S'il vous plaît	seel voo pleh	Please
Excusez-moi	eks-kew-zay mwah	Excuse me
Je ne comprends pas	zhuh nuh kohm-prohn pah	I don't understand
Où est la gare?	oo eh lah gahr	Where is the train station?
Combien ça coûte?	kohm-byen sah koot	How much does it cost?
Je m'appelle...	zhuh mah-pell...	My name is...
Parlez-vous anglais?	pahr-lay voo ahn-glay?	Do you speak English?

À quelle heure?	ah kell uhr	At what time?
Je voudrais...	zhuh voo-dray	I would like...

Exercises

Multiple-Choice Questions:

1. What is the most versatile French greeting?

      a) Salut
      b) Bonsoir
      c) Bonjour
      d) Au revoir

2. Which greeting is best used among friends in French?

      a) Bonsoir
      b) Salut
      c) Bonjour
      d) Au revoir

3. What does "Bonsoir" mean in English?

      a) Good night
      b) Good afternoon
      c) Good morning
      d) Good evening

4. Which phrase is the standard way to say goodbye in French?

      a) Salut
      b) Au revoir
      c) À bientôt
      d) Bonsoir

5. How do you pronounce "Salut" in French?

      a) bohn-zhoor
      b) seel voo pleh
      c) sa-loo
      d) ah kell uhr

6. What is the pronunciation of "Bonjour?"

      a) oh ruh-vwahr
      b) bohn-swahr
      c) sa-loo
      d) bohn-zhoor

7. Which phrase means "See you soon" in French?

      a) À bientôt

b) Salut
c) Au revoir
d) Je m'appelle

8. What does "Merci" translate to in English?

a) Please
b) Excuse me
c) Thank you
d) You're welcome

9. Which of the following is correctly matched with its translation?

a) "Je voudrais" – My name is...
b) "Combien ça coûte?" – How much does it cost?
c) "Excusez-moi" – Please
d) "Où est la gare?" – I don't understand

10. How is "Au revoir" pronounced?

a) kohm-byen sah koot
b) eks-kew-zay mwah
c) oh ruh-vwahr
d) pahr-lay voo ahn-glay

Answer Key

1. c) Bonjour

2. b) Salut

3. d) Good evening

4. b) Au revoir

5. c) sa-loo

6. d) bohn-zhoor

7. a) À bientôt

8. c) Thank you

9. b) "Combien ça coûte?" – How much does it cost?

10. c) oh ruh-vwahr

Chapter 2: Who Are You?

"Soyez vous-même, tous les autres sont déjà pris."

– Oscar Wilde

In this chapter, you'll discover how to introduce yourself and ask questions

Subject Pronouns

Subject pronouns are words used to replace the subject of a sentence: "I," "you," "he," "she," "we," and "they" in English. In French, subject pronouns are "je" (I), "tu" (you, informal), "il/elle" (he/she), "nous" (we), "vous" (you, singular formal or plural), and "ils/elles" (they).

French 3rd-person pronouns must agree with the gender of the subject, using "il" for masculine subjects and "elle" for feminine ones. Additionally, French has a formal "you" (vous) used in polite situations, whereas English uses the same "you" for both formal and informal contexts.

Person & Number	Pronoun	Pronunciation	Translation
1st Person Singular	Je	zhuh	I
1st Person Plural	Nous	noo	We
2nd Person Singular	Tu	tew	You (informal)
2nd Person Plural	Vous	voo	You (formal/plural)
3rd Person Singular (M)	Il	eel	He
3rd Person Singular (F)	Elle	ell	She
3rd Person Plural (M)	Ils	eel	They (masculine/mixed)

3rd Person Plural (F)	Elles	ell	They (feminine)

Gender and Number Agreement

Understanding Gender in French

In the French language, every noun is either masculine or feminine. For instance, the word for "book" (livre) is masculine, so it is referred to as un livre ("a book"). On the other hand, the word for "house" (maison) is feminine, and thus it is une maison ("a house"). This gender distinction extends to adjectives, articles, and even some verb forms, meaning that the form of these words will change depending on whether they are associated with a masculine or feminine noun.

The Influence of Gender on Adjectives

Adjectives in French must agree with the gender of the noun they describe. This agreement often results in different forms of an adjective depending on whether the noun is masculine or feminine. For example, the adjective "small" in French is petit when describing a masculine noun, as in un petit chien ("a small dog"), and petite when describing a feminine noun, as in une petite fille ("a small girl"). Additionally, plural forms also require agreement, meaning that the adjective may change further when describing more than one noun. This complexity requires learners to pay close attention to the gender of nouns and adjust the form of adjectives accordingly.

Number Agreement in French

In addition to gender, number plays a significant role in the structure of French sentences. For example, the singular form of "the" in French is le for masculine nouns and la for feminine nouns, as in le chat ("the cat") and la pomme ("the apple"). However, when these nouns are plural, the article changes to les for both genders, resulting in les chats ("the cats") and les pommes ("the apples"). This rule extends to adjectives, which must agree in number with the nouns they modify, often adding an "-s" to the end of the adjective in plural forms, such as in les petits chiens ("the small dogs").

Challenges and Tips for Mastering Gender and Number

One of the biggest challenges for learners of French is memorizing the gender of nouns, as there are few consistent rules to determine whether a noun is masculine or feminine. It often comes down to memorization and practice).

Getting to Know Someone

Now we'll begin going over some questions you can ask when meeting someone for the first time. Below is a list of basic questions, along with their pronunciation and English translations.

Question	Pronunciation	Translation

Comment vous appelez-vous?	koh-moh voo zah-peh-lay voo	What is your name?
Où habitez-vous?	oo ah-bee-tay voo	Where do you live?
Quel âge avez-vous?	kell ahzh ah-vay voo	How old are you?
Que faites-vous dans la vie?	kuh feht voo dahn lah vee	What do you do for a living?
D'où venez-vous?	doo veh-nay voo	Where are you from?
Parlez-vous anglais?	pahr-lay voo ahn-glay	Do you speak English?
Avez-vous des frères et sœurs?	ah-vay voo day frehr ay suhr	Do you have any brothers or sisters?
Quelle est votre nationalité?	kell eh voh-truh nah-syo-nah-lee-tay	What is your nationality?
Aimez-vous voyager?	eh-may voo vwoy-ah-zhay	Do you like to travel?
Quel est votre passe-temps préféré?	kell eh voh-truh pahss-tahmp preh-fay-ray	What is your favorite hobby?

Answering Questions

Phrase	Pronunciation	Translation
Je t'aime	zhuh tem	I love you
Merci beaucoup	mehr-see boh-coo	Thank you very much
S'il vous plaît	seel voo pleh	Please
Excusez-moi	eks-kew-zay mwah	Excuse me
Je suis désolé	zhuh swee day-zoh-lay	I'm sorry

À bientôt	ah byan-toh	See you soon
Je ne sais pas	zhuh nuh say pah	I don't know
Bonne journée	bohn zhoor-nay	Have a good day
Il fait beau	eel feh boh	The weather is nice
Où sont les toilettes?	oo sohn lay twah-let	Where are the restrooms?

Verbs: Être, Avoir, Aller

Person & Number	Pronoun	Être (To be)	Avoir (To have)	Aller (To go)
1st Person Singular	Je	suis (I am)	ai (I have)	vais (I go)
1st Person Plural	Nous	sommes (We are)	avons (We have)	allons (We go)
2nd Person Singular	Tu	es (You are)	as (You have)	vas (You go)
2nd Person Plural	Vous	êtes (You are)	avez (You have)	allez (You go)
3rd Person Singular (M/F)	Il/Elle	est (He/She is)	a (He/She has)	va (He/She goes)
3rd Person Plural (M/F)	Ils/Elles	sont (They are)	ont (They have)	vont (They go)

1. Être (to be):

- Je suis heureux de te voir.
- (I am happy to see you.)
- Nous sommes étudiants à l'université.
- (We are students at the university.)
- Elle est très gentille avec tout le monde.
- (She is very kind to everyone.)

2. Avoir (to have):

- J'ai un chien et un chat chez moi.
- (I have a dog and a cat at home.)
- Tu as un rendez-vous important aujourd'hui.
- (You have an important appointment today.)
- Ils ont beaucoup de travail à faire.
- (They have a lot of work to do.)

3. Aller (to go):

- Je vais à la bibliothèque après les cours.
- (I am going to the library after classes.)
- Nous allons en France cet été.
- (We are going to France this summer.)
- Ils vont au cinéma ce soir.
- (They are going to the movies tonight.)

Exercises

Multiple-Choice Questions:

1. What is the translation of "Comment vous appelez-vous?"

    a) Where do you live?
    b) What is your name?
    c) How old are you?
    d) Do you like to travel?

2. How do you pronounce "Où habitez-vous?" in French?

    a) kuh feht voo dahn lah vee
    b) oo sohn lay twah-let
    c) oo ah-bee-tay voo
    d) ah byan-toh

3. Which question in French means "How old are you?"

    a) Quel âge avez-vous?
    b) D'où venez-vous?
    c) Parlez-vous anglais?
    d) Avez-vous des frères et sœurs?

4. What is the pronunciation of "Je t'aime?"

    a) zhuh tem
    b) eks-kew-zay mwah
    c) seel voo pleh
    d) mehr-see boh-coo

5. How do you say "Please" in French?

    a) Merci beaucoup
    b) S'il vous plaît
    c) Excusez-moi
    d) Je suis désolé

6. Which of the following sentences means "I am happy to see you?"

    a) Je vais à la bibliothèque après les cours.
    b) Nous sommes étudiants à l'université.
    c) Je suis heureux de te voir.
    d) Ils vont au cinéma ce soir.

7. What is the translation of "Nous avons" in the context of the verb avoir?

    a) We go

b) We are
c) We have
d) We see

8. How do you say "They go" in French?

   a) Ils ont
   b) Ils sont
   c) Ils vont
   d) Ils aiment

9. What is the French verb for "to be?"

   a) Être
   b) Avoir
   c) Aller
   d) Venir

10. Which pronoun would you use with "es" in the present tense of être?

    a) Je
    b) Tu
    c) Il/Elle
    d) Nous

Answer Key

1. b) What is your name?
2. c) oo ah-bee-tay voo
3. a) Quel âge avez-vous?
4. a) zhuh tem
5. b) S'il vous plaît
6. c) Je suis heureux de te voir.
7. c) We have
8. c) Ils vont
9. a) Être
10. b) Tu

Chapter 3: Such a Beautiful Place!

"Un nom, c'est plus qu'un mot, c'est une identité." – Victor Hugo

In this chapter, we'll explore how to describe places using a variety of adjectives, and discuss the regular verb forms in the present tense, along with how to conjugate an irregular verb.

Nouns to Describe

Below is a list of nouns for items you might want to describe in a new setting.

Noun	Pronunciation	Translation
La maison	lah meh-zon	The house
Le livre	luh lee-vruh	The book
La voiture	lah vwah-tewr	The car
Le chien	luh shee-ehn	The dog
La table	lah tah-bluh	The table
Le jardin	luh zhar-dan	The garden
L'école	lay-kohl	The school
Le téléphone	luh teh-lay-fohn	The telephone
La fenêtre	lah fuh-netr	The window
Le chat	luh shah	The cat

Plural Forms

You might be wondering how to form plural nouns. In some cases, it's somewhat like English: you simply add an -s. However, in other cases, you need to add -es or -ces. Let's review the rules in the table below:

Combination	Rule	Examples
-s	For most nouns, simply add -s to form the plural.	Le livre (The book) → Les livres (The books)
-es	Nouns ending in -eau or -eu add -x instead of -s.	Le tableau (The painting) → Les tableaux (The paintings)
-ces	Nouns ending in -al change to -aux in the plural form.	Le journal (The newspaper) → Les journaux (The newspapers)
-x	Nouns ending in -eau, -eu, or -au often take -x in plural.	Le château (The castle) → Les châteaux (The castles)
-s	Nouns ending in -z, -x, or -s remain unchanged in plural.	Le nez (The nose) → Les nez (The noses)

Expressing Existence: Il y a

Understanding "Il y a" in French

The phrase "Il y a" is a French expression similar to the English expressions "there is" or "there are." For instance: Il y a un chat dans la maison ("There is a cat in the house") or Il y a des livres sur la table ("There are books on the table"). The phrase is always invariable, meaning it doesn't change regardless of whether the noun it references is singular or plural, masculine or feminine.

Using "Il y a" in Different Contexts

"Il y a" can be used in both affirmative and negative sentences. For example, in a negative sentence: Il n'y a pas de chat dans la maison ("There is no cat in the house") or Il n'y a pas de livres sur la table ("There are no books on the table").

The construction for negatives involves inserting "ne" before "y" and "pas" after "a," effectively negating the statement.

"Il y a" is frequently used in questions to inquire about the presence or absence of something: Y a-t-il un problème? ("Is there a problem?") or Est-ce qu'il y a des pommes? ("Are there any apples?").

The Temporal Use of "Il y a"

"Il y a" also has a temporal function, similar to the English phrase "ago." For instance: Il y a deux ans, j'ai visité Paris ("Two years ago, I visited Paris") or Il y a une heure, il a quitté la maison ("He left the house an hour ago"). In this usage, "Il y a" is always followed by an expression to convey how long ago the event occurred.

Examples of Il y a usage:

1. Il y a un chat dans le jardin.

   (There is a cat in the garden.)

2. Il y a des livres sur la table.

   (There are books on the table.)

3. Il n'y a pas de pain dans la cuisine.

   (There is no bread in the kitchen.)

4. Il y a une fête ce soir.

   (There is a party tonight.)

5. Il y a trois voitures devant la maison.

   (There are three cars in front of the house.)

6. Il y a eu un accident sur l'autoroute.

   (There was an accident on the highway.)

7. Il y a beaucoup de monde au marché.

   (There are a lot of people at the market.)

8. Il y a cinq ans, j'ai déménagé en France.

   (Five years ago, I moved to France.)

9. Il y a du vent aujourd'hui.

   (It is windy today.)

10. Il y a des pommes dans le réfrigérateur.

    (There are apples in the refrigerator.)

Expressing Location: Se Trouver

Understanding "Se Trouver" in French

The verb "se trouver" is a reflexive verb commonly used to express the location or position of someone or something. It can be translated into English as "to be located," "to be situated," or simply "to find oneself."

"Se trouver" specifically emphasizes the physical location or placement of an object or person. For example:La bibliothèque se trouve au centre-ville ("The library is located downtown") or Je me trouve dans un café ("I am in a café").

Additionally, "se trouver" can be used metaphorically to describe a person's situation or state of being, such as in Il se trouve dans une situation difficile ("He finds himself in a difficult situation").

"Se Trouver" in Relation to Other Verbs

While "être" is a general-purpose verb used in a wide range of contexts, "se trouver" is more specific and often carries a slightly formal tone.

"Se situer" is very similar to "se trouver" and is often used interchangeably, though "se trouver" is more commonly used in everyday speech. For example, L'école se situe près de la gare ("The school is located near the train station") could easily be replaced with L'école se trouve près de la gare without changing the meaning.

Examples of se trouve usage:

1. La maison se trouve au bout de la rue.

   (The house is located at the end of the street.)

2. L'hôtel se trouve à côté de la gare.

   (The hotel is situated next to the train station.)

3. Le parc se trouve en face de l'école.

   (The park is across from the school.)

4. Ma famille se trouve actuellement en vacances en Espagne.

   (My family is currently on vacation in Spain.)

5. Le musée se trouve près de la rivière.

   (The museum is located near the river.)

6. La bibliothèque se trouve au centre-ville.

   (The library is situated downtown.)

7. Le village se trouve dans une vallée.

   (The village is located in a valley.)

8. L'université se trouve à une heure de route d'ici.

(The university is an hour's drive from here.)

9. Je me trouve dans un café en ce moment.

(I am in a café at the moment.)

10. Le château se trouve au sommet de la colline.

(The castle is located at the top of the hill.)

Exercises

Multiple-Choice Questions:

1. What is the correct translation for "La maison" in English?

   a) The car
   b) The house
   c) The table
   d) The school

2. How do you say "The dog" in French?

   a) Le chat
   b) La table
   c) Le chien
   d) La voiture

3. What is the plural form of "Le château?"

   a) Les châteaux
   b) Les châteauxs
   c) Les châteaus
   d) Les châteux

4. Which of the following nouns remains unchanged in the plural form?

   a) Le tableau
   b) Le nez
   c) Le livre
   d) Le journal

5. How would you express "There are books on the table" in French?

   a) Il y a un livre sur la table
   b) Il y a des livres sur la table
   c) Il n'y a pas de livres sur la table
   d) Il y a des chats sur la table

6. Which sentence correctly uses "Il y a" in a temporal context?

   a) Il y a un problème dans la maison
   b) Il y a des voitures dans la rue
   c) Il y a cinq ans, j'ai déménagé en France
   d) Il y a un café au coin de la rue

7. How do you say "The library is located downtown" in French?

   a) La bibliothèque se trouve au centre-ville
   b) La bibliothèque est près de la gare

c) La bibliothèque est au centre-ville
d) La bibliothèque se situe au centre-ville

8. Which verb is similar in meaning to "se trouver" but is often used interchangeably?

a) Être
b) Avoir
c) Se situer
d) Aller

9. What is the meaning of "L'hôtel se trouve à côté de la gare?"

a) The hotel is in front of the station
b) The hotel is behind the station
c) The hotel is next to the station
d) The hotel is far from the station

10. Which of the following sentences correctly uses "Il y a" in a negative form?

a) Il y a un chat dans le jardin
b) Il n'y a pas de pain dans la cuisine
c) Il y a beaucoup de monde au marché
d) Il y a une fête ce soir

Answer Key

1. b) The house

2. c) Le chien

3. a) Les châteaux

4. b) Le nez

5. b) Il y a des livres sur la table

6. c) Il y a cinq ans, j'ai déménagé en France

7. a) La bibliothèque se trouve au centre-ville

8. c) Se situer

9. c) The hotel is next to the station

10. b) Il n'y a pas de pain dans la cuisine

Chapter 4: This or That?

"L'élégance est la seule beauté qui ne se fane jamais." – Coco Chanel

This chapter will be especially helpful when you're shopping. We'll cover various phrases and questions to use in a store, and we'll also delve into some grammatical structures, questions for identifying items, and relevant vocabulary.

Clothes and Vocabulary Related to Shopping

In the table below, you'll find a variety of clothing items and shopping terms, along with their corresponding articles, pronunciation, and translations.

Word	Pronunciation	Translation
Le pantalon	luh pahn-ta-lon	The pants
La robe	lah rob	The dress
Les chaussures	lay shoh-sur	The shoes
Le chapeau	luh shah-poh	The hat
La chemise	lah shuh-meez	The shirt
Le manteau	luh mahn-toh	The coat
Le sac	luh sahk	The bag
Les gants	lay gahn	The gloves
La jupe	lah zhup	The skirt

| Les lunettes | lay loo-net | The glasses |

Demonstratives

Understanding Demonstratives in French

Demonstratives are words used to point to specific objects, people, or places. In French, they function similarly to their English counterparts "this," "that," "these," and "those." However, in French, demonstratives change depending on the gender and number of the noun they modify.

The primary demonstrative adjectives in French are ce, cette, cet, and ces.

Singular Demonstratives: Ce, Cet, and Cette

- Ce is used before masculine singular nouns that begin with a consonant. For example: ce livre (this/that book).

- Cet is used before masculine singular nouns that start with a vowel or a silent "h." For instance: cet homme (this/that man) or cet hôtel (this/that hotel).

- Cette is used before all feminine singular nouns, regardless of whether they begin with a vowel or a consonant. For example: cette robe (this/that dress) or cette amie (this/that friend).

Plural Demonstratives: Ces

- Ces is used for all plural nouns, whether they are masculine or feminine, and regardless of the initial sound of the noun. For example: ces livres (these/those books) or ces chaussures (these/those shoes).

Emphasizing Demonstratives: Adding -ci and -là

In French, you can add -ci (here) or -là (there) after the noun to distinguish between "this" and "that" or "these" and "those" to be more specific about the object or person you're referring to. For example:

- Ce livre-ci (this book here) versus ce livre-là (that book there).

- Ces chaussures-ci (these shoes here) versus ces chaussures-là (those shoes there).

Usage in Sentences

- Je veux acheter ce pantalon. (I want to buy these pants.)

- Regarde cette chemise. (Look at this shirt.)

- Cet avion est en retard. (That plane is delayed.)

- Ces enfants jouent dans le parc. (Those children are playing in the park.)

Gender	Close to the Speaker	Close to the Addressee	Far from Both
Masculine	Ce livre-ci est à moi.	Ce livre que tu tiens est intéressant.	Ce livre-là sur l'étagère est ancien.
	(This book here is mine.)	(That book you're holding is interesting.)	(That book over there on the shelf is old.)
Feminine	Cette robe-ci me plaît beaucoup.	Cette robe que tu portes est jolie.	Cette robe-là dans la vitrine est chère.
	(This dress here pleases me a lot.)	(That dress you're wearing is pretty.)	(That dress over there in the shop window is expensive.)
Neuter	Cela-ci est important.	Ça que tu viens de dire est intéressant.	Cela-là me semble étrange.
	(This here is important.)	(That which you just said is interesting.)	(That over there seems strange to me.)

Definite Article + Adjective

Understanding Definite Articles in French

French definite articles correspond to the English word "the" and are used to refer to specific nouns. Unlike English, French has different forms of definite articles that must agree in gender and number with the noun they modify. There are four main definite articles in French:

1. Le – used for masculine singular nouns.

   Example: Le livre (The book)

2. La – used for feminine singular nouns.

   Example: La maison (The house)

3. L' – used before singular nouns (both masculine and feminine) that begin with a vowel or silent "h."

   Example: L'école (The school), L'homme (The man)

4. Les – used for all plural nouns, regardless of gender.

Example: Les livres (The books), Les maisons (The houses)

Using Adjectives in French

Adjectives are words that describe or modify nouns. However, unlike in English, French, adjectives must agree in gender and number with the noun they modify. This means that the form of the adjective changes depending on whether the noun is masculine, feminine, singular, or plural.

Position of Adjectives

- Before the noun: Some common adjectives, especially those that describe size, beauty, age, goodness, and quantity, are typically placed before the noun.

    o Example: Un beau livre (A beautiful book), Une petite maison (A small house)

- After the noun: In French, most adjectives are placed after the noun they describe.

    o Example: Un livre intéressant (An interesting book), Une maison bleue (A blue house)

Agreement in Gender and Number

- Masculine Singular: The default form of an adjective is typically masculine singular.

    o Example: Un chat noir (A black cat)

- Feminine Singular: To form the feminine singular, you usually add an "e" to the masculine form, unless the adjective already ends in "e."

    o Example: Une robe noire (A black dress)

- Masculine Plural: To form the masculine plural, you generally add an "s" to the masculine singular form.

    o Example: Des chats noirs (Black cats)

- Feminine Plural: To form the feminine plural, you add an "s" to the feminine singular form.

    o Example: Des robes noires (Black dresses)

Some adjectives have irregular forms that must be memorized, such as beau (beautiful), which becomes belle in the feminine singular, and beaux or belles in the plural.

Combining Definite Articles and Adjectives

When combining articles and adjectives in French, both must agree with the gender and number of the noun to convey the correct meaning. For instance:

- Le grand arbre (The tall tree) – masculine singular

- La petite fille (The little girl) – feminine singular

- Les vieux livres (The old books) – masculine plural
- Les belles maisons (The beautiful houses) – feminine plural

Expressing Likes, Dislikes, and Preferences

Likes and Dislikes

In French, the key verbs used for expressing likes and dislikes are aimer (to like, to love), adorer (to adore), and détester (to dislike, to hate).

Expressing Likes

1. Using "Aimer" (To Like/To Love):

- The verb aimer is the most common way to express liking something. It can mean "to like" or "to love," depending on the context. When used with a noun, aimer is followed by the definite article (le, la, l', les).

Example:

- J'aime le chocolat. (I like chocolate.)
- Il aime la musique. (He likes music.)
- Nous aimons les voyages. (We like traveling.)

2. Using "Adorer" (To Adore):

- The verb adorer is stronger than aimer and is used to express a deep liking or love for something. It is also followed by the definite article.

Example:

- J'adore le cinéma. (I adore the cinema.)
- Elle adore les fleurs. (She loves flowers.)
- Vous adorez les animaux. (You adore animals.)

Expressing Dislikes

1. Using "Détester" (To Dislike/To Hate):

- The verb détester is the standard way to express dislike or hatred toward something. Like aimer and adorer, it is also followed by the definite article.

Example:

- Je déteste les légumes. (I hate vegetables.)
- Il déteste la pluie. (He dislikes the rain.)
- Ils détestent les films d'horreur. (They hate horror movies.)

2. Negative Constructions with "Aimer":

- To express that you do not like something, you can use ne... pas with the verb aimer.

Example:

- Je n'aime pas le café. (I don't like coffee.)
- Elle n'aime pas les sports. (She doesn't like sports.)
- Nous n'aimons pas la danse. (We don't like dancing.)

Asking About Likes and Dislikes

1. Using "Qu'est-ce que":

- To ask someone what they like or dislike, you can use Qu'est-ce que followed by the like or dislike verb.

Example:

- Qu'est-ce que tu aimes? (What do you like?)
- Qu'est-ce que tu détestes? (What do you dislike?)

2. Using "Est-ce que":

- Another common way to ask about preferences is by using Est-ce que with the appropriate verb.

Example:

- Est-ce que tu aimes les chiens? (Do you like dogs?)
- Est-ce que vous préférez le vin ou la bière? (Do you prefer wine or beer?)

Person	Pronoun	Indirect Object Pronoun	Example Sentence	Translation
1st Person Singular	Je	Me	Il me parle.	(He is speaking to me.)
st Person Plural	Nous	Nous	Il nous donne un cadeau.	(He gives us a gift.)
2nd Person Singular	Tu	Te	Je te téléphone ce soir.	(I'm calling you tonight.)
2nd Person Plural	Vous	Vous	Je vous écris une lettre.	(I am writing you a letter.)
3rd Person Singular	Il/Elle	Lui	Elle lui parle doucement.	(She speaks to him/her softly.)

3rd Person Plural	Ils/Elles	Leur	Je leur explique la situation.	(I am explaining the situation to them.)

Explanation:

1. 1st Person Singular:

- Pronoun: Je (I)
- Indirect Object Pronoun: Me (to me, for me)

2. 1st Person Plural:

- Pronoun: Nous (We)
- Indirect Object Pronoun: Nous (to us, for us)

3. 2nd Person Singular:

- Pronoun: Tu (You - informal)
- Indirect Object Pronoun: Te (to you, for you)

4. 2nd Person Plural:

- Pronoun: Vous (You - formal or plural)
- Indirect Object Pronoun: Vous (to you, for you)

5. 3rd Person Singular:

- Pronoun: Il/Elle (He/She)
- Indirect Object Pronoun: Lui (to him, to her, for him, for her)

6. 3rd Person Plural:

- Pronoun: Ils/Elles (They - masculine/feminine)
- Indirect Object Pronoun: Leur (to them, for them)

Expressing Preferences in French

In French, the key verbs used for expressing preferences are préférer (to prefer), aimer mieux (to like better), and plaire (to please). Understanding how to use these verbs and their constructions allows you to clearly communicate your preferences in French.

Using "Préférer" (To Prefer)

The verb préférer is the most direct way to express a preference for one thing over another. It is conjugated like a regular -er verb with some slight spelling changes in certain forms.

Conjugation of Préférer (Present Tense):

- Je préfère (I prefer)

- Tu préfères (You prefer - informal)
- Il/Elle préfère (He/She prefers)
- Nous préférons (We prefer)
- Vous préférez (You prefer - formal or plural)
- Ils/Elles préfèrent (They prefer)

Examples:

- Je préfère le thé au café. (I prefer tea over coffee.)
- Nous préférons aller à la plage. (We prefer going to the beach.)
- Elle préfère ce film. (She prefers this movie.)

When expressing a preference between two things, you can use à (to) or que (than) to compare:

- Je préfère le chocolat à la vanille. (I prefer chocolate to vanilla.)
- Ils préfèrent lire que regarder la télévision. (They prefer reading to watching television.)

Using "Aimer Mieux" (To Like Better)

Another common way to express a preference is with the phrase aimer mieux, which translates to "to like better" or "to prefer." It is slightly less formal than préférer and can be used interchangeably in many contexts.

Examples:

- J'aime mieux rester à la maison. (I like staying at home better.)
- Il aime mieux ce livre que l'autre. (He likes this book better than the other one.)
- Nous aimons mieux ce restaurant. (We prefer this restaurant.)

Using "Plaire" (To Please)

The verb plaire is used less commonly but is still important for expressing when something pleases or is appealing to you. It is often used with indirect object pronouns to indicate who is pleased by something.

Conjugation of Plaire (Present Tense):

- Je plais (I please)
- Tu plais (You please)
- Il/Elle plaît (He/She pleases)
- Nous plaisons (We please)
- Vous plaisez (You please)
- Ils/Elles plaisent (They please)

Examples:

- Ce film me plaît beaucoup. (I like this movie a lot.)
- Cette robe lui plaît. (He/She likes this dress.)
- Les vacances en France nous plaisent. (We like vacations in France.)

In this construction, the thing that is liked is the subject of the sentence, and the person who likes it is indicated by the indirect object pronoun (me, lui, nous, etc.).

Asking About Preferences

To ask someone about their preferences, you can use the following structures:

- Qu'est-ce que tu préfères? (What do you prefer?)
- Est-ce que tu aimes mieux...? (Do you like... better?)
- Qu'est-ce qui te plaît le plus? (What do you like the most?)

Examples:

- Qu'est-ce que tu préfères, le cinéma ou le théâtre? (What do you prefer, the cinema or the theater?)
- Est-ce que tu aimes mieux la mer ou la montagne? (Do you like the sea or the mountains better?)
- Qu'est-ce qui te plaît le plus, cette robe ou cette jupe? (Which do you like more, this dress or this skirt?)

Pronoun	Conjugation of Préférer	Example Sentence	Translation
Je	préfère	Je préfère le thé au café.	(I prefer tea over coffee.)
Tu	préfères	Tu préfères le chocolat noir.	(You prefer dark chocolate.)
Il/Elle	préfère	Il préfère le football au basketball.	(He prefers football to basketball.)
Nous	préférons	Nous préférons voyager en train.	(We prefer traveling by train.)
Vous	préférez	Vous préférez ce restaurant.	(You prefer this restaurant.)
Ils/Elles	préfèrent	Elles préfèrent les films romantiques.	(You prefer this restaurant.)

At the Store

Questions To Ask Before Purchasing

French Question	Pronunciation	Translation
Combien ça coûte?	kohm-byen sah koot	How much does it cost?
Est-ce que c'est en solde?	ehs-kuh seh ahn sold	Is it on sale?
Quelle est la garantie?	kell eh lah gah-rahn-tee	What is the warranty?
Y a-t-il une réduction pour cet article?	yah-teel uhn ray-dook-syon poor seht ar-teek-luh	Is there a discount on this item?
Puis-je l'essayer?	pwee zhuh leh-say-yay	Can I try it on?
Quelle est la politique de retour?	kell eh lah poh-lee-teek duh ruh-toor	What is the return policy?
Quelle est la politique de retour?	kell eh lah poh-lee-teek duh ruh-toor	What is the return policy?
Est-ce que vous avez d'autres tailles?	ehs-kuh voo zah-vay dohtr tah-yuh	Do you have other sizes?
Acceptez-vous les cartes de crédit?	ahk-sep-tay voo lay kart duh cray-dee	Do you accept credit cards?
Est-ce que le prix inclut la TVA?	ehs-kuh luh pree ehn-kloot lah tay-vay-ah	Is tax included in the price?

Questions You Might Be Asked Before Purchasing

French Question	Pronunciation	Translation
Avez-vous trouvé ce que vous cherchiez?	ah-vay voo troo-vay suh kuh voo shair-shee-ay	Did you find what you were looking for?

Quelle taille faites-vous?	kell tah-yuh feht voo	What size do you wear?
Voulez-vous essayer cet article?	voo-lay voo eh-say-yay seht ar-teek-luh	Would you like to try this item?
Puis-je vous aider avec autre chose?	pwee zhuh voo zay-day ah-vek oh-truh shoz	Can I help you with anything else?
Avez-vous une préférence pour une couleur?	ah-vay voo uhn pray-fay-rahnss poor uhn koo-luhr	Do you have a preference for a color?
Souhaitez-vous payer en espèces ou par carte?	soo-eh-tay voo pay-yay ahn es-pehs oo par kart	Would you like to pay in cash or by card?
Désirez-vous un sac pour vos achats?	day-zee-ray voo uhn sahk poor voh zah-shah	Would you like a bag for your purchases?
Avez-vous besoin d'une garantie supplémentaire?	ah-vay voo buh-zwen doon gah-rahn-tee soo-pluh-men-tair	Do you need an additional warranty?
Voulez-vous recevoir le reçu par e-mail?	voo-lay voo ruh-swah-vwar luh ruh-su par ee-mehl	Would you like to receive the receipt by email?
Est-ce que je peux emballer ceci pour vous?	ehs-kuh zhuh puh ahn-bah-lay suh-see poor voo	Can I gift wrap this for you?

Questions To Ask At Check-Out

French Question	Pronunciation	Translation
Est-ce que je peux payer par carte?	ehs-kuh zhuh puh pay-yay par kart	Can I pay by card?
Est-ce que vous acceptez les espèces?	ehs-kuh voo zahk-sep-tay layz es-pehs	Do you accept cash?

Pouvez-vous me donner un reçu, s'il vous plaît?	poo-vay voo muh doh-nay uhn ruh-su, seel voo pleh	Can you give me a receipt, please?
Y a-t-il des frais supplémentaires?	yah-teel day fray soo-pluh-men-tair	Are there any additional fees?
Est-ce que je peux obtenir un sac?	ehs-kuh zhuh puh ob-teh-neer uhn sahk	Can I get a bag?
Puis-je payer en plusieurs fois?	pwee zhuh pay-yay ahn plew-zyur fwah	Can I pay in installments?
Est-ce que je peux retourner l'article si nécessaire?	ehs-kuh zhuh puh ruh-toor-nay l'ar-teek-luh see neh-seh-sair	Can I return the item if necessary?
Pouvez-vous me donner des informations sur la garantie?	poo-vay voo muh doh-nay dayz an-for-mah-syon sur lah gah-rahn-tee	Can you give me information about the warranty?
Est-ce que je peux avoir un emballage cadeau?	ehs-kuh zhuh puh ah-vwar uhn ahn-bah-lazh kah-doh	Can I have gift wrapping?
Puis-je payer en espèces?	pwee zhuh pay-yay ahn es-pehs	Can I pay in cash?

Questions You Might Be Asked At Check-Out

French Question	Pronunciation	Translation
Voulez-vous un sac?	voo-lay voo uhn sahk	Would you like a bag?
Comment souhaitez-vous payer?	koh-mahn soo-eh-tay voo pay-yay	How would you like to pay?
Avez-vous une carte de fidélité?	ah-vay voo uhn kart duh fee-day-lay-tay	Do you have a loyalty card?

Souhaitez-vous un reçu?	soo-eh-tay voo uhn ruh-su	Would you like a receipt?
Voulez-vous recevoir votre reçu par e-mail?	voo-lay voo ruh-swah-vwar voh-truh ruh-su par ee-mehl	Would you like to receive your receipt by email?
Est-ce que vous avez trouvé tout ce que vous cherchiez?	ehs-kuh voo zah-vay troo-vay too suh kuh voo shair-shee-ay	Did you find everything you were looking for?
Avez-vous besoin de quelque chose d'autre?	ah-vay voo buh-zwen duh kel-kuh shoz doh-truh	Do you need anything else?
Voulez-vous payer en espèces ou par carte?	oo-lay voo pay-yay ahn es-pehs oo par kart	Would you like to pay in cash or by card?
Souhaitez-vous une garantie supplémentaire?	soo-eh-tay voo uhn gah-rahn-tee soo-pluh-men-tair	Would you like an additional warranty?
Est-ce que je peux vous aider avec autre chose?	ehs-kuh zhuh puh voo zay-day ah-vek oh-truh shoz	Can I help you with anything else?

Exercises

Multiple-Choice Questions:

1. Which pronoun is correctly paired with the conjugation "préfère" in the present tense?

   a) Nous
   b) Vous
   c) Je
   d) Ils

2. What is the correct translation of "Tu préfères le chocolat noir?"

   a) You prefer white chocolate.
   b) You prefer milk chocolate.
   c) You prefer dark chocolate.
   d) You prefer hot chocolate.

3. What does the question "Combien ça coûte?" mean?

   a) Is it on sale?
   b) What is the warranty?
   c) How much does it cost?
   d) Do you accept credit cards?

4. Which of the following questions asks about the return policy?

   a) Quelle est la garantie?
   b) Est-ce que c'est en solde?
   c) Quelle est la politique de retour?
   d) Y a-t-il une réduction pour cet article?

5. How would you ask "Can I try it on?" in French?

   a) Puis-je l'essayer?
   b) Puis-je vous aider?
   c) Voulez-vous un sac?
   d) Voulez-vous essayer cet article?

6. If a store clerk asks "Avez-vous trouvé ce que vous cherchiez," what are they asking?

   a) Would you like a bag?
   b) Did you find what you were looking for?
   c) How would you like to pay?
   d) Do you have a loyalty card?

7. What is the meaning of "Est-ce que je peux payer par carte?"

   a) Can I pay by card?

b) Can I return the item?
c) Can I have gift wrapping?
d) Can I get a receipt?

8. Which question would you ask if you wanted to know if an item is on sale?

   a) Est-ce que je peux avoir un sac?
   b) Est-ce que le prix inclut la TVA?
   c) Est-ce que c'est en solde?
   d) Y a-t-il des frais supplémentaires?

9. How do you ask "Do you have a loyalty card?" in French?

   a) Souhaitez-vous un reçu?
   b) Voulez-vous un sac?
   c) Avez-vous une carte de fidélité?
   d) Est-ce que je peux payer en espèces?

10. What would a clerk mean if they ask "Voulez-vous payer en espèces ou par carte?"

    a) Do you need a bag?
    b) Would you like to pay in cash or by card?
    c) Can I help you with anything else?
    d) Do you want a gift receipt?

Answer Key

1. c) Je

2. c) You prefer dark chocolate.

3. c) How much does it cost?

4. c) Quelle est la politique de retour?

5. a) Puis-je l'essayer?

6. b) Did you find what you were looking for?

7. a) Can I pay by card?

8. c) Est-ce que c'est en solde?

9. c) Avez-vous une carte de fidélité?

10. b) Would you like to pay in cash or by card?

Chapter 5: It's Just Around the Corner

Les prépositions et les adverbes sont les ponts entre les mots, les liens subtils qui donnent du sens à nos pensées.– Victor Hugo

In this chapter, our aim is to learn how to ask for and give directions to reach a destination.

Prepositions and Adverbs of Place

In the table below, you'll find the preposition or adverb, its pronunciation, and its translation, as usual.

Preposition/Adverb	Pronunciation	Translation	Example Sentence	Translation of Example
Sur	syur	On	Le livre est sur la table.	The book is on the table.
Sous	soo	Under	Le chat est sous la chaise.	The cat is under the chair.
Devant	duh-vahn	In front of	La voiture est devant la maison.	The car is in front of the house.
Derrière	deh-ryehr	Behind	Le jardin est derrière la maison.	The garden is behind the house.
Entre	ahn-truh	Between	La lampe est entre le canapé et la table.	The lamp is between the sofa and the table.
À côté de	ah koh-tay duh	Next to	L'école est à côté de la bibliothèque.	The school is next to the library.

Près de	preh duh	Near	Le parc est près de l'église.	The park is near the church.
Loin de	lwahn duh	Far from	La station est loin du centre-ville.	The station is far from downtown.
Au-dessus de	oh duh-sue duh	Above	Le tableau est au-dessus du canapé.	The painting is above the sofa.
Au-dessous de	oh duh-soo duh	Below	Le sous-sol est au-dessous de la maison.	The basement is below the house.

Verbs: Aller and Vouloir

Pronoun	Aller (to go)	Example Sentence with Aller	Vouloir (to want)	Example Sentence with Vouloir
Je	vais	Je vais à l'école. (I am going to school.)	veux	Je veux un café. (I want a coffee.)
Tu	vas	Tu vas au marché. (You are going to the market.)	veux	Tu veux une pomme. (You want an apple.)
Il/Elle	va	Il va au cinéma. (He is going to the cinema.)	veut	Elle veut un livre. (She wants a book.)
Nous	allons	Nous allons à la plage. (We are going to the beach.)	voulons	Nous voulons des vacances. (We want a vacation.)
Vous	allez	Vous allez à Paris. (You are going to Paris.)	voulez	Vous voulez du thé. (You want tea.)
Ils/Elles	vont	Ils vont au restaurant. (They are going to the restaurant.)	veulent	Elles veulent des fleurs. (They want flowers.)

Asking for Directions

It's time to learn how to ask for directions to various places.

French Question	Pronunciation	Translation
Où est la gare, s'il vous plaît?	oo eh lah gahr, seel voo pleh	Where is the train station, please?
Comment puis-je aller à l'hôtel?	koh-mahn pwee zhuh ah-lay ah loh-tel	How can I get to the hotel?
Où se trouve la bibliothèque?	oo suh troov lah bee-blee-oh-tek	Where is the library located?
Pouvez-vous m'indiquer le chemin vers le musée?	poo-vay voo man-dee-kay luh shuh-mahn vehr luh myoo-zay	Can you show me the way to the museum?
Quelle est la direction pour aller au centre-ville?	kell eh lah dee-rek-syon poor ah-lay oh sahn-truh veel	What is the direction to downtown?
Y a-t-il un arrêt de bus près d'ici?	yah-teel uhn ah-ray duh boos preh dee-see	Is there a bus stop nearby?
Combien de temps faut-il pour aller à pied?	kohm-byen duh tahm fo-teel poor ah-lay ah pyeh	How long does it take to walk there?
Est-ce loin d'ici?	ehs-kuh lwahn dee-see	Is it far from here?
C'est à quelle distance d'ici?	seh tah kell dee-stahnss dee-see	How far is it from here?
Où puis-je trouver un taxi?	oo pwee zhuh troo-vay uhn tahk-see	Where can I find a taxi?

Exercises

Multiple-Choice Questions:

1. What does the preposition "sous" mean in English?

   a) On
   b) Under
   c) In front of
   d) Behind

2. Which of the following sentences correctly uses the preposition "sur?"

   a) Le chat est sous la chaise.
   b) La voiture est devant la maison.
   c) Le livre est sur la table.
   d) Le jardin est derrière la maison.

3. How do you say "The painting is above the sofa" in French?

   a) Le tableau est sous le canapé.
   b) Le tableau est derrière le canapé.
   c) Le tableau est devant le canapé.
   d) Le tableau est au-dessus du canapé.

4. What is the translation of the French question "Où est la gare, s'il vous plaît?"

   a) Where is the library, please?
   b) Where is the hotel, please?
   c) Where is the train station, please?
   d) Where is the museum, please?

5. Which pronoun matches with the conjugation "va" for the verb "aller?"

   a) Nous
   b) Il/Elle
   c) Je
   d) Vous

6. How do you ask "How can I get to the hotel?" in French?

   a) Où se trouve la bibliothèque?
   b) Pouvez-vous m'indiquer le chemin vers le musée?
   c) Comment puis-je aller à l'hôtel?
   d) Quelle est la direction pour aller au centre-ville?

7. What is the meaning of "Près de" in English?

   a) Next to

b) Near

c) Far from

d) Between

8. How do you say "Ils want flowers" in French?

a) Ils veulent des fleurs.

b) Elles veulent des fleurs.

c) Ils veulent du thé.

d) Elles vont des fleurs.

9. What does the French question "Y a-t-il un arrêt de bus près d'ici?" mean?

a) How long does it take to walk there?

b) Where is the bus station?

c) Is there a bus stop nearby?

d) How far is it from here?

10. Which of the following correctly translates "We prefer traveling by train" into French?

a) Nous préférons voyager en voiture.

b) Nous préférons voyager en train.

c) Vous préférez voyager en train.

d) Ils préfèrent voyager en train.

Answer Key

1. b) Under

2. c) Le livre est sur la table.

3. d) Le tableau est au-dessus du canapé.

4. c) Where is the train station, please?

5. b) Il/Elle

6. c) Comment puis-je aller à l'hôtel?

7. b) Near

8. a) Ils veulent des fleurs.

9. c) Is there a bus stop nearby?

10. b) Nous préférons voyager en train.

Chapter 6: My Family Is...

"Le foyer, c'est le nid de l'homme. Là est la lumière, là est l'amour, là est la vie."

- Victor Hugo

In this chapter, we'll explore topics such as family members, possessives, appearances, abilities, qualities, and flaws.

Family Members

In the table below, as always, you'll see the masculine and feminine terms for family members, along with their pronunciation and translation.

Noun	Pronunciation	Translation
Le père	luh pair	The father
La mère	lah mare	The mother
Le frère	luh frair	The brother
La sœur	lah sur	The sister
Le grand-père	luh grahn pair	The grandfather
La grand-mère	lah grahn mare	The grandmother
Le fils	luh fees	The son
La fille	lah fee	The daughter
L'oncle	lonkl	The uncle

La tante	lah tahnt	The aunt
Le cousin	luh koo-zan	The cousin (male)
La cousine	lah koo-zeen	The cousin (female)

Possessives

French possessive adjectives, such as "mon," "ma," and "mes," must agree with the noun they possess, depending on whether it is masculine, feminine, singular, or plural.

Possessive Adjectives

Person Who Possesses the Object	Singular Object (Masculine)	Singular Object (Feminine)	Plural Object (Masculine)	Plural Object (Feminine)
Je (I)	mon frère (my brother)	ma sœur (my sister)	mes livres (my books)	mes fleurs (my flowers)
Tu (You - singular informal)	ton chien (your dog)	ta maison (your house)	tes stylos (your pens)	tes chaises (your chairs)
Il/Elle (He/She)	son père (his/her father)	sa mère (his/her mother)	ses amis (his/her friends)	ses idées (his/her ideas)
Nous (We)	notre fils (our son)	notre fille (our daughter)	nos enfants (our children)	nos voitures (our cars)
Vous (You - singular formal or plural)	votre oncle (your uncle)	votre tante (your aunt)	vos projets (your projects)	vos photos (your photos)
Ils/Elles (They)	leur chat (their cat)	leur école (their school)	leurs problèmes (their problems)	leurs maisons (their houses)

Possessive Pronouns

Possessive pronouns in French are used to replace a noun that has already been mentioned and to indicate ownership. Examples in English include "mine," "yours," "his," "hers," "ours," and "theirs."

Person Who Possesses the Object	Object (Singular Masculine)	Object (Singular Feminine)	Object (Plural Masculine)	Object (Plural Feminine)
Je (I)	mon livre (my book)	ma table (my table)	mes chiens (my dogs)	mes voitures (my cars)
Tu (You - singular informal)	ton ami (your friend)	ta chambre (your room)	tes frères (your brothers)	tes sœurs (your sisters)
Il/Elle (He/She)	son stylo (his/her pen)	sa maison (his/her house)	ses cahiers (his/her notebooks)	ses robes (his/her dresses)
Nous (We)	notre jardin (our garden)	notre ville (our city)	nos enfants (our children)	nos écoles (our schools)
Vous (You - singular formal or plural)	votre fils (your son)	votre fille (your daughter)	vos arbres (your trees)	vos valises (your suitcases)
Ils/Elles (They)	leur chien (their dog)	leur famille (their family)	leurs livres (their books)	leurs idées (their ideas)

Describing People

Appearances

Adjective (French)	Pronunciation	Translation (English)
Beau	boh	Handsome (masculine)
Belle	bell	Beautiful (feminine)

Grand	grahn	Tall, Big (masculine)
Grande	grahnd	Tall, Big (feminine)
Petit	puh-tee	Short, Small (masculine)
Petite	puh-teet	Short, Small (feminine)
Mince	manhs	Slim
Gros	groh	Fat (masculine)
Grosse	gross	Fat (feminine)
Jeune	zhuhn	Young
Âgé	ah-zhay	Elderly (masculine)
Âgée	ah-zhay	Elderly (feminine)
Chauve	shov	Bald
Blond	blon	Blonde (masculine)
Blonde	blond	Blonde (feminine)
Brun	bruhn	Brown-haired (masculine)
Brune	breen	Brown-haired (feminine)

Personality

Adjective (French)	Pronunciation	Translation (English)
Aimable	eh-mahbl	Kind, Friendly

Sympathique	san-pa-teek	Nice, Pleasant
Drôle	drohl	Funny
Sérieux	ser-yuh	Serious (masculine)
Sérieuse	ser-yooz	Serious (feminine)
Intelligent	an-tay-lee-zhahn	Intelligent (masculine)
Intelligente	an-tay-lee-zhahnt	Intelligent (feminine)
Bavard	ba-var	Talkative (masculine)
Bavarde	ba-vard	Talkative (feminine)
Timide	tee-meed	Shy
Travailleur	tra-va-yur	Hardworking (masculine)
Paresseux	pa-ray-suh	Lazy (masculine)
Paresseuse	pa-ray-suz	Lazy (feminine)
Gentil	zhahn-tee	Gentle, Kind (masculine)
Gentille	zhahn-teel	Gentle, Kind (feminine)
Courageux	koo-ra-zhu	Courageous (masculine)
Courageuse	koo-ra-zhooz	Courageous (feminine)

Quantifiers

Quantifiers are words or phrases used to answer the questions "how much" or "how many."

French has its own set of quantifiers that function in specific ways depending on whether the noun is countable or uncountable. For instance, "beaucoup de" (a lot of) can be used with both countable nouns, like "beaucoup de livres" (a lot of books), and uncountable nouns, like "beaucoup d'eau" (a lot of water).

It's important to note the difference between countable and uncountable nouns, as some quantifiers change depending on the noun type. For example, "few" in English translates to "peu de" in French when referring to countable nouns, as in "peu de personnes" (few people). However, for uncountable nouns, such as "money," the French equivalent would still be "peu de," as in "peu d'argent" (little money).

"Some" and "any" in English translate to "du," "de la," or "des" in French, depending on the gender and number of the noun. For example, "some bread" translates to "du pain," while "some apples" becomes "des pommes."

French quantifiers that don't have direct English translations include: "plusieurs," which means "several" and is used with countable nouns ("plusieurs amis" (several friends)) and "quelques," which means "a few" ("quelques minutes" (a few minutes)).

No matter the situation, these quantifiers must agree in context and use with the noun they modify.

Exercises

1. Which possessive adjective would you use for "my brother" in French?

    a) Ma frère
    b) Mon frère
    c) Mes frère
    d) Mes frères

2. How do you say "their books" using the correct possessive adjective in French?

    a) Ses livres
    b) Vos livres
    c) Leurs livres
    d) Nos livres

3. Which possessive pronoun would replace "my car" in French?

    a) La mien
    b) Le mien
    c) La mienne
    d) Les miennes

4. What is the correct possessive adjective for "your (formal) son" in French?

    a) Ton fils
    b) Votre fils
    c) Vos fils
    d) Leur fils

5. Which of the following is the correct translation for "several friends" using a French quantifier?

    a) Beaucoup de amis
    b) Quelques amis
    c) Plusieurs amis
    d) Peu de amis

6. What is the correct possessive adjective for "our children" in French?

    a) Notre enfants
    b) Nos enfants
    c) Leur enfants
    d) Ses enfants

7. How do you translate "a lot of water" into French?

    a) Beaucoup d'eau
    b) Peu d'eau
    c) Plusieurs d'eau

d) Quelques d'eau

8. Which adjective would you use to describe a "tall" man in French?

   a) Grande
   b) Petit
   c) Grand
   d) Grosse

9. What is the French possessive pronoun for "yours" (feminine plural)?

   a) Les tiens
   b) Les tiennes
   c) Les siens
   d) Les nôtres

10. Which quantifier is used in French to express "a few minutes?"

   a) Plusieurs minutes
   b) Beaucoup de minutes
   c) Quelques minutes
   d) Peu de minutes

Answer Key

1. b) Mon frère
2. c) Leurs livres
3. c) La mienne
4. b) Votre fils
5. c) Plusieurs amis
6. b) Nos enfants
7. a) Beaucoup d'eau
8. c) Grand
9. b) Les tiennes
10. c) Quelques minutes

Chapter 7: Every Morning...

"Chaque matin, nous renaissons. Ce que nous faisons aujourd'hui est ce qui compte le plus."

- André Gid

In this chapter, we will explore another use of the present indicative: discussing habits and routines.

Expressing Frequency

In English, frequency is commonly expressed using adverbs, which are typically placed before the main verb (e.g., "She always eats breakfast.") or after the verb "to be" (e.g., "He is often late.").

French also uses adverbs to express frequency, but their placement can vary. For example, "toujours" (always), "souvent" (often), "parfois" (sometimes), "rarement" (rarely), and "jamais" (never) are used to convey how frequently something happens, and they are generally placed after the conjugated verb in a sentence (e.g., "Elle mange toujours le petit déjeuner").

In French, certain expressions are used to indicate frequency in specific contexts, for example, "chaque jour" (every day). These phrases usually come at the beginning or end of a sentence.

Adverb of Frequency (French)	Pronunciation	Translation (English)
Toujours	too-zhoor	Always
Souvent	soo-vahn	Often
Parfois	par-fwa	Sometimes
Rarement	rah-mahn	Rarely
Jamais	zhah-meh	Never
De temps en temps	duh tahnz ahn tahn	From time to time

Tous les jours	too lay zhoor	Every day
Une fois par semaine	uhn fwa par suh-men	Once a week
Quelquefois	kel-kuh-fwa	Occasionally
Presque toujours	presk too-zhoor	Almost always

Reflexive Verbs

Reflexive verbs are an important part of French grammar, used to indicate that the subject of a sentence is performing an action on itself. So they're commonly used in French to talk about daily routines

In French, reflexive verbs are constructed with a reflexive pronoun (me, te, se, nous, vous, se) that matches the subject of the sentence. For example, "se laver" means "to wash oneself," where "se" is the reflexive pronoun.

Reflexive verbs are easily identified by the "se" or "s'" before the infinitive form of the verb.

Remember that some verbs are reflexive in French for idiomatic reasons or to convey a particular nuance. For example, "s'en aller" means "to go away," and "s'ennuyer" means "to get bored." These verbs are considered pronominal verbs because they require reflexive pronouns but may not necessarily mean that the action is being performed on oneself.

Subject Pronoun (French)	Reflexive Pronoun	Verb (Infinitive Form)	Translation (English)
Je (I)	me (m')	se laver	to wash oneself
Tu (You - singular informal)	te (t')	se réveiller	to wake up
Il/Elle/On (He/She/One)	se (s')	se coucher	to go to bed
Nous (We)	nous	se brosser	to brush (e.g., one's hair, teeth)

Vous (You - singular formal or plural)	vous	s'habiller	to get dressed
Ils/Elles (They - masculine/feminine)	se (s')	s'amuser	to have fun

Present Indicative of Irregular Verbs

The present indicative tense in French is used to express actions that are currently happening, habitual actions, or general truths. While regular verbs follow predictable conjugation patterns (such as -er, -ir, or -re endings), irregular verbs must be memorized.

Some of the most frequently used irregular verbs in French include "être" (to be), "avoir" (to have), "aller" (to go), and "faire" (to do/make), "pouvoir" (to be able to/can), "vouloir" (to want), "venir" (to come), and "prendre" (to take).

Talking About Habits

The present indicative in French is equivalent to the simple present tense in English and is commonly used to talk about daily routines, personal habits, and general truths.

To express habits in French, adverbs of frequency are often used alongside verbs to indicate how often something happens.

Common adverbs of frequency include "toujours" (always), "souvent" (often), "parfois" (sometimes), "rarement" (rarely), and "jamais" (never). These adverbs are typically placed after the verb in French sentences. For example, "Il mange toujours des fruits le matin" translates to "He always eats fruits in the morning."

Examples:

1. "Je me lève tôt tous les jours."

    - Translation: "I wake up early every day."
    - This sentence uses the reflexive verb "se lever" in the present indicative to describe a daily habit.

2. "Elle lit un livre chaque soir avant de dormir."

    - Translation: "She reads a book every evening before sleeping."
    - The verb "lit" (reads) is in the present indicative, and "chaque soir" (every evening) indicates the frequency of the habit.

3. "Nous allons au marché le samedi."

    - Translation: "We go to the market on Saturdays."
    - Here, the verb "allons" (go) in the present indicative is used to express a habitual action.

4. "Ils prennent toujours le bus pour aller au travail."

- Translation: "They always take the bus to go to work."
- The verb "prennent" (take) is in the present indicative, and the adverb "toujours" (always) emphasizes the habitual nature of the action.

By using the present indicative along with frequency adverbs, French speakers can clearly communicate habits and routines.

Practice What We've Learned

Indirect Object (French)	Negation	Pronoun	Verb (Infinitive Form)	Quantifier	Direct Object (French)	Translation (English)
à lui (to him)	ne... pas	Il	donner (to give)	beaucoup de	livres (books)	He does not give him many books.
à elle (to her)	ne... jamais	Elle	envoyer (to send)	aucun	message (message)	She never sends her any messages.
à nous (to us)	ne... rien	Nous	montrer (to show)	plusieurs	photos (photos)	We do not show us any photos.
à eux (to them - masculine)	ne... plus	Ils	prêter (to lend)	beaucoup de	vêtements (clothes)	They no longer lend them many clothes.
à vous (to you - formal)	ne... jamais	Vous	dire (to tell)	quelques	histoires (stories)	You never tell you any stories.
à moi (to me)	ne... pas	Je	donner (to give)	un peu de	conseils (advice)	I do not give me a little advice.

à elle (to her)	ne... jamais	On	vendre (to sell)	assez de	produits (products)	We never sell her enough products.
à nous (to us)	ne... jamais	Nous	écrire (to write)	beaucoup de	lettres (letters)	We never write many letters.
à toi (to you - informal)	ne... rien	Tu	montrer (to show)	plusieurs	films (movies)	You do not show you any movies.
à eux (to them - masculine)	ne... plus	Ils	donner (to give)	trop de	informations (information)	They no longer give them too much information.

Exercises

1. Which adverb of frequency in French means "never?"

    a) Toujours
    b) Souvent
    c) Jamais
    d) Parfois

2. What is the correct placement of the adverb "souvent" in the French sentence "Elle ____ mange des légumes?"

    a) Elle mange souvent des légumes
    b) Elle souvent mange des légumes
    c) Souvent elle mange des légumes
    d) Elle mange des légumes souvent

3. Which reflexive pronoun is used with the subject pronoun "nous" in French?

    a) se
    b) vous
    c) nous
    d) te

4. How do you say "to wake up" using a reflexive verb in French?

    a) se laver
    b) se coucher
    c) se réveiller
    d) se brosser

5. What is the present indicative conjugation of the irregular verb "avoir" for "nous?"

    a) Nous sommes
    b) Nous allons
    c) Nous avons
    d) Nous faisons

6. Which sentence correctly uses the present indicative to talk about a habit in French?

    a) Je mange le déjeuner parfois
    b) Je parfois mange le déjeuner
    c) Je mange parfois le déjeuner
    d) Parfois je le déjeuner mange

7. Which reflexive verb form correctly completes the sentence: "Ils ____ habillent le matin?"

    a) se
    b) nous

c) vous
d) te

8. What is the English translation for the reflexive verb "s'amuser?"

    a) To wake up
    b) To have fun
    c) To go to bed
    d) To brush

9. How would you translate the phrase "once a week" to French?

    a) Tous les jours
    b) Une fois par semaine
    c) De temps en temps
    d) Tous les mois

10. Which verb is NOT an irregular verb in the present indicative in French?

    a) Être
    b) Avoir
    c) Parler
    d) Aller

Answer Key

1. c) Jamais

2. a) Elle mange souvent des légumes

3. c) nous

4. c) se réveiller

5. c) Nous avons

6. c) Je mange parfois le déjeuner

7. a) se

8. b) To have fun

9. b) Une fois par semaine

10. c) Parler

Chapter 8: Let's Grab A Bite

Le plaisir de la table est de toutes les conditions et de tous les âges, de toutes les contrées et de tous les jours.

- Jean Anthelme Brillat-Savarin

In this chapter, we'll explore various phrases that could come in handy when you're at a restaurant in France.

Useful Phrases At a Restaurant

Before Sitting Down

1. "Bonjour, avez-vous une table pour deux, s'il vous plaît?"

  - Pronunciation: bohn-zhoor, ah-vay voo uhn tab-luh poor duh, seel voo pleh
  - Translation: "Hello, do you have a table for two, please?"

2. "Je voudrais réserver une table, s'il vous plaît."

  - Pronunciation: zhuh voo-dreh reh-zair-vay uhn tab-luh, seel voo pleh
  - Translation: "I would like to reserve a table, please."

3. "Pour combien de personnes?"

  - Pronunciation:poor kohm-byen duh pair-son
  - Translation: "For how many people?"

4. "Est-ce que je peux avoir la carte, s'il vous plaît?"

  - Pronunciation: es kuh zhuh puh av-wahr lah kart, seel voo pleh
  - Translation: "Can I have the menu, please?"

5. "Avez-vous des places à l'intérieur ou en terrasse?"

  - Pronunciation: ah-vay voo duh plass ah l'an-teh-ryeur oo ahn teh-ras
  - Translation: "Do you have seats inside or on the terrace?"

6. "Pouvons-nous avoir une table près de la fenêtre?"

  - Pronunciation: poo-vohn noo av-wahr uhn tab-luh pray duh lah fuh-netr

- Translation: "Can we have a table near the window?"

7. "Y a-t-il un temps d'attente?"

   - Pronunciation: ee ya teel an tahn dah-tahnt
   - Translation: "Is there a waiting time?"

The Menu

1. "Qu'est-ce que vous recommandez?"

   - Pronunciation: kes kuh voo ruh-ko-mahn-day
   - Translation: "What do you recommend?"

2. "Quels sont les plats du jour?"

   - Pronunciation: kel sohn lay plah dew zhoor
   - Translation: "What are the daily specials?"

3. "Est-ce que ce plat est végétarien?"

   - Pronunciation: es kuh suh plah eh vay-zhay-tar-yen
   - Translation: "Is this dish vegetarian?"

4. "Avez-vous des options sans gluten?"

   - Pronunciation: ah-vay voo dez op-syon sahn glee-ten
   - Translation: "Do you have gluten-free options?"

5. "Pouvez-vous m'expliquer ce qu'est ce plat?"

   - Pronunciation: poo-vay voo mek-splee-kay suh keh suh plah
   - Translation: "Can you explain what this dish is?"

6. "Le plat est-il épicé?"

   - Pronunciation: luh plah ay-teel eh-pee-say
   - Translation: "Is the dish spicy?"

7. "Y a-t-il des plats sans viande?"

   - Pronunciation: ee ya teel duh plah sahn vyahnd
   - Translation: "Are there any dishes without meat?"

Asking About the Dishes

1. "Quels sont les ingrédients principaux de ce plat?"

   - Pronunciation: kel sohn lez an-gray-dee-yan prahn-see-po duh suh plah
   - Translation: "What are the main ingredients in this dish?"

2. "Ce plat contient-il des produits laitiers?"

- Pronunciation: suh plah kohn-tyen teel duh pro-dwee lay-tyay
- Translation: "Does this dish contain dairy products?"

3. "Est-ce que le poisson est frais?"

- Pronunciation: es kuh luh pwah-sohn eh freh
- Translation: "Is the fish fresh?"

4. "Comment est cuisiné ce plat?"

- Pronunciation: koh-mahn eh kwee-zee-nay suh plah
- Translation: "How is this dish prepared?"

5. "Le poulet est-il grillé ou frit?"

- Pronunciation: luh poo-lay ay-teel gree-yay oo free
- Translation: "Is the chicken grilled or fried?"

6. "Ce plat est-il servi avec un accompagnement?"

- Pronunciation: suh plah ay-teel sair-vee ah-vek en ah-kon-pa-nye-mahn
- Translation: "Is this dish served with a side?"

7. "Est-ce que ce plat est épicé?"

- Pronunciation: es kuh suh plah eh eh-pee-say
- Translation: "Is this dish spicy?"

Ordering

1. "Je voudrais..."

- Pronunciation: zhuh voo-dray
- Translation: "I would like..."

2. "Je prendrai..."

- Pronunciation: zhuh prahn-dray
- Translation: "I will have..."

3. "Pourriez-vous me donner..."

- Pronunciation: poor zhyuh voo muh doh-nay
- Translation: "Could you give me..."

4. "Nous aimerions commander maintenant."

- Pronunciation: noo zay-muh-ryon koh-mahn-day meht-nahn
- Translation: "We would like to order now."

5. "Est-ce que je peux avoir..."

- Pronunciation: es kuh zhuh puh av-wahr
- Translation: "Can I have..."

6. "Je vais prendre le menu du jour."

- Pronunciation: zhuh veh prahndruh luh muh-nyoo dy zhoor
- Translation: "I'll take the daily special."

7. "Pour commencer, je voudrais..."

- Pronunciation: poor koh-mahn-say, zhuh voo-dray
- Translation: "To start, I would like..."

Before You Leave

1. "L'addition, s'il vous plaît."

- Pronunciation: lah dee-syon, seel voo pleh
- Translation: "The bill, please."

2. "Est-ce que je peux payer par carte?"

- Pronunciation: es kuh zhuh puh pay-yay par kart
- Translation: "Can I pay by card?"

3. "Est-ce que le service est compris?"

- Pronunciation: es kuh luh sair-vees eh kohn-pree
- Translation: "Is the service included?"

4. "Pouvez-vous nous apporter l'addition?"

- Pronunciation: poo-vay voo noo zah-por-tay lah dee-syon
- Translation: "Can you bring us the bill?"

5. "Je voudrais laisser un pourboire."

- Pronunciation: zhuh voo-dray lay-say un poor-bwar
- Translation: "I would like to leave a tip."

6. "C'était délicieux, merci beaucoup !"

- Pronunciation: seh-teh deh-lee-syu, mehr-see boh-koo
- Translation: "It was delicious, thank you very much!"

7. "Nous reviendrons bientôt."

- Pronunciation: noo ruh-vyen-drohn byan-toh
- Translation: "We will come back soon."

Food, Meals, and Useful Words

Category	French	Pronunciation	Translation (English)
Food	Le pain	luh pan	Bread
	Le fromage	luh froh-mahzh	Cheese
	Les fruits	lay frwee	Fruits
	Les légumes	lay luh-geem	Vegetables
	Le poulet	luh poo-lay	Chicken
	Le poisson	luh pwah-sohn	Fish
	Le riz	luh ree	Rice
	Le bœuf	luh buhf	Beef
Meals	Le petit déjeuner	luh puh-tee day-zhuh-nay	Breakfast
	Le déjeuner	luh day-zhuh-nay	Lunch
	Le dîner	luh dee-nay	Dinner
	Le goûter	luh goo-tay	Afternoon snack
	Le dessert	luh day-sair	Dessert
Useful Words	Une boisson	uhn bwa-sohn	A drink
	L'eau	loh	Water
	Un verre	un vair	A glass
	Une assiette	uhn ah-syet	A plate

	Une fourchette	uhn foor-shet	A fork
	Un couteau	un koo-toh	A knife

Aussi and Non Plus

Aussi and non plus are two important words in French used to express agreement.

"Aussi" means "also" or "too" and is used to agree with a positive statement. For example, if someone says "J'aime le chocolat" (I like chocolate), you can reply with "Moi aussi" (Me too).

On the other hand, "non plus" means "neither" and is used to agree with a negative statement. If someone says "Je n'aime pas le café" (I don't like coffee), you would reply with "Moi non plus" (Me neither).

Comparatives and Superlatives

Comparative

Comparatives in French are used to compare two people, things, or ideas, indicating that one has more, less, or the same degree of a certain quality than the other.

There are three main types of comparatives in French: superiority, inferiority, and equality. These are constructed using the phrases "plus... que" (more... than), "moins... que" (less... than), and "aussi... que" (as... as), respectively. The adjective must agree in gender and number with the noun it describes, and the placement of these comparative phrases depends on whether they are modifying an adjective, adverb, or noun.

Examples of Comparatives in French:

1. Superiority (more than):

- "Marie est plus intelligente que Paul."
- Translation: "Marie is more intelligent than Paul."
- Here, "plus intelligente que" indicates that Marie is more intelligent in comparison to Paul. Note the agreement of the adjective "intelligente" with the feminine noun "Marie."

2. Inferiority (less than):

- "Ce film est moins intéressant que l'autre."
- Translation: "This movie is less interesting than the other one."
- "Moins intéressant que" shows that the movie being referred to is less interesting in comparison to another movie.

3. Equality (as... as):

- "Mon chien est aussi grand que le tien."
- Translation: "My dog is as big as yours."
- The phrase "aussi grand que" is used to express that both dogs are of the same size.

When comparing quantities, the construction changes slightly. For example, to say "more apples than" in French, you would say "plus de pommes que"; similarly, "moins de pommes que" means "fewer apples than," and "autant de pommes que" means "as many apples as."

Superlative

Superlatives in French are used to express the highest or lowest degree of a quality within a group. Just like in English, French superlatives are formed by combining the definite article (le, la, les) with "plus" (most) or "moins" (least), followed by an adjective or adverb.

The adjective in a superlative must agree in gender and number with the noun it describes. Additionally, the construction "le plus de" or "le moins de" is used to indicate the most or least amount of something when referring to nouns.

Examples of Superlatives in French:

1. Superlative of Superiority (most):

- "C'est le plus beau tableau du musée."
- Translation: "It is the most beautiful painting in the museum."
- Here, "le plus beau" is the superlative form, with "beau" agreeing in gender (masculine) with the noun "tableau."

2. Superlative of Inferiority (least):

- "Elle est la moins intéressée de la classe."
- Translation: "She is the least interested in the class."
- In this example, "la moins intéressée" is the superlative form, with "intéressée" agreeing in gender (feminine) and number (singular) with "elle."

3. Superlative with Plural Nouns:

- "Ce sont les étudiants les plus intelligents de l'école."
- Translation: "They are the most intelligent students in the school."
- The phrase "les plus intelligents" is the superlative, with "intelligents" agreeing in gender (masculine) and number (plural) with "les étudiants."

4. Superlative of Quantity (the most/the least of):

- "Il a le plus de livres."
- Translation: "He has the most books."

- "Elle a le moins de devoirs."

- Translation: "She has the least homework."

- Here, "le plus de" and "le moins de" are used to express the highest and lowest amounts of something.

Just like English, French has irregular superlatives, such as "le meilleur" (the best) for "bon" (good) and "le pire" (the worst) for "mauvais" (bad).

Adjectives to Describe Food

Let's take a look some adjectives you can use to describe food!

Adjective (French)	Pronunciation	Translation (English)
Délicieux	deh-lee-syoh	Delicious (masculine)
Délicieuse	deh-lee-syohz	Delicious (feminine)
Épicé	eh-pee-seh	Spicy (masculine)
Épicée	eh-pee-seh	Spicy (feminine)
Sucré	syu-kreh	Sweet (masculine)
Sucrée	syu-kreh	Sweet (feminine)
Salé	sah-leh	Salty (masculine)
Salée	sah-leh	Salty (feminine)
Amer	ah-mehr	Bitter (masculine)
Amère	ah-mehr	Bitter (feminine)
Frais	freh	Fresh (masculine)
Fraîche	fresh	Fresh (feminine)

Gras	grah	Fatty, Greasy (masculine)
Grasse	gras	Fatty, Greasy (feminine)
Acide	ah-seed	Sour
Moelleux	mwah-leu	Soft, Moist (masculine)
Moelleuse	mwah-leuz	Soft, Moist (feminine)
Croustillant	kroo-stee-yahn	Crunchy (masculine)
Croustillante	kroo-stee-yahnt	Crunchy (feminine)

Quantifiers

The final topic we'll cover in this chapter is quantifiers and how they can be used with food. As we've seen in a previous chapter, quantifiers vary based on the gender and number of the noun they quantify and always come before the noun.

Quantifier (French)	Pronunciation	Translation (English)
Beaucoup de	boh-kooh duh	A lot of, Much, Many
Un peu de	uh(n) puh duh	A little, A bit of
Trop de	troh duh	Too much, Too many
Assez de	ah-sey duh	Enough
Peu de	puh duh	Few, Little
Plusieurs	plee-zyuhr	Several
Quelques	kel-kuh	Some, A few
Aucun(e) de	oh-kuhn duh	None of

Tant de	tahn duh	So much, So many
Moins de	mwehn duh	Less, Fewer

Exercises

1. What is the French word for "Bread?"

   a) Le fromage
   b) Le pain
   c) Le poisson
   d) Le riz

2. Which French quantifier means "A little, A bit of?"

   a) Beaucoup de
   b) Un peu de
   c) Trop de
   d) Assez de

3. How do you say "Afternoon snack" in French?

   a) Le déjeuner
   b) Le dîner
   c) Le goûter
   d) Le dessert

4. What is the correct translation for "Elle a le moins de devoirs?"

   a) She has the most books.
   b) She has the least homework.
   c) She has some stories.
   d) She has more time.

5. What does the phrase "Moi non plus" mean?

   a) Me too
   b) I don't know
   c) Me neither
   d) Also me

6. Which adjective would you use in French to describe something "Soft, Moist" in the masculine form?

   a) Moelleuse
   b) Moelleux
   c) Croustillant
   d) Épicé

7. Which comparative form is used to express "as... as" in French?

   a) Plus... que
   b) Moins... que

c) Aussi... que
d) Autant... que

8. How would you express "Several" in French using a quantifier?

   a) Quelques
   b) Beaucoup de
   c) Plusieurs
   d) Trop de

9. What is the French superlative phrase for "the most beautiful?"

   a) Le plus beau
   b) Le moins beau
   c) Le meilleur
   d) Le pire

10. What is the French equivalent of the sentence "I do not give me a little advice?"

    a) Je ne donne pas beaucoup de conseils.
    b) Je ne donne pas un peu de conseils.
    c) Je ne donne jamais de conseils.
    d) Je ne prête pas de conseils.

Answer Key

1. b) Le pain

2. b) Un peu de

3. c) Le goûter

4. b) She has the least homework.

5. c) Me neither

6. b) Moelleux

7. c) Aussi... que

8. c) Plusieurs

9. a) Le plus beau

10. b) Je ne donne pas un peu de conseils.

Chapter 9: Can You Do It?

"Ce qui importe, ce n'est pas de voler, mais d'apprendre à se tenir debout."

- Antoine de Saint-Exupéry

In this chapter, we will learn how to discuss skills and the things you are capable of doing.

Talking About Abilities

Pronoun (French)	Savoir (to know)	Pouvoir (to be able to/can)
Je (I)	Je sais	Je peux
Tu (You - informal)	Tu sais	Tu peux
Il/Elle/On (He/She/One)	Il/Elle/On sait	Il/Elle/On peut
Nous (We)	Nous savons	Nous pouvons
Vous (You - formal/plural)	Vous savez	Vous pouvez
Ils/Elles (They - masculine/feminine)	Ils/Elles savent	Ils/Elles peuvent

Pronoun (French)	Savoir (to know) - Sentence Example	Pouvoir (to be able to/can) - Sentence Example
Je (I)	Je sais cuisiner des plats délicieux. (I know how to cook delicious dishes.)	Je peux venir à la fête ce soir. (I can come to the party tonight.)

Tu (You - informal)	Tu sais parler plusieurs langues. (You know how to speak several languages.)	Tu peux m'aider avec mes devoirs? (Can you help me with my homework?)
Il/Elle/On (He/She/One)	Il sait jouer de la guitare. (He knows how to play the guitar.)	Elle peut conduire une voiture. (She can drive a car.)
Nous (We)	Nous savons comment résoudre ce problème. (We know how to solve this problem.)	Nous pouvons voyager en France cet été. (We can travel to France this summer.)
Vous (You - formal/plural)	Vous savez où se trouve la bibliothèque. (You know where the library is.)	Vous pouvez réserver une table pour deux. (You can reserve a table for two.)
Ils/Elles (They - masculine/feminine)	Ils savent que c'est important de pratiquer tous les jours. (They know it's important to practice every day.)	Elles peuvent participer au concours de danse. (They can participate in the dance competition.)

Adverbs To Grade Our Abilities

Adverb (French)	Pronunciation	Translation (English)
Très bien	treh byeh	Very well/good
Assez bien	ah-seh byeh	Quite well/good, Fairly well/good
Plutôt bien	ploo-toh byeh	Rather well
Mal	mal	Badly, Poorly
Très mal	treh mal	Very badly
Couramment	koo-rah-mahn	Fluently

Parfaitement	par-fet-mahn	Perfectly
Un peu	uhn puh	A little
Moyennement	mwah-yen-mahn	Moderately
Pas du tout	pah dew too	Not at all

Talking About Abilities With *Etre*

In French, "être" (to be) is often used to describe abilities or capabilities. When using "être" to talk about abilities, it is typically followed by an adjective or an expression that describes the ability.

Common phrases using "être" to talk about abilities include "être capable de" (to be capable of), "être bon(ne) en" (to be good at), and "être fort(e) en" (to be strong in). These expressions can be followed by either a noun or an infinitive verb, depending on the context.

Examples:

1. "Il est capable de parler trois langues."

- Translation: "He is capable of speaking three languages."
- Here, "être capable de" is used to express someone's ability to do something (speak three languages).

2. "Elle est bonne en mathématiques."

- Translation: "She is good at mathematics."
- In this example, "être bon(ne) en" is used with a noun to indicate someone's skill or strength in a particular subject.

3. "Nous sommes forts en cuisine."

- Translation: "We are strong in cooking."
- "Être fort(e) en" is another way to describe someone's strength or proficiency in an activity, in this case, cooking.

4. "Je suis doué(e) pour le dessin."

- Translation: "I am gifted at drawing."
- "Être doué(e) pour" is another expression using "être" to describe someone's talent or aptitude in a particular area.

Talking AboutAbilities

Ability (French)	Pronunciation	Translation (English)
Être capable de	ehtr ka-pabl duh	To be capable of
Savoir danser	sa-vwar dan-say	To know how to dance
Pouvoir cuisiner	poo-vwar kwee-zee-nay	To be able to cook
Être bon(ne) en maths	ehtr bon ahn maths	To be good at math
Être fort(e) en sport	ehtr for ahn spor	To be strong in sports
Jouer du piano	jweh dew pya-no	To play the piano
Parler couramment l'anglais	par-lay koo-rah-mahn l'ahn-glay	To speak English fluently
Lire rapidement	leer ra-pee-duh-mahn	To read quickly
Dessiner parfaitement	deh-see-nay par-fet-mahn	To draw perfectly
Écrire sans fautes	eh-kreer san fot	To write without mistakes

Direct Object Pronouns

Direct object pronouns in French are used to replace a noun that is the direct object, the receiver, of a verb in a sentence. In French, using direct object pronouns helps to avoid repetition and makes sentences more concise and fluid. These pronouns must agree in gender and number with the noun they replace.

The French direct object pronouns are:

- me (m') - me
- te (t') - you (informal)
- le (l') - him/it (masculine singular)
- la (l') - her/it (feminine singular)

- nous - us
- vous - you (formal or plural)
- les - them (masculine or feminine plural)

Direct object pronouns in French are placed before the conjugated verb.

For example:

1. Je mange la pomme. (I eat the apple.)

   → Je la mange. (I eat it.)

2. Il regarde le film. (He watches the movie.)

   → Il le regarde. (He watches it.)

When there is an infinitive verb in a sentence, the direct object pronoun is placed before the infinitive:

3. Elle va lire le livre. (She is going to read the book.)

   → Elle va le lire. (She is going to read it.)

In negative sentences, the direct object pronoun is placed between "ne" and the conjugated verb:

4. Je ne vois pas Marie. (I do not see Marie.)

   → Je ne la vois pas. (I do not see her.)

Examples with Multiple Pronouns:

In sentences with both a direct and an indirect object pronoun, the direct object pronoun comes after the indirect object pronoun:

5. Je donne le livre à Marie. (I give the book to Marie.)

   → Je le lui donne. (I give it to her.)

Ability Adjectives

Mode + Number	Masculine (French)	Feminine (French)	Translation (English)
Singular Adjective	Petit	Petite	Small
	Heureux	Heureuse	Happy
	Doux	Douce	Sweet

	Intelligent	Intelligente	Intelligent
Plural Adjective	Grands	Grandes	Tall, Big
	Vieux	Vieilles	Old
Singular Noun	Un ami	Une amie	A friend
	Un étudiant	Une étudiante	A student
	Le directeur	La directrice	The director
Plural Noun	Des chats	Des chattes	Cats
	Les frères	Les sœurs	The brothers, The sisters
	Des voisins	Des voisines	Neighbors

Exercises

1. What is the correct conjugation of "savoir" (to know) for the pronoun "Nous" (We) in French?

   a) Nous sais
   b) Nous savons
   c) Nous savez
   d) Nous pouvez

2. Which sentence correctly uses "pouvoir" (to be able to/can) with the pronoun "Vous" (You - formal/plural)?

   a) Vous pouvez réserver une table pour deux.
   b) Vous pouvez cuisiner très bien.
   c) Vous savez cuisiner très bien.
   d) Vous savez réserver une table pour deux.

3. What is the French translation for "I know how to speak several languages?"

   a) Je sais parler plusieurs langues.
   b) Tu sais parler plusieurs langues.
   c) Ils savent parler plusieurs langues.
   d) Je peux parler plusieurs langues.

4. Which adverb in French means "Fluently?"

   a) Très bien
   b) Moyennement
   c) Couramment
   d) Parfaitement

5. What is the French expression to describe someone who is "good at math?"

   a) Être fort(e) en sport
   b) Être bon(ne) en maths
   c) Être capable de
   d) Savoir cuisiner

6. What is the direct object pronoun for "them" (masculine or feminine plural) in French?

   a) Le
   b) La
   c) Les
   d) Nous

7. Which sentence is correctly rewritten with the direct object pronoun? "Il regarde le film."

   a) Il la regarde.
   b) Il les regarde.

c) Il le regarde.

d) Il lui regarde.

8. Which adjective is the correct masculine form of "intelligent" in French?

a) Intelligente

b) Intelligent

c) Douce

d) Doux

9. How do you say "They are strong in sports" in French?

a) Ils sont forts en maths.

b) Elles peuvent jouer au sport.

c) Ils sont forts en sport.

d) Elles savent faire du sport.

10. Which French phrase means "I am gifted at drawing?"

a) Je suis doué(e) pour le dessin.

b) Je peux dessiner parfaitement.

c) Je sais dessiner très bien.

d) Je peux écrire sans fautes.

Answer Key

1. a) Vous pouvez réserver une table pour deux.

2. a) Je sais parler plusieurs langues.

3. c) Couramment

4. c) Couramment

5. b) Être bon(ne) en maths

6. c) Les

7. c) Il le regarde.

8. b) Intelligent

9. c) Ils sont forts en sport.

10. a) Je suis doué(e) pour le dessin.

Chapter 10: Other Uses of the Present Indicative

"L'existence précède l'essence."

- Jean-Paul Sartre.

In this chapter, we will explore some uses of the present indicative, like how to use the present tense to talk about future events, express the progressive tense, and discuss duration and reasons.

The Present to Talk About the Future

In French, the present indicative tense is often used to express future events, especially when referring to actions that are planned or scheduled to happen soon. This usage is similar to how the present continuous is used in English to talk about the future, such as in the sentence "I am meeting him tomorrow."

When using the present tense to talk about the future, it is common to use time expressions such as "demain" (tomorrow), "ce soir" (this evening), "la semaine prochaine" (next week), or "bientôt" (soon) to clarify that the action is set in the future. This method is particularly useful for informal conversation or when discussing events that are imminent or part of a scheduled plan.

Examples:

1. "Je vais au cinéma demain."

   - Translation: "I am going to the cinema tomorrow."
   - Here, the present tense "vais" (go) is used with "demain" (tomorrow) to indicate a future action.

2. "Nous partons en vacances la semaine prochaine."

   - Translation: "We are leaving on vacation next week."
   - The present tense "partons" (leave) is paired with "la semaine prochaine" (next week) to refer to a future event.

3. "Il arrive ce soir."

   - Translation: "He is arriving this evening."

- In this sentence, "arrive" (arrives) in the present tense is combined with "ce soir" (this evening) to express a future action.

4. "Ils se marient bientôt."

- Translation: "They are getting married soon."
- Here, "se marient" (get married) is in the present tense, while "bientôt" (soon) indicates that the action is in the near future.

The Present Progressive

The present progressive tense does not exist in French as a distinct grammatical tense. Instead, French uses the present indicative to express ongoing actions, often with context clues or additional phrases to indicate that the action is happening "right now."

To convey the present progressive meaning more precisely, French speakers often use the construction "être en train de" + infinitive verb. This phrase literally translates to "to be in the process of" and is the closest equivalent to the English "-ing" form to indicate an action in progress.

Examples:

1. Using the Present Indicative for Progressive Actions:

- "Je mange."
- Translation: "I am eating."
- Although this is the simple present tense in French, it can mean "I eat" or "I am eating" depending on context.

2. Using "Être en train de" for Emphasis:

- "Je suis en train de manger."
- Translation: "I am eating (right now)."
- This construction makes it clear that the action is taking place at the moment.

3. Other Examples of "Être en train de":

- "Elle est en train de lire un livre."
- Translation: "She is reading a book (right now)."
- Here, "est en train de lire" emphasizes the ongoing nature of the action.
- "Nous sommes en train de regarder un film."
- Translation: "We are watching a movie (right now)."
- Again, the phrase "sommes en train de" is used to indicate that the action is currently happening.

4. For Negative Form:

- "Je ne suis pas en train de travailler."
- Translation: "I am not working (right now)."

- The negative form is constructed by placing "ne" before the conjugated verb "suis" and "pas" after it.

Pronoun (French)	Present Simple (French)	Present Continuous (French)	Translation (English)
Je (I)	Je lis.	Je suis en train de lire.	I read. / I am reading (right now).
Tu (You - informal)	Tu manges.	Tu es en train de manger.	You eat. / You are eating (right now).
Il/Elle/On (He/She/One)	Il travaille.	Il est en train de travailler.	He works. / He is working (right now).
Nous (We)	Nous regardons la télé.	Nous sommes en train de regarder la télé.	We watch TV. / We are watching TV (right now).
Vous (You - formal/plural)	Vous écoutez de la musique.	Vous êtes en train d'écouter de la musique.	You listen to music. / You are listening to music (right now).
Ils/Elles (They - masculine/feminine)	Elles parlent.	Elles sont en train de parler.	They talk. / They are talking (right now).

Talking About Duration

In French, talking about how long something has been happening or will happen requires specific expressions and phrase constructions.

1. Using "depuis" (since, for)

The word "depuis" is commonly used to talk about an action that started in the past and is still continuing in the present. This is similar to the English use of "since" or "for."

- "Depuis" + a specific point in time: indicates when an action started (e.g., "since 2020").
- "Depuis" + a duration of time: indicates how long an action has been happening (e.g., "for three years").

Examples:

- "Je vis à Paris depuis 2015."

- Translation: "I have been living in Paris since 2015."
- "Elle étudie le français depuis deux ans."
- Translation: "She has been studying French for two years."

2. Using "il y a... que," "ça fait... que," and "voilà... que"

These three expressions can all be used to indicate that an action has been ongoing for a certain amount of time. They are often used interchangeably in spoken French, although "il y a... que" is more common.

Examples:

- "Il y a trois heures que je travaille."
- Translation: "I have been working for three hours."
- "Ça fait cinq ans qu'ils sont mariés."
- Translation: "They have been married for five years."
- "Voilà un mois que je suis en France."
- Translation: "I have been in France for a month."

3. Using "pendant" (during, for)

"Pendant" is used to describe the entire duration of an action that has been completed or that will happen in the future. It is similar to the English "for."

Examples:

- "J'ai dormi pendant huit heures."
- Translation: "I slept for eight hours."
- "Nous partirons en vacances pendant deux semaines."
- Translation: "We will go on vacation for two weeks."

4. Using "pour" (for) with the Future

"Pour" is often used to express the duration of a future action, particularly in planned activities.

Examples:

- "Je vais rester à Lyon pour trois jours."
- Translation: "I am going to stay in Lyon for three days."
- "Ils partiront en mission pour un mois."
- Translation: "They will go on a mission for a month."

5. Using "en" (in)

"En" is used to indicate the amount of time it takes to complete an action. This is the equivalent of "in" in English.

Examples:

- "J'ai fini mes devoirs en deux heures."

- Translation: "I finished my homework in two hours."
- "Il peut courir 10 kilomètres en une heure."
- Translation: "He can run 10 kilometers in an hour."

Talking About Motives and Motivation

In French, discussing motives and motivation involves using specific expressions and phrase structures.

1. Using "parce que" (because)

"Parce que" is the most common way to express a reason or motive in French. It is used to answer the question "Pourquoi?" (Why?). The phrase introduces a clause that explains why an action is being done.

Examples:

- "Je fais du sport parce que je veux rester en forme."
- Translation: "I exercise because I want to stay in shape."
- "Ils apprennent le français parce que c'est utile pour leur travail."
- Translation: "They are learning French because it is useful for their job."

2. Using "pour" + Infinitive (to, in order to)

"Pour" followed by an infinitive verb is used to express the purpose or goal of an action. It translates to "to" or "in order to" in English and provides a concise way to explain motives.

Examples:

- "Je travaille dur pour réussir mes examens."
- Translation: "I work hard to pass my exams."
- "Nous voyageons pour découvrir de nouvelles cultures."
- Translation: "We travel to discover new cultures."

3. Using "afin de" + Infinitive (in order to)

Similar to "pour," "afin de" is a more formal way to express purpose or intent. It is often used in written or formal contexts to indicate a more deliberate action.

Examples:

- "Elle économise de l'argent afin d'acheter une maison."
- Translation: "She is saving money in order to buy a house."
- "Il a pris des cours supplémentaires afin d'améliorer ses compétences."
- Translation: "He took extra classes in order to improve his skills."

4. Using "grâce à" (thanks to) and "à cause de" (because of, due to)

These expressions are used to discuss motives that are positive ("grâce à") or negative ("à cause de"). They are often followed by a noun or pronoun.

Examples:

- "J'ai réussi grâce à ton soutien."
- Translation: "I succeeded thanks to your support."
- "Ils sont en retard à cause du trafic."
- Translation: "They are late because of the traffic."

5. Using "motivés par" (motivated by)

"Motivés par" is specifically used to express what drives someone to act. It is often followed by a noun or a phrase that explains the source of the described motivation.

Examples:

- "Ils sont motivés par le désir de réussir."
- Translation: "They are motivated by the desire to succeed."
- "Je suis motivé par ma passion pour l'art."
- Translation: "I am motivated by my passion for art."

6. Using "pour que" + Subjunctive (so that)

"Pour que" is used when the motive or reason involves a different subject, requiring the use of the subjunctive mood. It translates to "so that" in English and is used to express purpose.

Examples:

- "Je t'aide pour que tu puisses finir à temps."
- Translation: "I help you so that you can finish on time."
- "Il a étudié tard pour que son projet soit parfait."
- Translation: "He studied late so that his project would be perfect."

Exercises

1. Which construction is used in French to emphasize an action happening right now?

    a) être en avance de
    b) être en train de
    c) être sur le point de
    d) être en mouvement de

2. What is the French translation of "I am eating (right now)" using the present continuous?

    a) Je mange.
    b) Je suis en train de manger.
    c) Je mange maintenant.
    d) Je vais manger.

3. Which phrase is used in French to indicate how long an action has been happening and is still ongoing?

    a) Pour
    b) Pendant
    c) Depuis
    d) En

4. What does "Ça fait cinq ans qu'ils sont mariés" mean?

    a) They got married five years ago.
    b) They will get married in five years.
    c) They have been married for five years.
    d) They are married since five years.

5. Which expression would you use to talk about a future action's duration in French?

    a) Pour
    b) Depuis
    c) Pendant
    d) En

6. How would you express "She is reading a book (right now)" in French?

    a) Elle lit un livre.
    b) Elle va lire un livre.
    c) Elle est en train de lire un livre.
    d) Elle lit le livre.

7. Which of the following phrases is NOT used to talk about motives in French?

    a) Pour que
    b) Grâce à

c) À cause de

d) Avant de

8. What is the meaning of "Je vis à Paris depuis 2015?"

a) I lived in Paris in 2015.

b) I have been living in Paris since 2015.

c) I am going to live in Paris in 2015.

d) I was living in Paris for three years.

9. How do you form a negative present continuous sentence in French?

a) Ne + verb + pas + être en train de

b) Ne + être + pas + en train de + verb

c) Être + en train de + ne + verb + pas

d) Ne + en train de + verb + pas + être

10. Which phrase is used to express purpose when involving a different subject in French, requiring the subjunctive?

a) Parce que

b) Afin de

c) Pour que

d) Depuis que

Answer Key

1. b) être en train de

2. b) Je suis en train de manger.

3. c) Depuis

4. c) They have been married for five years.

5. a) Pour

6. c) Elle est en train de lire un livre.

7. d) Avant de

8. b) I have been living in Paris since 2015.

9. b) Ne + être + pas + en train de + verb

10. c) Pour que

Cultural Annex

To keep on learning, here are ten French songs for you to add to your playlist:

1. "La Vie en rose" by Édith Piaf (Lyrics by Édith Piaf, Music by Louiguy)

2. "Aux Champs-Élysées" by Joe Dassin (Lyrics by Pierre Delanoë, Music by Mike Wilsh and Mike Deighan)

3. "Je te promets" by Johnny Hallyday (Lyrics by Jean-Jacques Goldman, Music by Jean-Jacques Goldman)

4. "Chanson Douce" by Henri Salvador (Lyrics by Maurice Pon, Music by Henri Salvador)

5. "Jardin d'hiver" by Henri Salvador (Lyrics by Keren Ann and Benjamin Biolay, Music by Keren Ann and Benjamin Biolay)

6. "Tous les mêmes" by Stromae (Lyrics and Music by Stromae)

7. "L'amour est un oiseau rebelle" from Carmen by Georges Bizet (Lyrics by Henri Meilhac and Ludovic Halévy, Music by Georges Bizet)

8. "Je l'aime à mourir" by Francis Cabrel (Lyrics and Music by Francis Cabrel)

9. "Sous le vent" by Garou and Céline Dion (Lyrics by Jacques Veneruso, Music by Jacques Veneruso)

10. "Papaoutai" by Stromae (Lyrics and Music by Stromae)

Conclusion

Congratulations on completing Part 1 of Learning French for Adult Beginners! Throughout this book, you've taken your first steps into the world of French language and culture. You've learned foundational grammar rules, such as the present indicative tense, basic sentence structures, and essential vocabulary for everyday conversations. From introducing yourself and discussing your daily routine to expressing likes, dislikes, and talking about future plans, you now have the tools to start engaging in basic conversations in French.

Keep immersing yourself in French to reinforce what you've learned.

BOOK 2

Complete French Workbook
for Adult Beginners

Essential French Words and Phrases You Need to Know

Explore to Win

Book 2 Description

Learning a new language, especially French, can seem incredibly intimidating for many students.

However, the advantages of learning French are truly astounding: it equips you with the tools to boost your happiness, sharpen your mind, preserve your memory, and enrich every part of your life—especially when it comes to socializing! The best part is, you can start enjoying these benefits right now by simply continuing your learning journey.

Chapter 1: Numbers

"Le cœur a ses raisons que la raison ne connaît point."

- Blaise Pascal

Numbers are all around us: in calendars, price tags, addresses, phone numbers, and more! So, they're essential when speaking French.

Cardinal Numbers

Number	French Cardinal Name	Pronunciation
1	Un	uhn
2	Deux	duh
3	Trois	trwah
4	Quatre	katr
5	Cinq	sank
6	Six	sees
7	Sept	set
8	Huit	weet
9	Neuf	nuhf
10	Dix	dees

Here are 10 example sentences using cardinal numbers in French:

1. Un: J'ai un chien et trois chats.

    - (I have one dog and three cats.)

2. Deux: Elle a deux enfants qui vont à l'école.

    - (She has two children who go to school.)

3. Trois: Nous allons partir en vacances dans trois semaines.

    - (We are going on vacation in three weeks.)

4. Quatre: Il y a quatre saisons dans une année.

    - (There are four seasons in a year.)

5. Cinq: Le concert commence à cinq heures.

    - (The concert starts at five o'clock.)

6. Six: Elle a acheté six roses pour son amie.

    - (She bought six roses for her friend.)

7. Sept: Ils ont sept jours pour terminer le projet.

    - (They have seven days to finish the project.)

8. Huit: J'ai huit verres à laver après le dîner.

    - (I have eight glasses to wash after dinner.)

9. Neuf: Mon fils a neuf ans aujourd'hui.

    - (My son is nine years old today.)

10. Dix: Il y a dix joueurs sur le terrain.

    - (There are ten players on the field.)

Ordinal Numbers

Number	French Ordinal Name	Pronunciation
1st	Premier/Première	pruh-myey (m), pruh-myer (f)
2nd	Deuxième	duh-zyem
3rd	Troisième	trwah-zyem

4th	Quatrième	ka-tree-yem
5th	Cinquième	sank-yem
6th	Sixième	see-zyem
7th	Septième	set-yem
8th	Huitième	weet-yem
9th	Neuvième	nuhv-yem
10th	Dixième	deez-yem

Here are 10 example sentences using ordinal numbers in French:

1. Premier/Première: C'est la première fois que je visite Paris.

    - (This is the first time I am visiting Paris.)

2. Deuxième: Elle est arrivée en deuxième position dans la course.

    - (She finished in second place in the race.)

3. Troisième: Nous habitons au troisième étage de l'immeuble.

    - (We live on the third floor of the building.)

4. Quatrième: Le quatrième chapitre du livre est le plus intéressant.

    - (The fourth chapter of the book is the most interesting.)

5. Cinquième: Son bureau est au cinquième étage.

    - (His office is on the fifth floor.)

6. Sixième: Elle a fêté son sixième anniversaire hier.

    - (She celebrated her sixth birthday yesterday.)

7. Septième: Le septième jour de la semaine est dimanche.

    - (The seventh day of the week is Sunday.)

8. Huitième: Il a terminé huitième dans la compétition de natation.

    - (He finished eighth in the swimming competition.)

9. Neuvième: Nous sommes au neuvième mois de l'année.

    -   (We are in the ninth month of the year.)

10. Dixième: C'est la dixième fois qu'il visite ce musée.

    -   (This is the tenth time he has visited this museum.)

Exercises

1. What is the French cardinal name for the number 3?

   a) Deux
   b) Trois
   c) Quatre
   d) Cinq

2. Which pronunciation corresponds to the French cardinal number 5?

   a) /set/
   b) /twah/
   c) /sank/
   d) /katr/

3. In the sentence, "J'ai huit verres à laver après le dîner," what does "huit" mean in English?

   a) Five
   b) Six
   c) Seven
   d) Eight

4. How do you say "second" in French using the ordinal form?

   a) Deuxième
   b) Troisième
   c) Quatrième
   d) Premier

5. What is the French ordinal name for 10th?

   a) Cinquième
   b) Sixième
   c) Dixième
   d) Septième

6. In French, how would you say "She finished in third place in the race?"

   a) Elle est arrivée en deuxième position dans la course.
   b) Elle est arrivée en troisième position dans la course.
   c) Elle est arrivée en quatrième position dans la course.
   d) Elle est arrivée en cinquième position dans la course.

7. What is the correct pronunciation for the French ordinal number 4th (quatrième)?

   a) /ka-tree-em/
   b) /doo-zyem/
   c) /trwa-zyem/

d) /nuhv-yem/

8. Which French ordinal number is used in the sentence: "Le septième jour de la semaine est dimanche?"

   a) Sixth
   b) Seventh
   c) Eighth
   d) Ninth

9. In the sentence, "Il y a dix joueurs sur le terrain," what does "dix" mean in English?

   a) Eight
   b) Nine
   c) Ten
   d) Eleven

10. What is the French ordinal form for 1st and its masculine pronunciation?

   a) Premier, /pruh-myeh/
   b) Première, /pruh-myehr/
   c) Deuxième, /duh-zyem/
   d) Troisième, /trwa-zyem/

Answer Key

1. B) Trois

2. C) /sank/

3. D) Eight

4. A) Deuxième

5. C) Dixième

6. B) Elle est arrivée en troisième position dans la course.

7. A) /ka-tree-em/

8. B) Seventh

9. C) Ten

10. A) Premier, /pruh-myeh/

Chapter 2: French Conversations

"Je pense donc je suis."

- René Descartes

In this chapter, we will explore what you need to know to carry on French conversations.

Conversation Vocabulary

Word	Pronunciation	Translation
Bonjour	bon-zhoor	Hello
Merci	mehr-see	Thank you
S'il vous plaît	seel voo pleh	Please
Chat	sha	Cat
Chien	shyen	Dog
Pomme	pom	Apple
Maison	meh-zon	House
Eau	oh	Water
Amour	ah-moor	Love
Voiture	vwa-tur	Car

Exercises

1. What is the French word for "Hello" and its pronunciation?

2. How do you say "Thank you" in French, and how is it pronounced?

3. What is the French word for "Dog," and what is its pronunciation?

4. How do you pronounce the French word for "Love?"

5. How do you say "Please" in French, and what is its pronunciation?

6. What is the French word for "House," and how do you pronounce it?

Answer Key

1. "Bonjour" - bon-zhoor

2. "Merci" - mehr-see

3. "Chien" - shyen

4. "Amour" - ah-moor

5. "S'il vous plaît" - seel voo pleh

6. "Maison" - meh-zohn

Chapter 3: Our Home

"Faire une maison, c'est bâtir un bonheur."

- Antoine de Saint-Exupéry

In everyday conversations, we often end up discussing topics related to our homes. In this chapter, we will focus primarily on specific vocabulary rather than on grammar or sentence structure.

Le salon - The Living Room

Object	Pronunciation	Translation
Le Canapé	/ka-na-pay/	Sofa
La Chaise	/shez/	Chair
La Table basse	/tab-l bah/	Coffee table
La Télévision	/tay-lay-vee-zyon/	Television
La Lampe	/lahmp/	Lamp
Le Tapis	/ta-pee/	Rug
Le Rideau	/ree-doh/	Curtain
L'Étagère	/ ay-ta-zhehr/	Shelf
L'Horloge	/or-lozh/	Clock
Le Tableau	/tab-loh/	Painting

La chambre - The Bedroom

Object	Pronunciation	Translation
Le Lit	lee	Bed
L'Oreiller	or-ray-yay	Pillow
La Couverture	koo-vair-teer	Blanket
L'Armoire	ar-mwar	Wardrobe
La Commode	ko-mod	Dresser
La Table de nuit	tab-l duh nwee	Nightstand
Le Tiroir	teer-war	Drawer
Le Miroir	meer-war	Mirror
La Lampe de chevet	lahmp duh shuh-veh	Bedside lamp
Le Placard	pla-kar	Closet

La salle à manger - The Dining Room

Object	Pronunciation	Translation
La Table	tabl	Table
La Chaise	shez	Chair
L'Assiette	ah-syet	Plate
Le Couteau	koo-toh	Knife

La Fourchette	foor-shet	Fork
La Cuillère	kwee-yer	Spoon
Le Verre	vair	Glass
La Serviette de table	sair-vyet duh tabl	Napkin
Le Buffet	byoo-feh	Sideboard/Buffet

La salle de bain - The Bathroom

Object	Pronunciation	Translation
Le Lavabo	lah-vah-bo	Sink
La Douche	doosh	Shower
La Baignoire	ben-wahr	Bathtub
La Serviette de bain	sair-vyet duh bah	Towel
Le Savon	sa-von	Soap
Le Miroir	meer-war	Mirror
Le Shampoing	shom-pwen	Shampoo
La Brosse à dents	bros ah don	Toothbrush
Le Dentifrice	don-tee-frees	Toothpaste
Le Papier toilette	pap-yay twa-let	Toilet paper

La cuisine - The Kitchen

Object	Pronunciation	Translation
La Cuisinière	kwee-zeen-yair	Stove
Le Four	foor	Oven
Le Réfrigérateur	ref-ree-zhay-ra-teur	Refrigerator
L'Évier	ev-yay	Sink
La Casserole	kas-rohl	Saucepan
Le Poêle	pwahl	Pan
Le Lave-vaisselle	lahv vay-sell	Dishwasher
La Planche à découper	plonsh ah day-koo-pay	Cutting board
Le Gobelet	goh-blay	Cup
Le Micro-ondes	meek-roh ond	Microwave

Exercises

1. What is the French word for "Sofa" and its pronunciation?

    a) Chaise, /shez/
    b) Canapé, /ka-na-pay/
    c) Tapis, /ta-pee/
    d) Table basse, /tab-l bahs/

2. Which object from "La chambre" (the bedroom) is translated as "Nightstand?"

    a) Tiroir
    b) Table de nuit
    c) Commode
    d) Armoire

3. How do you pronounce "Mirror" in French, and what is the word?

    a) /meer-wahr/, Miroir
    b) /ree-doh/, Rideau
    c) /lah-va-boh/, Lavabo
    d) /or-lozh/, Horloge

4. What is the French word for "Refrigerator" in "La cuisine" (the kitchen)?

    a) Cuisinière
    b) Four
    c) Réfrigérateur
    d) Micro-ondes

5. Which object is found in "La salle à manger" (the dining room) and is pronounced /fuʁʃɛt/?

    a) Assiette
    b) Verre
    c) Couteau
    d) Fourchette

6. What is the French translation for "Shampoo," and how is it pronounced?

    a) Shampoing, /shahn-pwang/
    b) Savon, /sah-vohn/
    c) Serviette, /sair-vyet/
    d) Douche, /doosh/

7. What is "Placemat" in French, and how is it pronounced?

    a) Verre, /vehr/
    b) Serviette de table, /sair-vyet duh tab-l/
    c) Napperon, /nah-prohn/

    d) Assiette, /ah-syet/

8. In "Le salon" (the living room), what is "Horloge," and what does it mean?

    a) /or-lozh/, Clock
    b) /lahmp/, Lamp
    c) /tay-lay-vee-zyon/, Television
    d) /tab-loh/, Painting

9. How do you say "Toothbrush" in French, and how is it pronounced?

    a) Savon, /sah-vohn/
    b) Brosse à dents, /bross ah dahn/
    c) Dentifrice, /dahn-tee-freess/
    d) Papier toilette, /pah-pyay twah-let/

10. What does "Poêle" mean in English, and what is its pronunciation in French?

    a) Oven, /fur/
    b) Frying pan, /pwal/
    c) Cutting board, /plan-sh ah day-koo-pay/
    d) Dishwasher, /lav vay-sel/

Answer Key

1. B) Canapé, /kanape/

2. B) Table de nuit

3. A) /meer-wahr/, Miroir

4. C) Réfrigérateur

5. D) Fourchette

6. A) Shampoing, /shahn-pwang/

7. C) Napperon, /nah-prohn/

8. A) /or-lozh/, Clock

9. B) Brosse à dents, /bross ah dahn/

10. B) Frying pan, /pwal/

Chapter 4: Work and Relationships

"Aimer, ce n'est pas se regarder l'un l'autre, c'est regarder ensemble dans la même direction."

- Antoine de Saint-Exupéry

In today's globalized world, speaking another language, like French, enables us to work from any location and opens up numerous opportunities.

Telling Time

Telling time in French involves understanding the specific vocabulary, expressions, and structure used to convey hours and minutes:

1. Hours (Heures):

The word "heure" (hour) is used to indicate the time. For example:

- 1:00 - Il est une heure. (It is one o'clock.)
- 3:00 - Il est trois heures. (It is three o'clock.)

2. Minutes (Minutes):

To add minutes, the number is simply stated after the hour:

- 1:10 - Il est une heure dix. (It is one ten.)
- 3:25 - Il est trois heures vingt-cinq. (It is three twenty-five.)

Key Expressions:

Quarter Past (et quart):

To indicate a quarter past the hour, use "et quart."

- 2:15 - Il est deux heures et quart. (It is a quarter past two.)

Half Past (et demie):

To say "half past," use "et demie."

- 4:30 - Il est quatre heures et demie. (It is half past four.)

Quarter To (moins le quart):

To indicate a quarter to the next hour, use "moins le quart."

- 5:45 - Il est six heures moins le quart. (It is a quarter to six.)

Additional Points:

Midnight (Minuit) and Noon (Midi):

Special terms are used for midnight and noon:

- 12:00 a.m. - Il est minuit. (It is midnight.)
- 12:00 p.m. - Il est midi. (It is noon.)

24-Hour Clock Format:

The French commonly use the 24-hour clock, especially in formal contexts like transportation schedules, business hours, and television programming. For example:

- 14:00 - Il est quatorze heures. (It is two o'clock in the afternoon.)
- 20:30 - Il est vingt heures trente. (It is eight thirty in the evening.)

Omitting "Heure":

When it's obvious you're referring to the time, "heure" can be omitted, especially in casual speech.

Practice Examples:

- 7:05 - Il est sept heures cinq.
- 11:15 - Il est onze heures et quart.
- 13:45 - Il est quatorze heures moins le quart.
- 8:30 - Il est huit heures et demie.

Time	Translation	Pronunciation
1:00	Il est une heure.	/eel et uhn uhr/
2:15	Il est deux heures et quart.	/eel eh dohz uhr ay kar/
3:30	Il est trois heures et demie.	/eel eh trwa-z uhr ay duh-mee/
4:45	Il est cinq heures moins le quart.	/eel eh sank uhr mwen luh kar/
5:10	Il est cinq heures dix.	/eel eh sank uhr dees/
6:20	Il est six heures vingt.	/eel eh seess uhr vahn/

7:05	Il est sept heures cinq.	/eel eh set uhr sank/
8:50	Il est neuf heures moins dix.	/eel eh nuhf uhr mwen dees/
12:00	Il est midi.	/eel eh mee-dee/
23:00	Il est vingt-trois heures.	/ eel eh vant trwa uhr/

Professions

Note: The base term for the following professions is masculine (le and l' articles). When applicable, the feminine version (la and l' articles) will also be listed.

Profession	Pronunciation	Translation
Médecin	/med-san/	Doctor
Enseignant(e)	/ahn-seh-nyan(t)/	Teacher
Ingénieur	/an-zhen-yeur/	Engineer
Avocat(e)	/ah-voh-kah(t)/	Lawyer
Infirmier/Infirmière	/an-feer-myay (m), an-feer-myair (f)/	Nurse
Policier/Policière	/poh-lees-yay (m), poh-lees-yair (f)/	Police officer
Architecte	/ar-shee-tekt/	Architect
Coiffeur/Coiffeuse	/kwah-fur (m), kwah-fuz (f)/	Hairdresser
Pompier	/pom-pyay/	Firefighter
Comptable	/kon-tab-l/	Accountant

Exercises

1. How do you say "It is half past four" in French?

    a) Il est quatre heures et quart.
    b) Il est quatre heures et demie.
    c) Il est quatre heures moins le quart.
    d) Il est quatre heures dix.

2. What is the French phrase for "It is a quarter to six," and how is it pronounced?

    a) Il est cinq heures et quart, /eel eh sank uhr ay kar/
    b) Il est six heures moins le quart, /eel eh seess uhr mwen luh kar/
    c) Il est six heures et demie, /eel eh seess uhr ay duh-mee/
    d) Il est six heures moins dix, / eel eh seess uhr mwen dees/

3. What time is Il est vingt-trois heures in a 12-hour clock format?

    a) 11:00 a.m.
    b) 1:00 p.m.
    c) 11:00 p.m.
    d) 1:00 a.m.

4. Which profession in French translates to "Nurse" and has the pronunciation /ɛ̃fiʁmjɛʁ/?

    a) Enseignant(e)
    b) Infirmier/Infirmière
    c) Comptable
    d) Avocat(e)

5. How would you say "It is a quarter past two" in French?

    a) Il est deux heures dix.
    b) Il est deux heures et demie.
    c) Il est deux heures et quart.
    d) Il est deux heures moins le quart.

6. What is the French translation for the profession "Firefighter," and how is it pronounced?

    a) Policier/Policière, /poh-lees-yay (m), poh-lees-yair (f)/
    b) Coiffeur/Coiffeuse, /kwah-fur (m), kwah-fuz (f)/
    c) Pompier, /pom-pyay/
    d) Comptable, /kon-tab-l/

7. If someone says Il est neuf heures moins dix in French, what time is it in English?

    a) 8:50
    b) 9:50
    c) 10:10

d) 9:10

8. What is the pronunciation of the French word "Architect," and what does it translate to in English?

   a) /an-zhen-yeur/, Engineer
   b) /ar-shee-tekt/, Architect
   c) /ah-voh-kah/, Lawyer
   d) /kwah-fuz/, Hairdresser

9. How do you say "It is one o'clock" in French, and how is it pronounced?

   a) Il est deux heures, /eel eh duh zur/
   b) Il est midi, /eel eh mee-dee/
   c) Il est une heure, /eel et oon uhr/
   d) Il est minuit, /eel eh meen-wee/

10. Which profession is described as /kwaføz/ in French, and what is its translation?

   a) Doctor
   b) Teacher
   c) Hairdresser
   d) Police officer

Answer Key

1. B) Il est quatre heures et demie.

2. B) Il est six heures moins le quart, /eel eh seess uhr mwen luh kar/

3. C) 11:00 p.m.

4. B) Infirmier/Infirmière

5. C) Il est deux heures et quart.

6. C) Pompier, /pom-pyay/

7. A) 8:50

8. B) /ar-shee-tekt/, Architect

9. C) Il est une heure, /eel et uhn uhr/

10. C) Hairdresser

Cultural Annex

Here are some songs in French to add to your playlist for more practice. Enjoy!

1. "Parler à mon père" by Céline Dion

2. "Le Pénitencier" by Johnny Hallyday

3. "Moi... Lolita" by Alizée

4. "Mon Précieux" by Soprano

Conclusion

After reading this section, we can confidently say that you are on your way to confidently speaking French and can start practicing to retain what you've learned. Are you ready to embark on this exciting adventure?

BOOK 3

Learn French with Short Stories for Adult Beginners

Shortcut Your French Fluency!
(Fun & Easy Reads)

Explore to Win

Book 3 Description

If you've recently started learning French, you may have noticed a lack of suitable reading materials. That's why we've created Learning French with Short Stories for Adult Beginners.

Elevate your French with our carefully crafted short stories designed specifically for adults. With this book, you'll find:- Captivating stories.

- Rich vocabulary and practical everyday phrases.
- Stories focused on specific sentence structures to challenge your French at every level.
- Examples of verb conjugations.
- Simplified explanations of the present and present progressive tenses.
- Descriptions of weather, people, and places.
- Helpful glossaries.
- Exercises to test your reading skills (answer keys are included).

So, let's dive in!

How to use this book

Each of the following stories follows the same structure:

- A short story in French

- A summary in French

- A summary in English

- A glossary with French words and phrases and their English translations

- Quizzes to test your comprehension

- Answer keys to check your work

To make the most of our stories:

1. Read the story all the way through. Focus on following the storyline as much as possible, using the context to fill in any gaps.

2. Read the French summary and compare it with your own understanding of the story. If the French summary feels too challenging, read the English version.

3. Read the story again, this time concentrating on the details you might have missed during your first reading.

4. Review the glossary context of all unfamiliar terms.

5. Test your understanding by answering the quizzes. Remember to check your answers. Don't worry if you don't get everything right the first time around. Just keep practicing.

6. Celebrate your progress! Remember that the key to learning a new language is consistent practice.

Chapter 1: Les courses – The grocery shopping

"Il faut cultiver notre jardin."

- Voltaire, Candide

Omar fait généralement ses courses le dimanche, car c'est mieux parce qu'il n'y a pas trop de monde. Il écoute de la musique pendant qu'il choisit quoi acheter. Il ne fait jamais de liste, donc il oublie souvent certains articles. Il se dirige vers le rayon des fruits et choisit quelques pommes. Il y a aussi des poires et des bananes. Il n'y a pas de fraises ni de myrtilles, ce qui est dommage parce que les fraises sont ses préférées. Omar prépare des smoothies aux fruits presque tous les jours et, pour cela, il a besoin d'acheter beaucoup de fruits. Dans le rayon des légumes, il y a des tomates juteuses. Il y a aussi des pommes de terre, des oignons, des concombres et de la laitue. Il y a quelques carottes mais elles sont pourries. Omar demande à l'un des employés du supermarché s'il y a plus de carottes et celui-ci lui demande d'attendre un moment.

Omar se demande ce qu'il lui manque encore. Il n'a pas encore cherché le lait, les céréales ni le pain. Il se rappelle que le pain ici est un peu cher. Il y a un autre endroit près de chez lui où le pain est moins cher, et parfois il y a de bonnes réductions ou des promotions de deux articles pour le prix d'un. Le jeune homme donne à Omar quelques carottes en très bon état et il continue de faire ses courses.

Les cuisses de poulet sont à moitié prix, alors il en prend 2 kilos. Il a déjà du saumon chez lui et donc il n'en achète pas.

Omar rencontre sa voisine.

- Toi aussi tu fais les courses le dimanche? Il te manque encore quelque chose?

- Non, je pense qu'il ne me manque que les pâtes et le riz, répond Omar.

- Tu vas préparer un plat spécial?

- Non, rien de spécial. Et toi?

- J'achète les ingrédients pour le gâteau d'anniversaire de ma sœur. Demain, c'est son anniversaire. Tu es invité.

- Merci, à quelle heure est la fête?

- À 20 heures. Ce n'est qu'une petite réunion.

- Bien, on se voit demain.

Il y a deux étagères avec beaucoup de riz. Il a seulement besoin d'un paquet d'un kilo. Il prend un paquet et deux paquets de pâtes d'un kilo, puis il se dirige vers la caisse pour payer.

- C'est tout? demande le caissier.

- Oui, s'il vous plaît.

- Parfait, ça fait 3 500 pesos.

- Vous acceptez les cartes de crédit?

- Oui, nous acceptons aussi les cartes de débit et les espèces.

À ce moment-là, Omar se rend compte que sa carte n'est pas dans sa poche. Il s'excuse auprès du caissier et appelle sa petite amie.

- Je pense que j'ai oublié ma carte de crédit à la maison.
- Vraiment? Je suis chez ma mère et je ne peux pas aller la chercher.
- Oui, je sais.
- Bon, tu feras les courses un autre jour.
- Non, ne t'inquiète pas, je fais tout aujourd'hui.

Omar est en colère contre lui-même. Il se sent stupide. Il prend un taxi jusqu'à chez lui qui lui coûte 200 pesos et cherche sa carte. Quelques minutes passent et il ne la trouve pas. Elle n'est pas sur la table de nuit comme il le pensait, ni sur la table de la salle à manger. Il trouve la carte sur le dessus du réfrigérateur, ce qui est étrange. En une demi-heure, il est déjà de retour au supermarché. Le caissier a son chariot avec la nourriture à côté de lui. Omar paie tout et rentre chez lui avec les sacs de provisions.

Résumé

Omar va au supermarché pour faire les courses un dimanche. Il prend quelques fruits et légumes tout en essayant de se rappeler ce qui lui manque à la maison. Il rencontre une voisine et ils discutent pendant quelques minutes. Lorsqu'il se dirige vers la caisse, il se rend compte qu'il n'a pas sa carte de crédit dans sa poche et qu'il l'a probablement laissée à la maison. Très embarrassé, il prend un taxi pour rentrer chez lui, cherche la carte et retourne au supermarché pour finalement payer ses achats.

Summary

Omar goes to the supermarket to get some groceries on a Sunday. He picks up some fruits and vegetables as he tries to remember what he needs at home. He runs into a neighbor and talks to her for a few minutes. When he gets to the cash register, he realizes he doesn't have his credit card in his pocket, and he probably left it at home. Feeling embarrassed, he takes a taxi home, looks for his card, and returns to the supermarket to finally pay for his groceries.

Glossaire – Glossary

- Il fait habituellement les courses: He usually goes grocery shopping

- Le dimanche: On Sundays

- Il n'y a pas tant de monde: There aren't that many people

- Il écoute de la musique: He listens to music

- Pendant qu'il choisit quoi acheter: As he selects what to buy

- Il ne fait jamais de liste: He never makes a list

- Il oublie souvent certains articles: He often forgets some items

- Le rayon des fruits: The fruit section

- Il choisit quelques pommes: He chooses a couple of apples

- Il y a des poires et des bananes: There are pears and bananas

- Il n'y a pas de fraises ni de myrtilles: There aren't any strawberries or cranberries

- Ce qui est dommage: Which is a pity

- Ce sont ses préférées: They are his favorite

- Il prépare des smoothies aux fruits: He makes smoothies

- Presque tous les jours: Almost every day

- Le rayon des légumes: The vegetable section

- Tomates juteuses: Juicy tomatoes

- Il y a des pommes de terre, des oignons, des concombres et de la laitue: There are potatoes, onions, cucumbers, and lettuce

- Carottes: Carrots

- Elles sont pourries: They are rotten

- L'un des employés du supermarché: One of the employees of the supermarket

- Il lui demande d'attendre une minute: He asks him to wait a minute

- Il se demande ce qu'il lui manque encore: He wonders what else he's missing

- Il n'a pas encore cherché le lait ni les céréales: He still hasn't looked for milk or cereals

- Le pain: The bread

- Un peu cher: A bit expensive

- Un autre endroit: Another place

- Moins cher: Cheaper

- De bonnes réductions: Good discounts

- Promotions de deux articles pour le prix d'un: Special offers of two items for the price of one

- En bon état: In good shape

- Les cuisses de poulet: The chicken thighs

- Ils sont à moitié prix: They are half off

- Il prend 2 kilos: He takes 2 kilograms

- Il a déjà du saumon chez lui: He already has salmon at home

- Il rencontre sa voisine: He runs into his neighbor

- Toi aussi: You too

- Il te manque encore quelque chose?: Do you need anything else?

- Je pense que: I think that

- Il ne me manque que les pâtes et le riz: I'm only missing pasta and rice

- Tu vas préparer un plat spécial?: Are you going to make a special dish?

- Et toi?: And you?

- Les ingrédients: The ingredients

- Gâteau d'anniversaire: Birthday cake

- Tu es invité: You are invited

- Merci: Thank you

- Ce n'est qu'une petite réunion: It is just a little get-together

- Bien, on se voit demain: Good, see you tomorrow

- Deux étagères: Two shelves

- Un paquet d'un kilo: A package of 1 kilogram

- La caisse: The cash register

- C'est tout?: Is that all?

- S'il vous plaît: Please

- Ça fait 3.500 pesos: It is 3,500 pesos

- Vous acceptez les cartes de crédit?: Do you take credit cards?

- Carte de débit et espèces: Debit card and cash

- À ce moment-là: In that moment

- Il n'est pas dans sa poche: It is not in his pocket

- Il s'excuse auprès du caissier: He apologizes to the cashier

- J'ai oublié: I forgot

- Vraiment?: Really?

- Je ne peux pas aller la chercher: I can't look for it

- Oui, je sais: Yes, I know

- Un autre jour: Another day

- Non, ne t'inquiète pas: No, don't worry

- Je fais tout aujourd'hui: I will get it all done today

- Il est en colère contre lui-même: He is angry at himself

- Il se sent stupide: He feels stupid

- Il prend un taxi jusqu'à chez lui: He takes a taxi home

- Il lui demande 200 pesos: He charges him 200 pesos

- Quelques minutes passent: A few minutes go by

- Il ne la trouve pas: He can't find it

- La table de nuit: The nightstand

- Comme il pensait: As he thought

- La table de la salle à manger: The dining table

- Sur le réfrigérateur: On the fridge

- Ce qui est étrange: Which is weird

- Une demi-heure: Half an hour

- Chariot avec de la nourriture: Shopping cart with food

- Il paie tout: He pays for everything

- Les sacs: The bags

Exercice 1

Répondez aux questions suivantes – Answer the following questions.

1. French: Pourquoi Omar fait-il les courses le dimanche?

   English: Why does Omar do the grocery shopping on Sundays?

   _____

2. French: Quel est le fruit préféré d'Omar?

   English: What is Omar's favorite fruit?

   _____

3. French: Quelles légumes y a-t-il dans le rayon des légumes?

   English: What vegetables are there in the vegetable section?

   _____

4. French: Pourquoi Omar n'achète-t-il pas de pain là-bas?

   English: Why doesn't Omar buy bread there?

   _____

5. French: Combien de kilos de cuisses de poulet Omar achète-t-il?

   English: How many kilograms of chicken thighs does Omar buy?

   _____

6. French: Qu'est-ce que sa voisine achète?

   English: What is his neighbor buying?

   _____

Exercice 2

Choisissez entre "vrai" ou "faux" – choose "true" or "false"

1. French: Omar n'oublie jamais aucun article.

   English: Omar never forgets any items.

___

2. French: Il n'y a pas de bananes dans le rayon des fruits.

   English: There are no bananas in the fruit section.

___

3. French: Les carottes sont pourries.

   English: The carrots are rotten.

___

4. French: Omar achète 1 kilo de saumon.

   English: Omar buys 1 kilogram of salmon.

___

5. French: Omar décline l'invitation de sa voisine.

   English: Omar turns down his neighbor's invitation.

___

6. French: Omar achète 2 kilos de pâtes.

   English: Omar buys 2 kilograms of pasta.

___

Réponses– Answers

Exercice 1:

1. Omar fait les courses le dimanche parce qu'il n'y a pas tant de monde.

2. La fraise est le fruit préféré d'Omar.

3. Dans le rayon des légumes, il y a des tomates, des pommes de terre, des oignons, des concombres, de la laitue et des carottes.

4. Omar n'achète pas de pain là-bas parce qu'il est un peu cher.

5. Omar achète 2 kilos de cuisses de poulet.

6. La voisine d'Omar achète les ingrédients pour le gâteau d'anniversaire de sa sœur.

Exercice 2:

1. Faux

2. Faux

3. Vrai

4. Faux

5. Faux

6. Vrai

Chapter 3: Le rendez-vous – The date

La vie, c'est le présent ; le passé, ce n'est plus ; l'avenir, ce n'est pas encore."

- Victor Hugo

Daniela est célibataire et Cristina adore lui présenter de nouveaux garçons. Bien qu'elles soient de très bonnes amies, Cristina ne sait pas vraiment quel type d'hommes plaît à Daniela, c'est pourquoi les rendez-vous sont toujours un désastre complet. Pour éviter ces moments gênants, Daniela a téléchargé une application de rencontres appelée Cupidon pour trouver un garçon qui lui semble intéressant. Elle ne sait pas si elle veut une relation ou quelque chose de plus décontracté. Pour l'instant, l'idée est de s'amuser.

Cristina et Daniela se réunissent pour regarder les différents profils des garçons et en trouvent certains plus intéressants que d'autres. Il y a de nombreux profils avec peu de photos, d'autres sans description ni information sur le candidat potentiel. Elles écartent immédiatement ce type de profils. Daniela aime les hommes qui prennent le temps de se décrire au moins un peu. Elles trouvent aussi quelques garçons très charmants et séduisants. Parmi ces garçons, il y en a deux que Daniela aime beaucoup : l'un s'appelle Juan et l'autre, Sebastián.

Juan est avocat, ce que Cristina n'aime pas car elle pense que cela signifie que Juan est ennuyeux. Mais Daniela aime que Juan ait un côté créatif. Juan dit qu'il aime chanter et écrire des poèmes. Il semble que Juan soit un garçon sensible, ce qui est bien pour Daniela. Juan dit qu'il est introverti, qu'il préfère rester à la maison à regarder un film plutôt que de sortir dans un bar pour boire. Daniela aime regarder des films à la maison, mais elle aime aussi sortir et aimerait sortir avec Juan de temps en temps, donc elle ne sait pas si leurs personnalités sont compatibles.

Sebastián a deux ans de moins que Daniela et étudie l'économie. Pour l'instant, il ne travaille pas et ses parents l'aident financièrement. Daniela préfère les hommes qui sont indépendants, mais Sebastián a d'autres qualités. Il aime beaucoup cuisiner et semble très attentionné.

Il aime aussi explorer de nouveaux endroits, il a beaucoup de photos à la montagne, sur différentes plages, à faire du vélo. Daniela aime les activités de plein air et elle pense que leurs personnalités pourraient être compatibles.

Juan a cinq ans de plus que Sebastián et il est aussi plus grand. Sebastián est plus musclé que Juan et aussi plus extraverti et direct. Sebastián semble moins mature que Juan, mais il est aussi poli que Juan. Daniela pense que Juan est plus séduisant que Sebastián, mais Juan flirte mieux que Sebastián.

Sebastián habite plus loin que Juan, ce qui peut être un problème si Daniela veut faire des plans avec lui. Juan aime les animaux et Sebastián non, et Daniela a un chat, donc cela pourrait être un problème.

Daniela est très indécise.

- Qui te plaît le plus? – demande Cristina.

- Franchement, je ne sais pas. Ils ont tous les deux de bonnes et de mauvaises qualités.

- Tu aimes les garçons drôles. Qui est le plus drôle?

- Je pense que Sebastián est plus drôle que Juan.

- Juan est-il plus attirant que Sebastián?

- Les deux sont très mignons.

- Qui est le plus respectueux?

- Je pense que c'est Juan.

- Qui est le moins attentionné?

- Je pense que c'est Sebastián.

- Juan est-il plus intelligent que Sebastián?

- Non, je pense que Sebastián est aussi intelligent que Juan. C'est une décision très difficile.

Dans les jours qui suivent, Daniela a un rendez-vous avec les deux garçons. Le jeudi, Daniela va au cinéma avec Juan, et le samedi, elle va dans un bar avec Sebastián. Le dimanche matin, Daniela voit Cristina et lui raconte tout.

- Tu sais déjà qui tu préfères? – demande Cristina.

- Je suis plus confuse que jamais – répond Daniela.

- Pourquoi?

- Je pense que les deux me plaisent autant. Juan est très galant et c'est aussi un bon embrasseur. Sebastián est un bon danseur et je passe un très bon moment avec lui, et on voit qu'il a un côté sensible. Que dois-je faire?

- Eh bien, apprends à les connaître un peu mieux, et avec le temps, décide de ce que tu veux faire. Pour l'instant, profite de leur compagnie. Tu n'as pas besoin de te presser.

- Tu as tout à fait raison, il est trop tôt pour prendre une décision. Merci pour tes conseils.

Résumé

Daniela cherche à rencontrer des garçons intéressants, alors elle télécharge une application de rencontres appelée Cupidon. Son amie Cristina l'aide à passer en revue les profils de nombreux garçons et à choisir les meilleurs pour un rendez-vous. Parmi tous ces profils, elles trouvent deux garçons qui semblent prometteurs : Juan et Sebastián. Daniela et Cristina discutent des attributs des deux garçons et de leur compatibilité potentielle avec Daniela. Plus tard dans la semaine, Daniela a un rendez-vous avec chacun d'eux, et à la fin, elle décide de prendre son temps pour apprendre à les connaître.

Summary

Daniela is looking to meet interesting guys, so she downloads a dating app called Cupid. Her friend Cristina helps her check the profiles and choose the best ones to go on a date with. Among all the profiles, they find two guys that seem promising: Juan and Sebastián. Daniela and Cristina talk about the attributes of both guys and whether they think they would be a good match with Daniela. Later that week, Daniela has a date with each of the guys, and in the end, she decides she wants to get to know them in no rush.

Glossaire – Glossary

- **Cristina adore lui présenter de nouveaux garçons:** Cristina loves to introduce new guys to her

- **Bonnes amies:** Good friends

- **Elle ne sait pas très bien:** She doesn't know that well

- **Quel type d'hommes plaît à Daniela:** What type of men Daniela likes

- **C'est pourquoi:** That's why

- **Les rendez-vous:** The dates

- **Un désastre total:** A total disaster

- **Pour éviter:** To avoid

- **Ces moments gênants:** Those awkward moments

- **Elle a téléchargé une application de rencontres:** She downloaded a dating app

- **Cupidon:** Cupid

- **Pour trouver:** To find

- **Un garçon qu'elle trouve intéressant:** A guy she finds interesting

- **Elle ne sait pas si elle veut:** She doesn't know if she wants

- **Une relation:** A relationship

- **Quelque chose de plus décontracté:** Something more casual

- **Pour l'instant:** For the time being

- **L'idée est de s'amuser:** The idea is to have fun

- **Elles se réunissent:** They get together

- **Les profils des garçons:** The guys' profiles

- **Certains plus intéressants que d'autres:** Some more interesting than others

- **Avec peu de photos:** With few pictures

- **Sans aucune description ni information:** With no description or information

- **Sur le candidat potentiel:** About the possible candidate

- **Elles écartent:** They rule out

- **Les hommes qui prennent le temps:** The men who take the time

- **Pour au moins se décrire un peu:** To at least describe themselves a bit

- **Beaux et charmants:** Handsome and charming

- **Parmi ceux-là:** Among those

- **Il y en a deux que Daniela adore:** There are two that Daniela loves

- **Ce que Cristina n'aime pas:** Which Cristina doesn't like

- **Cela signifie que:** It means

- **Juan est ennuyeux:** Juan is boring

- **Il a un côté créatif:** He has a creative side

- **Il dit qu'il aime chanter et écrire des poèmes:** He says he likes to sing and to write poems

- **Il semble que:** It seems that

- **Sensible:** Tender

- **Ce qui est bon pour Daniela:** Which is good for Daniela

- **Introverti:** Introverted

- **Il préfère:** He prefers

- **Rester à la maison à regarder un film:** To stay home watching a movie

- **Plutôt que de sortir dans un bar pour boire:** Rather than going out to a bar to drink

- **Elle aime sortir:** She likes to go out

- **Elle aimerait:** She would like

- **De temps en temps:** Once in a while

- **Elle ne sait pas si:** She doesn't know if

- **Leurs personnalités sont compatibles:** Their personalities are compatible

- **Sebastián a deux ans de moins que Daniela:**

- Sebastián is two years younger than Daniela

- **Il étudie l'économie:** He studies economics

- **Pour l'instant:** For the moment

- **Ses parents l'aident:** His parents help him

- **Financièremen:** Financially

- **Indépendants: Independent- D'autres bonnes qualités:** Other good qualities

- **Attentionné:** Thoughtful

- **Explorer de nouveaux endroits:** To explore new places

- **Montagnes:** Mountains

- **Plages:** Beaches

- **Faire du vélo:** Riding a bike

- **Activités de plein air:** Outdoor activities

- **Ils peuvent être:** They might be

- **Cinq ans de plus que:** Five years older than

- **Plus grand:** Taller

- **Plus musclé que:** More muscular than

- **Plus extraverti et direct:** More extroverted and direct

- **Moins mature que:** Less mature than

- **Sebastián est aussi poli que Juan:** Sebastián is as polite as Juan

- **Plus séduisant:** More handsome

- **Il flirte mieux:** He flirts better

- **Il habite plus loin:** He lives farther

- **Faire des plans avec lui:** To make plans with him

- **Il aime les animaux:** He likes animals

- **Chats:** Cats
- **Peut-être que c'est:** That might be
- **Indécise:** Indecisive
- **Qui te plaît le plus?:** Who do you like more?
- **Honnêtement:** Honestly
- **Les deux:** They both
- **Mauvaises:** Bad
- **Tu aimes:** You like
- **Drôles:** Funny
- **Qui est le plus drôle?:** Who is funnier?
- **Plus attirant:** More attractive
- **Plus respectueux:** More respectful
- **Qui est le moins attentionné?:** Who is less thoughtful?
- **Plus intelligent:** Smarter
- **Aussi intelligent que:** As smart as
- **Dans les jours suivants:** In the following days
- **Elle va au cinéma:** She goes to the movies
- **Elle lui raconte tout:** She tells her everything
- **Je suis plus confuse que jamais:** I'm more confused than ever before
- **J'aime les deux autant:** I like them both the same
- **Galant:** Chivalrous
- **C'est un bon embrasseur:** He is a good kisser
- **Il est bon danseur:** He is a great dancer
- **Je passe un très bon moment avec lui:** I have a great time with him
- **On voit qu'il a un côté sensible:** You can tell he has a sensitive side
- **Que dois-je faire?:** What should I do?
- **Eh bien, apprends à les connaître un peu mieux:** Well, get to know them a little better
- **Avec le temps:** With time
- **Décide de ce que tu vas faire:** Decide what you're going to do

- **Profite de leur compagnie:** Enjoy their company
- **Tu n'as pas besoin de te presser:** You don't have to rush
- **Tu as tout à fait raison:** You're totally right
- **Il est trop tôt:** It's too early
- **Pour prendre une décision:** To make a decision
- **Conseils:** Advice

Exercice 1

Répondez aux questions suivantes – Answer the following questions.

1. French: Pourquoi ses rendez-vous sont-ils si mauvais?

   English: Why are her dates so bad?

   _____

2. French: Qu'est-ce que Cupidon?

   English: What is Cupid?

   _____

3. French: Que cherche Daniela en ce moment?

   English: What is Daniela looking for right now?

   _____

4. French: Quel type de profils Daniela n'aime-t-elle pas?

   English: What kinds of profiles doesn't Daniela like?

   _____

5. French: Pourquoi Cristina n'aime-t-elle pas que Juan soit avocat?

   English: Why doesn't Cristina like Juan being a lawyer?

   _____

6. French: Quel est le côté créatif de Juan?

   English: What is Juan's creative side?

   _____

Exercice 2

Choisissez entre "vrai" ou "faux" – Choose "true" or "false."

1. French: Daniela et Cristina sont cousines.

   English: Daniela and Cristina are cousins.

   _____

2. French: Daniela aime le côté créatif de Juan.

   English: Daniela likes Juan's creative side.

   _____

3. French: Sebastián est plus jeune que Daniela.

   English: Sebastián is younger than Daniela.

   _____

4. French: Sebastián est plus grand que Juan.

   English: Sebastián is taller than Juan.

   _____

5. French: Juan n'aime pas les animaux.

   English: Juan doesn't like animals.

   _____

6. French: Juan est plus attentionné que Sebastián.

   English: Juan is more thoughtful than Sebastián.

   _____

Réponses– Answers

Exercice 1:

1. Les rendez-vous de Daniela sont mauvais parce que son amie ne sait pas quel type d'homme elle aime.

2. Cupidon est une application de rencontres.

3. Pour l'instant, Daniela cherche à s'amuser.

4. Daniela n'aime pas les profils sans photos ou avec peu d'informations.

5. Cristina n'aime pas que Juan soit avocat parce qu'elle pense qu'il peut être ennuyeux.

6. Le côté créatif de Juan est qu'il aime chanter et écrire.

Exercice 2:

1. Faux

2. Vrai

3. Vrai

4. Faux

5. Faux

6. Vrai

Chapter 4: Sortir faire du jogging – Going out for a jog

"La vie est une course de fond. L'important n'est pas d'arriver le premier, mais de courir avec passion et persévérance."

- Albert Camus

Cristina vit avec son petit ami depuis quelques mois. Il part très tôt au travail, donc la plupart du temps, il n'est plus là quand elle se lève. Cristina commence son travail à 9 heures du matin, ce qui lui laisse le temps de tout faire calmement. Son réveil sonne à 7 heures et demie, et Cristina se lève pour se brosser les dents. Elle se prépare une arepa qu'elle accompagne d'un café au lait. Elle regarde la télévision pendant quelques minutes, puis se prépare à sortir pour faire un jogging. Elle préfère courir à cette heure-là parce qu'il n'y a pas trop de monde dans la rue. Elle court à son rythme, respirant profondément et appréciant le paysage. La journée est belle, le ciel est dégagé et il fait soleil. Il y a un parc avec beaucoup d'arbres dans le quartier de Cristina, qu'elle adore parce qu'il est magnifique et qu'il y a toujours des écureuils qui grimpent aux arbres. Parfois, elle nourrit les écureuils avec des fraises ou des bananes.

Avant de quitter le parc, Cristina s'arrête un moment pour prendre un peu de soleil et apprécier les sons de la nature. Elle vérifie l'heure sur son téléphone et se dépêche de rentrer chez elle pour ne pas être en retard à son travail. Elle doit encore prendre une douche et s'habiller. En arrivant devant la porte de sa maison, elle ne trouve pas ses clés. Elles ne sont ni dans ses poches, ni dans sa banane. Peut-être a-t-elle laissé les clés à la maison, ou les a-t-elle perdues dans le parc.

Un peu angoissée, elle appelle son petit ami, mais il ne répond pas au téléphone. Peut-être est-il en réunion importante ou simplement occupé. Cristina ne sait pas quoi faire, car elle ne veut pas être irresponsable et arriver en retard au travail. Elle retourne au parc, à l'endroit où elle s'est assise il y a quelques minutes, et cherche les clés. Elle va même jusqu'à fouiller dans un buisson, mais ne voit les clés nulle part. Elle retourne devant sa porte, et sa voisine lui demande si tout va bien et l'invite chez elle pour une tasse de café. Le ciel s'assombrit un peu et il fait froid, alors Cristina accepte. C'est mieux que d'attendre dans la rue. Cristina envoie un courriel à son patron pour expliquer la situation, en espérant qu'il comprenne.

Cristina est en colère contre elle-même d'être si distraite et d'avoir perdu ses clés. Sa voisine lui dit de ne pas s'inquiéter, que ça arrive à tout le monde.

Quelques minutes plus tard, le petit ami de Cristina finit par répondre au téléphone. Il lui dit qu'il est très occupé en ce moment et qu'il ne peut pas quitter le bureau, mais qu'il pourra rentrer à la maison dans une heure. Cristina se résigne et accepte la situation. En attendant, elle joue avec le chien de la voisine, un vieux chien mais très joueur. Elle lance la balle et le chien la rapporte. Elle joue avec lui jusqu'à ce que son petit ami arrive. Cristina court à la salle de bain, se déshabille et prend une douche. Elle met une blouse et une jupe, et son petit ami la dépose au travail. Cristina s'excuse auprès de son patron pour son retard, mais celui-ci lui dit de ne pas s'inquiéter et qu'il n'est pas fâché parce qu'elle arrive toujours à l'heure au bureau. Cela la rassure un peu.

Le soir, sans pression, Cristina cherche ses clés mais ne les trouve pas. C'est très étrange. Le lendemain, elle va chez le serrurier pour faire de nouvelles clés.

Résumé

Cristina se leva un matin, prête pour une journée normale. Elle prend son petit déjeuner, regarde la télévision et sort faire un jogging au parc près de chez elle. Quand elle revient à la maison, elle se rend compte que les clés ne sont pas dans ses poches. Elle appelle son petit ami, mais il est déjà au travail et ne répond pas. Sa voisine l'invite à attendre chez elle avec une tasse de café. Elle se divertit un moment en jouant avec le chien de sa voisine. Quand son petit ami arrive, elle se dépêche de prendre une douche et de s'habiller pour partir au travail. Cristina est très embarrassée, mais son patron lui dit de ne pas s'inquiéter. Le lendemain, elle va chez le serrurier pour faire de nouvelles clés.

Summary

Cristina wakes up one morning, ready to have a normal day. She has breakfast, watches TV, and goes jogging for a while at the park near her house. When she returns home, she realizes her keys are not in her pockets. She calls her boyfriend, but he's at work so he doesn't pick up the phone. Her neighbor invites her over to her house for a cup of coffee while she waits. She distracts herself playing with her neighbor's dog for a while. When her boyfriend gets home, she rushes to take a shower and gets dressed for work. Cristina feels embarrassed, but her boss tells her not to worry. The next day, she goes to the locksmith for new keys.

Glossaire – Glossary

- **Elle vit avec son petit ami depuis quelques mois.**: She's been living with her boyfriend for a couple of months.

- **Il commence le travail très tôt.**: He starts work pretty early.

- **La plupart du temps.**: Most of the time.

- **Elle se lève.**: She gets up.

- **Il est déjà parti.**: He's already gone.

- **Ce qui lui laisse le temps.**: Which gives her time.

- **De tout faire calmement.**: To do everything calmly.

- **Son réveil sonne à 7h30.**: Her alarm goes off at 7:30.

- **Elle se lève du lit.**: She gets out of bed.

- **Elle se brosse les dents.**: She brushes her teeth.

- **Elle se prépare une arepa.**: She makes herself an arepa.

- **Elle l'accompagne d'un café au lait.**: She pairs it with a coffee with milk.

- **Elle regarde la télévision pendant quelques minutes.**: She watches TV for a few minutes.

- **Elle se prépare à aller courir.**: She gets ready to go jogging.

- **Elle préfère courir à cette heure-ci.**: She prefers to jog at this time.

- **Il n'y a pas trop de monde dans la rue.**: There aren't that many people on the street.

- **Elle court à son rythme.**: She jogs at her own pace.

- **En respirant profondément.**: Breathing deeply.

- **En appréciant le paysage.**: Taking in the view.

- **Il fait beau.**: It's a nice day outside.

- **Le ciel est dégagé.**: The sky is clear.

- **Il fait soleil.**: It's sunny.

- **Un parc avec beaucoup d'arbres.**: A park with lots of trees.

- **Dans le quartier de Cristina.**: In Cristina's neighborhood.

- **Il y a toujours des écureuils.**: There's always squirrels.

- **Qui grimpent aux arbres.**: Climbing the trees.

- **Elle nourrit parfois les écureuils.**: She sometimes feeds the squirrels.

- **Elle s'arrête un moment.**: She stops for a moment.

- **Pour prendre un peu de soleil.**: To take in the sun.

- **Pour apprécier les sons de la nature.**: To take in the sounds of nature.

- **Elle vérifie l'heure.**: She checks the time.

- **Elle se dépêche de rentrer chez elle.**: She rushes back home.

- **Pour ne pas être en retard au travail.**: To not be late for work.

- **Elle doit encore prendre une douche.**: She still has to take a shower.

- **S'habiller.**: To get dressed.
- **Elle arrive à la porte de la maison.**: She gets to her front door.
- **Elle ne trouve pas ses clés.**: She can't find her keys.
- **Dans ses poches.**: In her pockets.
- **Sa banane.**: Her fanny pack.
- **Elle a laissé les clés.**: She left her keys.
- **Elle les a perdues dans le parc.**: She lost them in the park.
- **Angoissée.**: Worried.
- **Il ne répond pas au téléphone.**: He doesn't pick up the phone.
- **Il est en réunion.**: He's in a meeting.
- **Elle ne sait pas quoi faire.**: She doesn't know what to do.
- **Irresponsable.**: Irresponsible.
- **Elle retourne au parc.**: She walks back to the park.
- **À l'endroit où elle s'est assise.**: To the place where she sat down.
- **Il y a quelques minutes.**: A few minutes ago.
- **Un buisson.**: A bush.
- **Nulle part.**: Nowhere.
- **Sa voisine.**: Her neighbor (female).
- **Si tout va bien.**: If everything is alright.
- **Elle l'invite chez elle.**: She invites her into her house.
- **Pour une tasse de café.**: For a cup of coffee.
- **Le ciel s'assombrit.**: The sky gets dark.
- **Il fait froid.**: It's cold.
- **Elle accepte.**: She accepts.
- **C'est mieux que.**: It's better than.
- **Attendre dans la rue.**: Waiting on the street.
- **Elle envoie un courriel à son patron.**: She emails her boss.
- **Expliquant la situation.**: Explaining the situation.
- **En espérant qu'il comprenne.**: Hoping he will understand.

- **Elle est en colère contre elle-même.**: She's angry at herself.

- **D'être si distraite.**: For being so absent-minded.

- **Perdre ses clés.**: Losing her keys.

- **Elle lui dit de ne pas s'inquiéter.**: She tells her not to worry.

- **Que ces choses arrivent à tout le monde.**: That those things happen to everyone.

- **Quelques minutes plus tard.**: A few minutes later.

- **Trop occupé pour quitter le bureau.**: Too busy to leave the office.

- **Il peut.**: He can.

- **Elle se résigne.**: She gives up.

- **Pendant qu'elle attend.**: While she waits.

- **Elle commence à jouer avec le chien.**: She starts playing with the dog.

- **Joueur.**: Playful.

- **Elle lance la balle.**: She throws the ball.

- **Il va la chercher.**: He goes for it.

- **Il la rapporte.**: He brings it back.

- **Elle court à la salle de bain.**: She runs to the bathroom.

- **Elle se déshabille.**: She undresses.

- **Elle met une blouse et une jupe.**: She puts on a blouse and a skirt.

- **Il lui donne un coup de pouce.**: He gives her a ride.

- **Elle s'excuse.**: She apologizes.

- **Pour son retard.**: For her tardiness.

- **Il n'est pas fâché contre elle.**: He's not mad at her.

- **Elle arrive toujours au bureau à temps.**: She always gets to the office on time.

- **Cela la fait se sentir mieux.**: That makes her feel better.

- **Maintenant sans pression.**: Now, without pressure.

- **C'est très étrange.**: It's very strange.

- **Elle va chez le serrurier.**: She goes to the locksmith.

Exercice 1

Répondez aux questions suivantes – Answer the following questions.

1. À quelle heure Cristina se lève-t-elle? – What time does Cristina wake up?

_____

2. Que prend Cristina pour le petit-déjeuner? – What does Cristina have for breakfast?

_____

3. Pourquoi Cristina préfère-t-elle courir à cette heure-ci? – Why does Cristina prefer to go jogging at that time?

_____

4. Quel animal voit-elle dans le parc? – What animal does she see at the park?

_____

5. Que fait Cristina avant de quitter le parc? – What does Cristina do before leaving the park?

_____

6. Qu'est-ce que Cristina perd? – What does Cristina lose?

_____

Exercice 2

Choisissez entre "vrai" ou "faux" – Choose "true" or "false"

1. Cristina vit avec son petit ami depuis quelques années. – Cristina has been living with her boyfriend for a few years.

_____

2. Le petit ami de Cristina se lève avant elle. – Cristina's boyfriend wakes up before her.

_____

3. C'est un matin froid. – It's a cold morning.

_____

4. Le parc est près de chez elle. – The park is near her home.

_____

5. Cristina nourrit parfois les écureuils. – Cristina sometimes feeds the squirrels.

_____

6. Sa voisine lui offre une tasse de café. – Her neighbor offers her a cup of coffee.

_____

Réponses– Answers

Exercice 1:

1. Cristina se lève à 7h30.

2. Cristina prend une arepa avec un café au lait pour le petit-déjeuner.

3. Cristina préfère courir à cette heure-là parce qu'il n'y a pas de monde dans la rue.

4. Cristina voit beaucoup d'écureuils dans le parc.

5. Avant de partir, Cristina s'arrête un moment pour prendre le soleil et apprécier les sons de la nature.

6. Cristina perd ses clés.

Exercice 2:

1. Faux

2. Vrai

3. Faux

4. Vrai

5. Vrai

6. Vrai

BOOK 4

Learn Intermediate French for Adults Workbook:

Go from French Beginner to Intermediate in 30 Days!

Explore to Win

Book 4 Description

Are you ready to elevate your understanding of French to the next level?

If so, you're ready for your next workbook.

In this comprehensive workbook, you will find:

- Simplified explanations of past, present, and future tenses.

- Clear and concise grammar explanations.

- Tips and tricks for mastering French conjugations.

- Easy-to-follow pronunciation guides.

- Everyday phrases that are practical and useful.

- Techniques for mixing different tenses seamlessly.

- Guidance on forming hypotheses in French.

- Detailed explanations of the subjunctive and imperative moods.

- Insight into using impersonal constructions.

- Exercises and answer keys designed to reinforce every topic covered.

Chapter 1: Blast from the past

"Le passé est une lanterne allumée dans nos mains qui éclaire le chemin derrière nous."

- Victor Hugo

The past tense in French, known as "le passé," is used to describe actions or events that have already occurred. French utilizes several forms of past tense, each serving a distinct purpose. The most commonly used is the "passé composé," which conveys completed actions or events. Another form, the "imparfait," expresses continuous, habitual, or incomplete actions in the past, often setting a scene or describing background conditions.

Talking About Events in the Past

Le passé simple

Le Passé Simple is used to express actions that were completed in the past. Unlike the Passé Composé, which is commonly used in everyday conversation, the Passé Simple is more formal and is rarely used in spoken French today.

1. Purpose and Usage of the Passé Simple

- Literary and Formal Contexts: The Passé Simple is primarily used in literature (novels, short stories, poetry), historical narratives, and formal writing such as academic papers or articles. It helps create a sense of distance and formality, making the text feel more sophisticated or classical.

- Narration and Temporal clarity of Completed Actions: This tense narrates actions that were completed in the past and have no direct connection to the present. It's often used to sequence events in a story.

2. Conjugation of the Passé Simple

The Passé Simple has unique conjugation patterns, which vary according to the verb group (1st, 2nd, or 3rd group verbs).

- 1st Group Verbs (-er verbs like "chanter"):

Pronoun	Conjugation of "chanter" (to sing)

Je	chantai
Tu	chantas
Il/Elle/On	chanta
Nous	chantâmes
Vous	chantâtes
Ils/Elles	chantèrent

- 2nd Group Verbs (-ir verbs like "finir"):

Pronoun	Conjugation of "finir" (to finish)
Je	finis
Tu	finis
Il/Elle/On	finit
Nous	finîmes
Vous	finîtes
Ils/Elles	finirent

- 3rd Group Verbs (irregular verbs like "vivre"):

Pronoun	Conjugation of "vivre" (to live)
Je	vécus
Tu	vécus

Il/Elle/On	vécut
Nous	vécûmes
Vous	vécûtes
Ils/Elles	vécurent

3. Examples of the Passé Simple in Context

- Literary Example:

    o Il chanta une dernière fois avant de partir.

    o (He sang one last time before leaving.)

- Historical Example:

    o Napoléon Bonaparte devint empereur en 1804.

    o (Napoleon Bonaparte became emperor in 1804.)

- Formal Writing Example:

    o Les chercheurs découvrirent une nouvelle méthode pour traiter la maladie.

    o (The researchers discovered a new method to treat the disease.)

4. Differences Between Passé Simple and Passé Composé

- Usage in Spoken French:

    o The Passé Composé is used in everyday conversation to describe past actions that have relevance to the present or are simply part of a story or dialogue. The Passé Simple is not often used in spoken French since it's considered to be formal and old-fashioned.

- Style and Tone:

    o The Passé Simple conveys a more formal, literary, or poetic tone, which adds a level of sophistication or distance to the narrative. In contrast, the Passé Composé is neutral and more common in modern communication.

- Regional and Cultural Context:

    o Passé Simple may be less familiar in other Francophone regions outside of France where the Passé Composé may be more used culturally.

5. Common Verbs in the Passé Simple

Some verbs in the Passé Simple are highly irregular and need to be memorized separately. Here are a few common ones:

- Être (to be): je fus, tu fus, il/elle/on fut, nous fûmes, vous fûtes, ils/elles furent

- Avoir (to have): j'eus, tu eus, il/elle/on eut, nous eûmes, vous eûtes, ils/elles eurent

- Faire (to do/make): je fis, tu fis, il/elle/on fit, nous fîmes, vous fîtes, ils/elles firent

- Aller (to go): j'allai, tu allas, il/elle/on alla, nous allâmes, vous allâtes, ils/elles allèrent

Talking About Past Experiences

Passé Composé

Le passé composé is one of the most commonly used past tenses in French, primarily used to describe actions that are completed and have specific time frames or definitive results in the past. It is equivalent to the English simple past (e.g., "I ate") or present perfect (e.g., "I have eaten") and is essential for everyday communication.

To form the passé composé, you need an auxiliary verb — either "avoir" (to have) or "être" (to be) — conjugated in the present tense, followed by the past participle of the main verb.

Most verbs use "avoir," but some, particularly those indicating motion or change of state (like "aller" – to go, "venir" – to come, "naître" – to be born, "mourir" – to die), use "être."

When using "être" as the auxiliary, remember that the past participle must agree in gender and number with the subject, making the tense more nuanced and reflective of the sentence's context.

For example, the sentence "J'ai mangé" means "I ate" or "I have eaten," using "avoir" as the auxiliary. In contrast, "Elle est allée" means "She went," using "être" and showing agreement with the subject ("elle" – she).

Infinitive (French)	Present Tense Conjugation (French)	Sample Sentences (French)	Translation (English)
Chanter	Je chante, Tu chantes, Il/Elle chante, Nous chantons, Vous chantez, Ils/Elles chantent	Elle chante une belle chanson.	She sings a beautiful song.
		Nous chantons tous les jours dans la chorale.	We sing every day in the choir.

Manger	Je mange, Tu manges, Il/Elle mange, Nous mangeons, Vous mangez, Ils/Elles mangent	Je mange une pomme.	I am eating an apple.
		Ils mangent au restaurant ce soir.	They are eating at the restaurant tonight.
Vivre	Je vis, Tu vis, Il/Elle vit, Nous vivons, Vous vivez, Ils/Elles vivent	Nous vivons dans une petite ville.	We live in a small town.
		Tu vis près de la mer.	You live near the sea.

Talking About Past Habits

Imparfait

The Imparfait is used to describe past actions or situations that were ongoing, habitual, repeated, or used to set the scene in a narrative. It often provides background information or describes what was happening when another action occurred (often expressed in the Passé Composé).

1. Purpose and Usage of the Imparfait

The Imparfait is used in several contexts in French:

- Describing past habits or repeated actions.
  - Quand j'étais enfant, je jouais au football tous les jours.
  - (When I was a child, I used to play football every day.)
- Setting the scene to provide background information or describe conditions in the past.
  - Il faisait froid et il pleuvait.
  - (It was cold and raining.)
- Describing ongoing actions in the past:.
  - Elle lisait un livre quand je suis entré.
  - (She was reading a book when I entered.)

- Describing simultaneous actions in the past.
    - Pendant que tu cuisinais, je regardais la télévision.
    - (While you were cooking, I was watching TV.)

2. Conjugation of the Imparfait

Here are the conjugation patterns for the verbs "chanter" (to sing), "manger" (to eat), and "vivre" (to live) in the Imparfait:

- 1st Group Verb (-er verbs like "chanter"):

Pronoun	Conjugation of "chanter" (to sing)
Je	chantais
Tu	chantais
Il/Elle/On	chantait
Nous	chantions
Vous	chantiez
Ils/Elles	chantaient

- 2nd Group Verb (-ir verbs like "finir"):

Pronoun	Conjugation of "finir" (to finish)
Je	finissais
Tu	finissais
Il/Elle/On	finissait
Nous	finissions
Vous	finissiez

- 3rd Group Verb (irregular verbs like "vivre"):

Pronoun	Conjugation of "vivre" (to live)
Je	vivais
Tu	vivais
Il/Elle/On	vivait
Nous	vivions
Vous	viviez
Ils/Elles	vivaient

Examples of the Imparfait in Context

- Describing a Habitual Action in the Past:
    - Quand j'étais petit, je chantais souvent dans la chorale.
    - (When I was young, I often sang in the choir.)
- Setting the Scene:
    - Il pleuvait et le vent soufflait fort quand nous sommes arrivés.
    - (It was raining, and the wind was blowing hard when we arrived.)
- Describing an Ongoing Action Interrupted by Another:
    - Elle mangeait quand le téléphone a sonné.
    - (She was eating when the phone rang.)
- Simultaneous Actions in the Past:
    - Pendant que je vivais à Paris, tu étudiais à Londres.
    - (While I was living in Paris, you were studying in London.)

3. Differences Between Imparfait and Passé Composé

- Imparfait:
    - Describes actions that were ongoing, habitual, or repetitive in the past.
    - Used to provide background information, set the scene, or describe situations.
    - Focuses on the duration or continuity of the past action.
- Passé Composé:
    - Describes actions that were completed in the past.
    - Used to express specific events or actions that occurred once or at a particular point in time.
    - Focuses on the completion of the action.

For example:

- Il lisait un livre (Imparfait) quand elle est entrée (Passé Composé).
- (He was reading a book when she entered.)

Time Markers for the Past

There are several words and phrases that trigger the past tenses by letting us know beforehand that what follows is an event in the past.

Time markers for the Passé Simple

1. Verb: Chanter (to sing)

- Il chanta une chanson magnifique à la fin du concert.
- (He sang a beautiful song at the end of the concert.)
- Nous chantâmes tous ensemble lors de la cérémonie.
- (We all sang together during the ceremony.)

2. Verb: Manger (to eat)

- Elle mangea rapidement son dîner avant de partir.
- (She ate her dinner quickly before leaving.)
- Ils mangèrent tout le gâteau en quelques minutes.
- (They ate the whole cake in a few minutes.)

3. Verb: Vivre (to live)

- Ils vécurent en France pendant dix ans avant de déménager.
- (They lived in France for ten years before moving.)
- Je vécus une aventure incroyable lors de mon voyage en Afrique.
- (I lived an incredible adventure during my trip to Africa.)

4. Verb: Avoir (to have)

- Il eut un succès immense après la publication de son livre.
- (He had immense success after the publication of his book.)
- Nous eûmes une réunion productive avec les investisseurs.
- (We had a productive meeting with the investors.)

5. Verb: Être (to be)

- Elle fut très contente de recevoir ce prix prestigieux.
- (She was very happy to receive that prestigious award.)
- Vous fûtes les premiers à arriver à la fête.
- (You were the first to arrive at the party.)

6. Verb: Faire (to do/make)

- Ils firent tout leur possible pour résoudre le problème.
- (They did everything they could to solve the problem.)
- Je fis une longue promenade dans le parc hier.
- (I took a long walk in the park yesterday.)

7. Verb: Aller (to go)

- Elle alla au marché pour acheter des fruits frais.
- (She went to the market to buy fresh fruit.)
- Nous allâmes à Paris pour les vacances d'été.
- (We went to Paris for summer vacation.)

8. Verb: Prendre (to take)

- Il prit le train pour aller à Lyon.
- (He took the train to go to Lyon.)
- Elles prirent la décision de partir en voyage.

- (They made the decision to go on a trip.)

Time markers for the Passé Composé

1. Verb: Chanter (to sing)

   - J'ai chanté une chanson pour ma mère hier soir.

   - (I sang a song for my mother last night.)

   - Ils ont chanté dans le parc tout l'après-midi.

   - (They sang in the park all afternoon.)

2. Verb: Manger (to eat)

   - Nous avons mangé un délicieux repas au restaurant.

   - (We ate a delicious meal at the restaurant.)

   - Elle a mangé du chocolat avant de dormir.

   - (She ate some chocolate before sleeping.)

3. Verb: Vivre (to live)

   - Il a vécu en Italie pendant trois ans.

   - (He lived in Italy for three years.)

   - J'ai vécu une expérience incroyable pendant mon voyage.

   - (I had an incredible experience during my trip.)

4. Verb: Aller (to go)

   - Je suis allé(e) au cinéma avec mes amis hier soir.

   - (I went to the cinema with my friends last night.)

   - Ils sont allés à la montagne pour le week-end.

   - (They went to the mountains for the weekend.)

5. Verb: Faire (to do/make)

   - Nous avons fait nos devoirs après le dîner.

   - (We did our homework after dinner.)

   - Elle a fait une belle peinture pour le concours.

   - (She made a beautiful painting for the contest.)

6. Verb: Prendre (to take)

- J'ai pris le train ce matin pour aller au travail.

- (I took the train this morning to go to work.)

- Ils ont pris une décision importante pour l'avenir de l'entreprise.

- (They made an important decision for the future of the company.)

7. Verb: Voir (to see)

- Elle a vu un film intéressant hier soir.

- (She saw an interesting film last night.)

- Nous avons vu les étoiles dans le ciel clair.

- (We saw the stars in the clear sky.)

8. Verb: Être (to be)

- Ils ont été très heureux de nous revoir.

- (They were very happy to see us again.)

- J'ai été surpris par la nouvelle.

- (I was surprised by the news.)

Time markers for the Imparfait

1. Verb: Chanter (to sing)

- Je chantais dans la chorale tous les dimanches.

- (I used to sing in the choir every Sunday.)

- Ils chantaient ensemble dans le jardin.

- (They were singing together in the garden.)

2. Verb: Manger (to eat)

- Nous mangions toujours à 20 heures.

- (We always ate at 8 p.m.)

- Elle mangeait une pomme quand le téléphone a sonné.

- (She was eating an apple when the phone rang.)

3. Verb: Vivre (to live)

- Ils vivaient en France pendant plusieurs années.

- (They lived in France for several years.)

- Je vivais chez mes parents à l'époque.
- (I was living with my parents at that time.)

4. Verb: Aller (to go)

- Chaque été, nous allions à la plage.
- (Every summer, we used to go to the beach.)
- Il allait souvent au marché le dimanche matin.
- (He often went to the market on Sunday mornings.)

5. Verb: Faire (to do/make)

- Quand j'étais enfant, je faisais du vélo tous les jours.
- (When I was a child, I used to ride my bike every day.)
- Elle faisait ses devoirs pendant que nous regardions la télévision.
- (She was doing her homework while we were watching TV.)

6. Verb: Avoir (to have)

- Nous avions beaucoup de travail à faire cette semaine-là.
- (We had a lot of work to do that week.)
- Il avait toujours faim après l'école.
- (He was always hungry after school.)

7. Verb: Être (to be)

- Il était très timide quand il était petit.
- (He was very shy when he was little.)
- Les rues étaient pleines de monde ce jour-là.
- (The streets were full of people that day.)

8. Verb: Regarder (to watch)

- Nous regardions souvent des films ensemble le soir.
- (We often watched movies together in the evening.)
- Tu regardais par la fenêtre quand il est arrivé.
- (You were looking out the window when he arrived.)

Duration of an Action

Duration of an Action:

- **Imperfect:** Used to express the duration of an action.

  ○ *Il pleuvait toute la journée.* (It rained all day.)

- **Past Continuous:** Formed using the auxiliary verb *être* and the present participle.

  ○ *J'étais en train de lire un livre.* (I was reading a book.)

- **Past Simple:** Can also indicate duration, especially when paired with expressions like *pendant* (for) or *tout* (all).

  ○ *Nous avons attendu pendant deux heures.* (We waited for two hours.)

Choice of Tense:

The choice between the imperfect and past continuous often depends on the nuance of meaning you want to convey.

- **Imperfect:** Focuses on the ongoing nature of the action.
- **Past Continuous:** Emphasizes the action in progress at a specific point in the past.

Example:

- *Hier soir, je regardais la télévision.* (Last night, I was watching TV.) - Emphasizes the action in progress.
- *Hier soir, je regardais toujours la télévision.* (Last night, I was still watching TV.) - Emphasizes the ongoing nature of the action.

Additional Considerations:

- **Past Simple:** Often used for completed actions or a sequence of events.
- **Passé Composé:** Can also be used for completed actions, especially when emphasizing the result.
- **Future Perfect:** Used to express actions that will be completed by a certain time in the future.

Exercises

1. **The Passé Simple is primarily used for:**
   a) Ongoing actions in the past
   b) Completed actions in the past
   c) Future actions
   d) Habitual actions in the past

2. **The Passé Simple is most commonly found in:**
   a) Everyday conversations
   b) Spoken French
   c) Formal writing
   d) Casual conversations

3. **Which tense is used to describe actions that were completed in the past and have no direct connection to the present?:**
   a) Imparfait
   b) Passé Composé
   c) Passé Simple
   d) Future Perfect

4. **To form the Passé Composé, you need:**
   a) An auxiliary verb and the present participle
   b) An auxiliary verb and the past participle
   c) The present tense and the future participle
   d) The past tense and the past participle

5. **The auxiliary verb "être" is typically used with verbs related to:**
   a) Actions
   b) States
   c) Emotions
   d) Thoughts

6. **The Imparfait is used to describe:**
   a) Completed actions
   b) Ongoing or habitual actions
   c) Future actions
   d) Specific events

7. **Which tense is used to set the scene or provide background information in a narrative?:**

   a) Passé Simple

   b) Passé Composé

   c) Imparfait

   d) Future Perfect

8. **Which tense is more common in spoken French?:**

   a) Passé Simple

   b) Passé Composé

   c) Imparfait

   d) All of the above

9. **The Passé Simple and Passé Composé are both used to talk about the past. How do they differ in terms of their usage?:**

   a) The Passé Simple is more formal and literary.

   b) The Passé Composé is more formal and literary.

   c) There is no difference in their usage.

   d) The Passé Simple is used for ongoing actions, while the Passé Composé is used for completed actions.

10. **Which tense would you use to describe an action that was happening in the past when another action interrupted it?:**

    a) Passé Simple

    b) Passé Composé

    c) Imparfait

    d) Future Perfect

Answer Key

1. b) Completed actions in the past
2. c) Formal writing
3. c) Passé Simple
4. b) An auxiliary verb and the past participle
5. b) States
6. b) Ongoing or habitual actions
7. c) Imparfait
8. b) Passé Composé
9. a) The Passé Simple is more formal and literary.
10. c) Imparfait

Chapter 2: Describing People, Places, and Things

"To describe a thing is to know it; to know a thing is to love it."

- Victor Hugo

Relative Pronouns

Relative pronouns are words that connect dependent clauses to independent clauses.

Here are the most common relative pronouns in French:

Who/Whom

- **Qui** (masculine and feminine, singular, and plural): Used for people and things.
  - *Le livre **qui** est sur la table est à moi.* (The book **that** is on the table is mine.)
  - *La femme **qui** tu as rencontrée est ma sœur.* (The woman **whom** you met is my sister.)

Which

- **Que** (neutral, singular, and plural): Used for things.
  - *La maison **que** j'ai achetée est très grande.* (The house **which** I bought is very big.)
  - *Les fleurs **que** tu m'as offertes sont magnifiques.* (The flowers **which** you gave me are beautiful.)

Whose

- **Dont** (neutral, singular, and plural): Used to indicate possession.
  - *Le garçon **dont** le père est médecin étudie la médecine.* (The boy **whose** father is a doctor is studying medicine.)
  - *La voiture **dont** j'ai parlé est à vendre.* (The car **whose** I talked about is for sale.)

Where

- **Où** (neutral, singular, and plural): Used to indicate place.
  - *Le restaurant **où** nous avons mangé était délicieux.* (The restaurant **where** we ate was delicious.)

- *La ville **où** je suis né est très petite.* (The city **where** I was born is very small.)

When

- **Quand** (neutral, singular, and plural): Used to indicate time.

  - *Le jour **quand** nous sommes arrivés, il faisait beau.* (The day **when** we arrived, it was sunny.)

  - *L'heure **quand** le concert commence est 20h.* (The time **when** the concert starts is 8 pm.)

Why

- **Pourquoi** (neutral, singular, and plural): Used to indicate reason.

  - *La raison **pourquoi** je suis en retard est que j'ai eu un accident.* (The reason **why** I'm late is that I had an accident.)

Note: In French, relative pronouns often begin a relative clause. However, in certain constructions, the relative pronoun can be omitted if it is the direct object of the verb in the relative clause.

- **Example:**

  - *Le livre **que** je lis est très intéressant.* (The book **that** I'm reading is very interesting.)

  - *Le livre je lis est très intéressant.* (The book I'm reading is very interesting.)

French Relative Pronoun	English Translation	Usage Example	English Example
qui	who, that, which	Le livre qui est sur la table est rouge.	The book that is on the table is red.
que	whom, that, which	C'est la fille que j'ai vue hier.	That's the girl whom I saw yesterday.
dont	whose, of whom, of which	Voici l'homme dont je t'ai parlé.	Here is the man whom I told you about.
où	where, when	C'est l'endroit où nous nous sommes rencontrés.| It's the place where we met.	

lequel (masc. sing.)	which	Le livre pour lequel j'ai payé est perdu.	The book which I paid for is lost.
laquelle (fem. sing.)	which	La maison dans laquelle ils vivent est grande.	The house in which they live is big.
lesquels (masc. pl.)	which	Les films pour lesquels ils sont célèbres.	The movies for which they are famous.
lesquelles (fem. pl.)	which	Les idées avec lesquelles nous travaillons.	The ideas with which we are working.
ce qui	what (subject)	Ce qui m'intéresse est la littérature.	What interests me is literature.
ce que	what (object)	Dis-moi ce que tu veux.	Tell me what you want.
ce dont	what (of which)	Ce dont j'ai besoin, c'est de vacances.	What I need is a vacation.

Relative Clauses

Relative Clauses in French

Relative clauses provide additional information about a noun or pronoun in the main clause. They are introduced by relative pronouns, such as *qui* (who/that), *que* (which/that), *dont* (whose), *où* (where), *quand* (when), and *pourquoi* (why).

Basic Structure:

- **Main clause + relative pronoun + relative clause**

Examples:

- **Qui** (who/that):
    - *Le garçon **qui** a gagné le prix est très intelligent.* (The boy **who** won the prize is very intelligent.)
    - *La femme **qui** tu as rencontrée est ma sœur.* (The woman **whom** you met is my sister.)

- **Que** (which/that):
    - *Le livre **que** j'ai acheté est très intéressant.* (The book **which** I bought is very interesting.)
    - *Les fleurs **que** tu m'as offertes sont magnifiques.* (The flowers **which** you gave me are beautiful.)
- **Dont** (whose):
    - *Le garçon **dont** le père est médecin étudie la médecine.* (The boy **whose** father is a doctor is studying medicine.)
    - *La voiture **dont** j'ai parlé est à vendre.* (The car **whose** I talked about is for sale.)
- **Où** (where):
    - *Le restaurant **où** nous avons mangé était délicieux.* (The restaurant **where** we ate was delicious.)
    - *La ville **où** je suis né est très petite.* (The city **where** I was born is very small.)
- **Quand** (when):
    - *Le jour **quand** nous sommes arrivés, il faisait beau.* (The day **when** we arrived, it was sunny.)
    - *L'heure **quand** le concert commence est 20h.* (The time **when** the concert starts is 8 pm.)
- **Pourquoi** (why):
    - *La raison **pourquoi** je suis en retard est que j'ai eu un accident.* (The reason **why** I'm late is that I had an accident.)

Subject-Verb Agreement:

In French, the verb in a relative clause must agree in number and gender with the antecedent (the noun or pronoun it refers to).

- **Example:**
    - *Les garçons **qui** jouent au football sont très sportifs.* (The boys **who** play football are very sporty.)

Defining relative clauses

Defining relative clauses in French provide essential information to identify or define the noun or pronoun in the main clause. They are not set off by commas.

Structure:

- **Main clause + relative pronoun + defining relative clause**

Examples:

- **Qui** (who/that):
    - *Le garçon **qui** a gagné le prix est très intelligent.* (The boy **who** won the prize is very intelligent.)
    - *La femme **qui** tu as rencontrée est ma sœur.* (The woman **whom** you met is my sister.)

- **Que** (which/that):
    - *Le livre **que** j'ai acheté est très intéressant.* (The book **which** I bought is very interesting.)
    - *Les fleurs **que** tu m'as offertes sont magnifiques.* (The flowers **which** you gave me are beautiful.)

- **Dont** (whose):
    - *Le garçon **dont** le père est médecin étudie la médecine.* (The boy **whose** father is a doctor is studying medicine.)
    - *La voiture **dont** j'ai parlé est à vendre.* (The car **whose** I talked about is for sale.)

- **Où** (where):
    - *Le restaurant **où** nous avons mangé était délicieux.* (The restaurant **where** we ate was delicious.)
    - *La ville **où** je suis né est très petite.* (The city **where** I was born is very small.)

- **Quand** (when):
    - *Le jour **quand** nous sommes arrivés, il faisait beau.* (The day **when** we arrived, it was sunny.)
    - *L'heure **quand** le concert commence est 20h.* (The time **when** the concert starts is 8 pm.)

- **Pourquoi** (why):
    - *La raison **pourquoi** je suis en retard est que j'ai eu un accident.* (The reason **why** I'm late is that I had an accident.)

Note: In French, relative pronouns can often be omitted in defining relative clauses when they are the direct object of the verb in the relative clause.

- **Example:**
    - *Le livre **que** je lis est très intéressant.* (The book **that** I'm reading is very interesting.)
    - *Le livre je lis est très intéressant.* (The book I'm reading is very interesting.)

Non-defining relative clauses

Non-defining relative clauses in French provide additional information about the noun or pronoun in the main clause, but they are not essential to the meaning of the sentence. They are set off by commas.

Structure:

- **Main clause** + **comma** + **relative pronoun** + **non-defining relative clause** + **comma**

Examples:

- **Qui** (who/that):
    - *Marie, **qui** est ma meilleure amie, vient me voir ce soir.* (Marie, **who** is my best friend, is coming to see me tonight.)
    - *Le professeur, **qui** est très compétent, a expliqué la leçon clairement.* (The professor, **who** is very competent, explained the lesson clearly.)

- **Que** (which/that):
    - *Le livre, **que** j'ai acheté hier, est très intéressant.* (The book, **which** I bought yesterday, is very interesting.)
    - *Les fleurs, **que** tu m'as offertes pour mon anniversaire, sont magnifiques.* (The flowers, **which** you gave me for my birthday, are beautiful.)

- **Dont** (whose):
    - *Pierre, **dont** le père est médecin, étudie la médecine.* (Pierre, **whose** father is a doctor, is studying medicine.)
    - *La voiture, **dont** j'ai parlé hier, est à vendre.* (The car, **whose** I talked about yesterday, is for sale.)

- **Où** (where):
    - *Le restaurant, **où** nous avons mangé hier soir, était délicieux.* (The restaurant, **where** we ate last night, was delicious.)
    - *La ville, **où** je suis né, est très petite.* (The city, **where** I was born, is very small.)

- **Quand** (when):
    - *Le jour, **quand** nous sommes arrivés, il faisait beau.* (The day, **when** we arrived, it was sunny.)
    - *L'heure, **quand** le concert commence, est 20h.* (The time, **when** the concert starts, is 8 pm.)

- **Pourquoi** (why):

- *La raison, **pourquoi** je suis en retard, est que j'ai eu un accident.* (The reason, **why** I'm late, is that I had an accident.)

Exercises

1. Which relative pronoun is used to introduce a relative clause that refers to a person?

    a) que
    b) qui
    c) dont
    d) où

2. Which relative pronoun is used to introduce a relative clause that refers to a thing?

    a) qui
    b) que
    c) dont
    d) où

3. Which relative pronoun is used to indicate possession in a relative clause?

    a) qui
    b) que
    c) dont
    d) où

4. Which relative pronoun is used to indicate place in a relative clause?

    a) qui
    b) que
    c) dont
    d) où

5. Which relative pronoun is used to indicate time in a relative clause?

    a) qui
    b) que
    c) dont
    d) quand

6. Which relative pronoun is used to indicate reason in a relative clause?

    a) qui
    b) que
    c) dont
    d) pourquoi

7. In which construction can the relative pronoun be omitted in a French relative clause?

    a) When it is the subject of the relative clause

    b) When it is the direct object of the verb in the relative clause

    c) When it is the indirect object of the verb in the relative clause

    d) Always

8. Which relative pronoun is used to introduce a non defining relative clause?

    a) qui

    b) que

    c) dont

    d) où

9. What is the difference between a defining relative clause and a non-defining relative clause?

    a) Defining relative clauses provide essential information, while non-defining relative clauses provide additional information.

    b) Defining relative clauses are set off by commas, while non-defining relative clauses are not.

    c) Defining relative clauses use different relative pronouns than non-defining relative clauses.

    d) There is no difference between defining and non-defining relative clauses in French.

10. In which of the following sentences is the relative pronoun used correctly?

    a) Le livre qui je lis est très intéressant.

    b) La femme que tu as rencontrée est ma sœur.

    c) Le garçon dont le père est médecin étudie la médecine.

    d) Le restaurant où nous avons mangé était délicieux.

Answer Key

1. b) qui

2. b) que

3. c) dont

4. d) où

5. d) quand

6. d) pourquoi

7. b) When it is the direct object of the verb in the relative clause

8. a) qui

9. a) Defining relative clauses provide essential information, while non-defining relative clauses provide additional information.

10. c) Le garçon dont le père est médecin étudie la médecine.

Chapter 3: Present Subjunctive in Use

""Le style est l'homme même.""

- Georges-Louis Leclerc, Comte de Buffon

Up until now, we have only covered the indicative mood, which is used to describe real and factual situations. Now, we will explore scenarios that are hypothetical, uncertain, or not yet realized—contexts where the **subjunctive** mood is employed.

In French, there are several tenses within the subjunctive mood: le subjonctif présent (present subjunctive), le subjonctif passé (past subjunctive), le subjonctif imparfait (imperfect subjunctive), and le subjonctif plus-que-parfait (pluperfect subjunctive). Each of these tenses serves to convey different nuances of doubt, wish, emotion, or uncertainty.

Le Subjonctif Présent

The present subjunctive can be used to express possibility, desire, impressions, and hypothetical situations and for giving opinions and recommendations.

French Equivalent	Infinitive Form	Present Tense	Past Tense (Passé Composé)	Future Tense	Subjunctive Present	Conditional Present
Chanter	Je chanter	Je chante (I sing)	J'ai chanté (I sang)	Je chanterai (I will sing)	Il est important que je chante	Je chanterais (I would sing)
	Tu chanter	Tu chantes (You sing)	Tu as chanté (You sang)	Tu chanteras (You will sing)	Il faut que tu chantes	Tu chanterais (You would sing)
	Il/elle/on chanter	Il chante (He sings)	Il a chanté (He sang)	Il chantera (He will sing)	Bien qu'il chante	Il chanterait (He would sing)

	Nous chanter	Nous chantons (We sing)	Nous avons chanté (We sang)	Nous chanterons (We will sing)	Il est essentiel que nous chantions	Nous chanterions (We would sing)
Manger	Je manger	Je mange (I eat)	J'ai mangé (I ate)	Je mangerai (I will eat)	Il est crucial que je mange	Je mangerais (I would eat)
	Tu manger	Tu manges (You eat)	Tu as mangé (You ate)	Tu mangeras (You will eat)	Il faut que tu manges	Tu mangerais (You would eat)
	Il/elle/on manger	Il mange (He eats)	Il a mangé (He ate)	Il mangera (He will eat)	Bien qu'il mange	Il mangerait (He would eat)
	Nous manger	Nous mangeons (We eat)	Nous avons mangé (We ate)	Nous mangerons (We will eat)	Que nous mangions	Nous mangerions (We would eat)
Vivre	Je vivre	Je vis (I live)	J'ai vécu (I lived)	Je vivrai (I will live)	Il est important que je vive	Je vivrais (I would live)
	Tu vivre	Tu vis (You live)	Tu as vécu (You lived)	Tu vivras (You will live)	Que tu vives	Tu vivrais (You would live)
	Il/elle/on vivre	Il vit (He lives)	Il a vécu (He lived)	Il vivra (He will live)	Bien qu'il vive	Il vivrait (He would live)
	Nous vivre	Nous vivons (We live)	Nous avons vécu (We lived)	Nous vivrons (We will live)	Il est nécessaire	Nous vivrions

					que nous vivions	(We would live)

Uses of the Present Subjunctive

As we noted earlier, the present subjunctive is used to convey possibility, desire, impressions, hypothetical situations, and to express opinions and recommendations. Now, let's explore how to apply it.

Expressing desire

To express desire, the present subjunctive is often used in conjunction with the verb *vouloir* (to want) or *désirer* (to desire).

Examples:

- **Simple desire:**
  - *Je veux **qu'il vienne**.* (I want him to come.)
  - *Nous désirons **qu'elle réussisse**.* (We desire her to succeed.)
- **Desire with a negative:**
  - *Je ne veux pas **qu'ils partent**.* (I don't want them to leave.)
  - *Nous ne désirons pas **qu'elle échoue**.* (We don't want her to fail.)
- **Desire with *il faut* (it's necessary):**
  - *Il faut **qu'ils étudient** davantage.* (It's necessary for them to study more.)
  - *Il faut **que tu te dépêches**.* (It's necessary for you to hurry.)
- **Desire with *je voudrais* (I would like):**
  - *Je voudrais **qu'elle m'appelle**.* (I would like her to call me.)
  - *Nous voudrions **qu'ils viennent** à la fête.* (We would like them to come to the party.)

Expressing necessity

To express necessity, the present subjunctive is often used in conjunction with the verb *il faut* (it's necessary).

Examples:

- **Simple necessity:**
  - *Il faut **qu'ils étudient** davantage.* (It's necessary for them to study more.)

- *Il faut **que tu te dépêches***. (It's necessary for you to hurry.)
- **Necessity with a negative:**
  - *Il ne faut pas **qu'ils partent** maintenant*. (It's not necessary for them to leave now.)
  - *Il ne faut pas **que tu te fâches***. (It's not necessary for you to get angry.)
- **Necessity with *il est important* (it's important):**
  - *Il est important **qu'elle arrive** à l'heure*. (It's important for her to arrive on time.)
  - *Il est important **que nous soyons** ponctuels*. (It's important for us to be punctual.)

Expressing interests and feelings

To express interests, the present subjunctive is often used in conjunction with the verb *il est important* (it's important) or *je souhaite* (I wish).

Examples:

- **Expressing interest:**
  - *Il est important **que tu apprennes** le français*. (It's important for you to learn French.)
  - *Je souhaite **qu'ils viennent** nous voir*. (I wish they would come visit us.)
- **Expressing feelings of surprise or indignation:**
  - *Il est étonnant **qu'elle ne soit pas venue***. (It's surprising that she didn't come.)
  - *Il est scandaleux **qu'ils aient menti***. (It's scandalous that they lied.)
- **Expressing feelings of relief or disappointment:**
  - *Je suis soulagée **qu'il soit arrivé** à l'heure*. (I'm relieved that he arrived on time.)
  - *Je suis déçu **qu'ils n'aient pas accepté** notre proposition*. (I'm disappointed that they didn't accept our proposal.)

Expressing doubt and probability

To express doubt, the present subjunctive is often used in conjunction with the verbs *il est possible* (it's possible), *il est probable* (it's probable), *il est douteux* (it's doubtful), or *je doute que* (I doubt that).

Examples:

- **Expressing doubt:**
  - *Il est possible **qu'il pleuve** demain*. (It's possible that it will rain tomorrow.)
  - *Il est douteux **qu'ils arrivent** à l'heure*. (It's doubtful that they will arrive on time.)

- Je doute **qu'elle accepte** notre proposition. (I doubt that she will accept our proposal.)

To express probability, the present subjunctive is often used in conjunction with the verbs *il est probable* (it's probable), *il est certain* (it's certain), or *je suis sûr que* (I'm sure that).

Examples:

- **Expressing probability:**
  - *Il est probable **qu'ils viennent** à la fête.* (It's probable that they will come to the party.)
  - *Il est certain **qu'elle réussira**.* (It's certain that she will succeed.)
  - *Je suis sûr **qu'ils vont gagner** le match.* (I'm sure that they will win the match.)

Giving advice and orders and asking someone to do something

To give advice, the present subjunctive is often used in conjunction with the verbs *il faut* (it's necessary), *il est important* (it's important), or *je te conseille* (I advise you).

Examples:

- **Giving advice:**
  - *Il faut **que tu étudies** davantage.* (It's necessary for you to study more.)
  - *Il est important **que tu te dépêches**.* (It's important for you to hurry.)
  - *Je te conseille **que tu consultes** un médecin.* (I advise you to see a doctor.)

To give orders, the present subjunctive is often used with the imperative mood, especially in formal or polite contexts.

Examples:

- **Giving orders:**
  - *Il faut **que tu arrives** à l'heure.* (You must arrive on time.)
  - *Je veux **qu'il parte** immédiatement.* (I want him to leave immediately.)

To ask someone to do something, the present subjunctive is often used in conjunction with the verbs *pouvoir* (can), *devoir* (must), or *vouloir* (want).

Examples:

- **Asking someone to do something:**
  - *Peux-tu **m'aider** à porter ces valises?* (Can you help me carry these suitcases?)

- ○ *Tu dois **finir** ton travail avant de partir.* (You must finish your work before leaving.)
- ○ *Veux-tu **venir** avec moi?* (Do you want to come with me?)

Expressing purpose

To express purpose, the present subjunctive is often used in conjunction with the conjunction *afin que* (in order that) or *pour que* (so that).

Examples:

- **Expressing purpose:**
  - ○ *Je travaille dur **afin qu'elle réussisse**.* (I work hard **in order that** she succeeds.)
  - ○ *Il étudie beaucoup **pour que ses parents soient fiers de lui**.* (He studies a lot **so that** his parents are proud of him.)
  - ○ *Nous faisons de notre mieux **afin que le projet réussisse**.* (We do our best **in order that** the project succeeds.)

Other Words and Phrases that Trigger the Subjunctive

In addition to the structures and verbs we've discussed, there are several other words and phrases in French that can trigger the use of the present subjunctive:

Expressions of Emotion:

- **Il est étonnant que...** (It's surprising that...)
- **Il est dommage que...** (It's a shame that...)
- **Il est important que...** (It's important that...)
- **Il est triste que...** (It's sad that...)
- **Il est heureux que...** (It's happy that...)

Expressions of Doubt and Uncertainty:

- **Je doute que...** (I doubt that...)
- **Il est possible que...** (It's possible that...)
- **Il est probable que...** (It's probable that...)
- **Il est peu probable que...** (It's unlikely that...)

Expressions of Wishes and Desires:

- **Je souhaite que...** (I wish that...)
- **Je voudrais que...** (I would like that...)

- **Je préfère que...** (I prefer that...)

Imperative Sentences:

- **Il faut que...** (It's necessary that...)
- **Il est nécessaire que...** (It's necessary that...)
- **Il est indispensable que...** (It's indispensable that...)

Exercises

1. Which of the following verbs is conjugated correctly in the present subjunctive for the first person singular (je)?

    A. Je mange

    B. Je mangeons

    C. Je mangez

    D. Je mange

2. In the present subjunctive, the verb "vivre" (to live) is conjugated for the third person plural as follows:

    A. Ils vivent

    B. Ils vivons

    C. Ils vivent

    D. Ils vivrez

3. To express a desire that someone succeeds, you would use the present subjunctive with which verb?

    A. Vouloir

    B. Avoir

    C. Être

    D. Faire

4. Which phrase triggers the use of the present subjunctive to express doubt?

    A. Il est certain que...

    B. Je suis sûr que...

    C. Je doute que...

    D. Il est évident que...

5. The present subjunctive is used to express opinions and recommendations. Which of the following phrases is an example of this usage?

    A. Il est important que tu étudies.

    B. Je mange une pomme.

    C. Nous avons fini le travail.

    D. Je vais au cinéma.

6. To express a wish that someone arrives on time, you would use the present subjunctive with which verb?

    A. Pouvoir

B. Devoir

C. Vouloir

D. Falloir

7. Which of the following phrases is an example of the present subjunctive being used to express a hypothetical situation?

A. Il fait beau.

B. Je suis allé au restaurant.

C. S'il pleut, je resterai à la maison.

D. Nous avons mangé.

8. The present subjunctive is often used with the conjunction "afin que" to express:

A. Possibility

B. Desire

C. Purpose

D. Necessity

9. Which of the following verbs is conjugated correctly in the present subjunctive for the second person singular (tu)?

A. Tu chantes

B. Tu chantons

C. Tu chantez

D. Tu chanter

10. To express surprise that someone has not arrived, you would use the present subjunctive with which phrase?

A. Il est normal que...

B. Il est évident que...

C. Il est étonnant que...

D. Il est certain que...

Answer Key

1. A. Je mange

2. C. Ils vivent

3. A. Vouloir

4. C. Je doute que…

5. A. Il est important que tu étudies.

6. C. Vouloir

7. C. S'il pleut, je resterai à la maison.

8. C. Purpose

9. A. Tu chantes

10. C. Il est étonnant que…

Chapter 4: Anecdotes

"Les anecdotes ne sont jamais insignifiantes : elles révèlent les vérités cachées de notre âme."

- Marcel Proust

In this chapter, we will focus on learning how to narrate anecdotes in French using the plus-que-parfait tense in our storytelling.

Plus-que-parfait

Plus-que-parfait is a French verb tense that is used to express an action that was completed **before another action in the past**.

Here's a breakdown of its usage:

Structure:

- **Auxiliary Verb:** *avoir* or *être* (depending on the verb's conjugation)
- **Past Participle:** The past participle form of the main verb

Examples:

- **Avant de partir, j'avais mangé.** (Before leaving, I had eaten.)
- **Quand je suis arrivé, il avait déjà fini.** (When I arrived, he had already finished.)

Key points to remember:

- **Timeframe:** The plus-que-parfait places the action in a time before another past action.
- **Sequence:** It emphasizes the sequence of events.
- **Completion:** The action expressed in the plus-que-parfait is always completed.

Common uses:

- **Narrating past events:** To describe a series of past actions, especially when emphasizing the order in which they occurred.
- **Expressing wishes or regrets:** To convey a wish or regret about something that didn't happen in the past.

- **Hypothetical situations:** To describe hypothetical situations or actions that could have happened but didn't.

Verb	Present	Passé Composé	Imparfait	Futur Simple	Subjonctif Présent
Chanter	Je chante	J'ai chanté	Je chantais	Je chanterai	Que je chante
Manger	Je mange	J'ai mangé	Je mangeais	Je mangerai	Que je mange
Vivre	Je vis	J'ai vécu	Je vivais	Je vivrai	Que je vive

Combining Past Tenses

Combining past tenses in French allows you to express nuanced relationships between past actions and events. Here's a breakdown of some common combinations:

1. Passé Composé and Imparfait

- **Contrast:** The *passé composé* is used for completed actions, while the *imparfait* describes ongoing or habitual actions in the past.
- **Example:** *Hier, il **pleuvait** quand je **suis sorti**.* (Yesterday, it **was raining** when I **went out**.)

2. Passé Simple and Imparfait

- **Literary Style:** These tenses are often used in literary or formal writing.
- **Example:** *Il **vint** et **me dit** qu'il **avait** faim.* (He **came** and **told** me that he **was** hungry.)

3. Plus-que-parfait and Passé Composé

- **Sequence:** The *plus-que-parfait* indicates an action that was completed before another past action.
- **Example:** *Avant de partir, j'**avais** déjà **mangé**.* (Before leaving, I had already eaten.)

4. Plus-que-parfait and Imparfait

- **Background:** The *plus-que-parfait* can provide background information for an action described in the *imparfait*.
- **Example:** *Quand il **arriva**, il **avait** déjà **plu** toute la journée.* (When he arrived, it had already been raining all day.)

5. Passé Composé and Futur dans le Passé

- **Hypothetical Past:** The *futur dans le passé* is used to express a future action from the perspective of a past moment.

- **Example:** *Je **pensais** qu'il **arriverait** bientôt.* (I thought he would arrive soon.)

How to Narrate Anecdotes

Starting an anecdote

1. Direct Introduction:

- **Simple and straightforward:** Start with a clear statement of the main event or situation.

- **Example:** *"Il y a quelques années, je me suis retrouvé dans une situation plutôt inhabituelle."* (A few years ago, I found myself in a rather unusual situation.)

2. Setting the Scene:

- **Descriptive language:** Paint a picture of the setting, time, and atmosphere.

- **Example:** *"C'était un soir d'hiver, il faisait très froid et il neigeait."* (It was a winter evening, it was very cold and it was snowing.)

3. Questioning the Listener:

- **Engaging:** Pose a question to involve the listener and create anticipation.

- **Example:** *"Avez-vous déjà eu peur de l'inconnu?"* (Have you ever been afraid of the unknown?)

4. Using a Quotation:

- **Memorable:** Start with a relevant quote to set the tone.

- **Example:** *"Comme disait le proverbe français, 'Qui veut voyager loin doit partir de près'."* (As the French proverb says, "He who wants to travel far must start close.")

5. Creating Intrigue:

- **Mysterious:** Start with a hint or a cliffhanger to pique the listener's curiosity.

- **Example:** *"Je me souviens encore de cette journée où tout a changé."* (I still remember that day when everything changed.)

Sequence words

Sequence words, also known as connectors of order, are used to indicate the sequence or order of events, ideas, or items in a sentence or paragraph. Here are some common connectors of order in French:

Temporal Connectors (Time Sequence):

- **Avant que:** before
- **Après que:** after
- **En premier lieu:** in the first place
- **Ensuite:** then
- **Puis:** then
- **Finalement:** finally

Numerical Connectors:

- **Premier(ère):** first
- **Deuxième:** second
- **Troisième:** third
- **Quatrième:** fourth
- **Cinquième:** fifth

Other Connectors:

- **D'abord:** first
- **Ensuite:** then
- **Enfin:** finally
- **Par la suite:** subsequently
- **Plus tard:** later
- **Avant de partir, j'ai mangé.** (Before leaving, I ate.)
- **En premier lieu, il faut étudier.** (First, you need to study.)
- **Ensuite, nous avons joué au football.** (Then, we played football.)
- **Finalement, nous sommes allés au cinéma.** (Finally, we went to the cinema.)

Adding new or similar ideas

When adding new or similar ideas to a French text, it's important to use appropriate connectors to maintain the flow and coherence of your writing. Here are some common connectors you can use:

To introduce new ideas:

- **De plus:** Moreover
- **En outre:** Besides
- **Par ailleurs:** Furthermore
- **D'ailleurs:** Besides
- **De même:** Similarly

To show similarity:

- **De même:** Similarly
- **Pareillement:** Likewise
- **De la même manière:** In the same way
- **Semblablement:** Similarly

To show contrast:

- **Au contraire:** On the contrary
- **Cependant:** However
- **Néanmoins:** Nevertheless
- **Malgré cela:** Despite that
- **En revanche:** On the other hand

Examples:
- **De plus,** il est important de manger sainement. (Moreover, it's important to eat healthy.)
- **De même,** les chats sont aussi des animaux de compagnie populaires. (Similarly, cats are also popular pets.)
- **Au contraire,** je préfère les films d'horreur. (On the contrary, I prefer horror movies.)

Limit or contradict an idea

When you want to limit or contradict an idea in French, you can use various connectors to express the relationship between ideas. Here are some common ones:

To limit an idea:

- **Cependant:** However
- **Néanmoins:** Nevertheless
- **Malgré cela:** Despite that
- **Toutefois:** However
- **Pourtant:** Yet

To contradict an idea:

- **Au contraire:** On the contrary
- **Au lieu de cela:** Instead
- **Contrairement à cela:** Contrary to that
- **D'ailleurs:** Besides

Examples:

- **Cependant,** il y a aussi des inconvénients. (However, there are also disadvantages.)
- **Au contraire,** je préfère les films d'action. (On the contrary, I prefer action movies.)

Connectors of cause and consequence

Connectors of cause and consequence are used to indicate a relationship between two events or ideas. Here are some common connectors used in French:

To indicate cause:

- **Parce que:** because
- **Puisque:** since
- **Comme:** as
- **Étant donné que:** given that
- **Grâce à:** thanks to

To indicate consequence:

- **Donc:** therefore
- **Ainsi:** thus
- **Par conséquent:** consequently
- **De ce fait:** as a result

- **C'est pourquoi:** that's why

Examples:

- **Parce qu'il pleut,** je vais rester à la maison. (Because it's raining, I'm going to stay home.)
- **Grâce à son travail acharné, elle a réussi ses examens.** (Thanks to her hard work, she passed her exams.)
- **Il fait chaud, donc je vais porter des shorts.** (It's hot, so I'm going to wear shorts.)
- **Par conséquent, nous avons décidé de reporter le voyage.** (Consequently, we decided to postpone the trip.)

Temporal references to tell an anecdote

When telling an anecdote in French, temporal references are crucial to help the listener or reader understand the sequence of events. Here are some common temporal references you can use:

Specific time references:

- **Heures:** heures (hours), minutes (minutes), secondes (seconds)
- **Jours:** jours (days), semaines (weeks), mois (months), années (years)
- **Saisons:** printemps (spring), été (summer), automne (autumn), hiver (winter)
- **Fêtes:** Noël (Christmas), Pâques (Easter), etc.

Relative time references:

- **Hier:** yesterday
- **Aujourd'hui:** today
- **Demain:** tomorrow
- **Avant-hier:** the day before yesterday
- **Après-demain:** the day after tomorrow
- **La semaine dernière:** last week
- **La semaine prochaine:** next week
- **Le mois dernier:** last month
- **Le mois prochain:** next month
- **L'année dernière:** last year
- **L'année prochaine:** next year

Time expressions:

- **Le matin:** in the morning
- **L'après-midi:** in the afternoon
- **Le soir:** in the evening
- **La nuit:** at night
- **Pendant:** during
- **Avant:** before
- **Après:** after
- **En même temps:** at the same time

Examples:

- **Hier soir, vers 22 heures, j'ai entendu un bruit étrange.** (Last night, around 10 o'clock, I heard a strange noise.)
- **Pendant l'été, nous sommes allés à la plage.** (During the summer, we went to the beach.)
- **Avant de partir, j'ai vérifié mes bagages.** (Before leaving, I checked my luggage.)

Exercises

1. **Which tense is used to express an ongoing or habitual action in the past?**

    A. Passé Composé

    B. Imparfait

    C. Futur Simple

    D. Subjonctif Présent

2. **What is the correct conjugation of the verb "chanter" in the present tense, first person singular?**

    A. Je chante

    B. J'ai chanté

    C. Je chantais

    D. Je chanterai

3. **Which tense is used to express a completed action in the past?**

    A. Passé Composé

    B. Imparfait

    C. Futur Simple

    D. Subjonctif Présent

4. **What is the correct conjugation of the verb "vivre" in the future simple tense, first person singular?**

    A. Je vis

    B. J'ai vécu

    C. Je vivais

    D. Je vivrai

5. **Which two tenses are often used in literary or formal writing?**

    A. Passé Composé and Imparfait

    B. Passé Simple and Imparfait

    C. Plus-que-parfait and Passé Composé

    D. Plus-que-parfait and Imparfait

6. **Which tense indicates an action that was completed before another past action?**

    A. Passé Composé

    B. Imparfait

C. Plus-que-parfait

D. Futur dans le Passé

7. **Which tense can provide background information for an action described in the imparfait?**

    A. Passé Composé

    B. Imparfait

    C. Plus-que-parfait

    D. Futur dans le Passé

8. **Which tense is used to express a future action from the perspective of a past moment?**

    A. Passé Composé

    B. Imparfait

    C. Plus-que-parfait

    D. Futur dans le Passé

9. **Which technique involves starting an anecdote with a clear statement of the main event or situation?**

    A. Direct Introduction

    B. Setting the Scene

    C. Questioning the Listener

    D. Using a Quotation

10. **Which technique involves painting a picture of the setting, time, and atmosphere?**

    A. Direct Introduction
    B. Setting the Scene
    C. Questioning the Listener
    D. Using a Quotation

Answer Key

1. B. Imparfait

2. A. Je chante

3. A. Passé Composé

4. D. Je vivrai

5. B. Passé Simple and Imparfait

6. C. Plus-que-parfait

7. C. Plus-que-parfait

8. D. Futur dans le Passé

9. A. Direct Introduction

10. B. Setting the Scene

Chapter 5: Hypotheses

"C'est par la logique que nous prouvons, mais par l'intuition que nous trouvons."

- Henri Poincaré

What do you think the earth will look like in the year 2500? Do you believe we'll be driving flying cars a few decades from now? And what about you? What are your plans for the future? After this chapter, you'll be able to express hypotheses like these and many others in French!

Futur Simple

Futur Simple is a verb tense used to express future actions or events, including predictions, promises, and plans.

Conjugation Patterns:

- **Regular verbs:**
  - **-er verbs:** Add "-ai," "-as," "-a," "-ons," "-ez," "-ont" to the infinitive, depending on the subject .
  - **-ir verbs:** Add "-ai," "-as," "-a," "-ons," "-ez," "-ont" to the infinitive, depending on the subject.
  - **-re verbs:** Add "-ai," "-as," "-a," "-ons," "-ez," "-ont" to the infinitive, depending on the subject.
- **Irregular verbs:** These verbs have unique conjugation patterns. Some examples include:
  - **avoir:** j'aurai, tu auras, il aura, nous aurons, vous aurez, ils auront
  - **être:** je serai, tu seras, il sera, nous serons, vous serez, ils seront
  - **aller:** j'irai, tu iras, il ira, nous irons, vous irez, ils iront

Uses of Futur Simple:

- **Predictions:** To make predictions about future events.
- **Promises:** To make promises or commitments.

- **Plans:** To talk about future plans or intentions.
- **Hypothetical situations:** To describe hypothetical situations or actions that might happen in the future.

Examples:

- **Demain, je vais au cinéma.** (Tomorrow, I'm going to the cinema.)
- **Il fera beau demain.** (It will be nice tomorrow.)
- **Nous mangerons à la maison ce soir.** (We will eat at home tonight.)

Verb	Present	Passé Composé	Imparfait	Futur Simple	Subjonctif Présent
Avoir	J'ai	J'ai eu	J'avais	J'aurai	Que j'aie
Pouvoir	Je peux	J'ai pu	Je pouvais	Je pourrai	Que je puisse
Dire	Je dis	J'ai dit	Je disais	Je dirai	Que je dise
Faire	Je fais	J'ai fait	Je faisais	Je ferai	Que je fasse

Conditionnel Simple

Conditionnel Simple is a verb tense used to express hypothetical or conditional actions or events. It's often used to talk about things that could happen, might have happened, or are unlikely to happen.

Conjugation Patterns:

- **Regular verbs:**
  - **-er verbs:** Add "-ais," "-ais," "-ait," "-ions," "-iez," "-aient" to the infinitive, depending on the subject.
  - **-ir verbs:** Add "-ais," "-ais," "-ait," "-ions," "-iez," "-aient" to the infinitive, depending on the subject.
  - **-re verbs:** Add "-ais," "-ais," "-ait," "-ions," "-iez," "-aient" to the infinitive, depending on the subject.
- **Irregular verbs:** These verbs have unique conjugation patterns. Some examples include:
  - **avoir:** j'aurais, tu aurais, il aurait, nous aurions, vous auriez, ils auraient
  - **être:** je serais, tu serais, il serait, nous serions, vous seriez, ils seraient

○ **aller:** j'irais, tu irais, il irait, nous irions, vous iriez, ils iraient

Uses of the simple conditional

1. **Hypothetical Situations:**
   ○ **If clauses:** Often used with "si" (if) to express hypothetical conditions.
     ■ Example: *Si j'avais le temps, je voyagerais.* (If I had the time, I would travel.)
2. **Politeness:** Used to make requests or suggestions more polite.
   ○ Example: Voulez-vous venir dîner avec nous? (Would you like to come to dinner with us?)
3. **Unlikely Events:** Used to talk about things that are unlikely to happen.
   ○ Example: *Il pleuvrait demain, je resterais à la maison.* (If it rained tomorrow, I would stay at home.)

Examples:

- **Regular verb:** *Je parlerais français.* (I would speak French.)
- **Irregular verb:** *Nous irions à la plage.* (We would go to the beach.)
- **Hypothetical situation:** *Si tu avais de l'argent, tu achèterais une nouvelle voiture.* (If you had money, you would buy a new car.)

How to form the simple conditional

Verb in French	Infinitive Form	Conditional Form Example	English Translation
Chanter	chanter	Je chanterais	I would sing
Manger	manger	Je mangerais	I would eat
Vivre	vivre	Je vivrais	I would live

Conditionnel Passé

Uses of the compound conditional

The conditionnel passé in French is used to express actions that would have happened in the past under certain conditions. It conveys ideas related to hypothetical scenarios, regrets, unfulfilled actions, polite expressions, or speculations about past events. Here are the main ways to use the conditionnel passé:

1. Expressing Hypothetical Situations in the Past:

The conditionnel passé is used to describe an action that would have occurred if a certain condition had been met. These sentences often follow a "if... then..." structure.

Structure:

- Si (if) + Plus-que-parfait (Past Perfect) → Conditionnel Passé

Examples:

- Si j'avais su, j'aurais agi autrement.

- ("If I had known, I would have acted differently.")

- Si tu étais venu plus tôt, nous serions partis ensemble.

- ("If you had come earlier, we would have left together.")

2. Expressing Regret or Reproach:

The conditionnel passé is used to express regret about something that did not happen or a reproach for something that should have been done.

Examples:

- J'aurais aimé te voir avant ton départ.

- ("I would have liked to see you before you left.")

- Tu aurais dû me prévenir!

- ("You should have warned me!")

3. Expressing Politeness or Softening Statements:

It is used to make a statement more polite or less direct, especially when expressing doubt or uncertainty about past events.

Examples:

- J'aurais voulu vous parler plus tôt, mais je n'ai pas eu l'occasion.

- ("I would have wanted to speak to you earlier, but I didn't have the opportunity.")

- On m'a dit que vous auriez accepté l'offre.

- ("I was told that you might have accepted the offer.")

4. Expressing Speculation or Uncertainty about the Past:

The conditionnel passé can express doubt, rumors, or speculation about something that might have happened in the past.

Examples:

- Il aurait eu un accident hier soir.

- ("He is said to have had an accident last night.")

- Ils auraient terminé le projet, mais ce n'est pas certain.

- ("They would have finished the project, but it's not certain.")

5. Expressing an Unfulfilled Action or a Missed Opportunity:

It describes actions or events that could have happened but did not because a certain condition was not met.

Examples:

- Nous serions allés au concert, mais il pleuvait trop.

- ("We would have gone to the concert, but it was raining too much.")

- Elle aurait réussi son examen si elle avait étudié davantage.

- ("She would have passed her exam if she had studied more.")

Step-by-Step Formation:

1. Auxiliary Verb in Conditional Present:

- Use avoir (to have) or être (to be) in the conditional present form.

- Most verbs use avoir as the auxiliary verb.

- Verbs that are reflexive or show movement without an object use être.

2. Past Participle of the Main Verb:

- Regular -er verbs: Replace -er with -é (e.g., manger → mangé).

- Regular -ir verbs: Replace -ir with -i (e.g., finir → fini).

- Regular -re verbs: Replace -re with -u (e.g., vendre → vendu).

- Irregular verbs have unique past participles that must be memorized (e.g., être → été, avoir → eu).

Auxiliary Verb Forms in Conditional Present:

Pronoun	Avoir (to have)	Être (to be)
Je	aurais	serais

Tu	aurais	serais
Il/Elle/On	aurait	serait
Nous	aurions	serions
Vous	auriez	seriez
Ils/Elles	auraient	seraient

Examples of the Conditionnel Passé:

Verb (Infinitive)	Auxiliary Verb (Conditional Present)	Past Participle	Conditionnel Passé Example	English Translation
Manger (to eat)	aurais	mangé	J'aurais mangé	I would have eaten
Aller (to go)	serais	allé(e)	Je serais allé(e)	I would have gone
Finir (to finish)	aurais	fini	Tu aurais fini	You would have finished
Partir (to leave)	serais	parti(e)	Nous serions parti(e)s	We would have left
Voir (to see)	aurais	vu	Vous auriez vu	You would have seen

Propositions Conditionnelles

Propositions conditionnelles (conditional sentences) in French express hypothetical or conditional situations.

Typical Structure:

1. **The if clause (clause si):** This clause introduces the condition using the conjunction "si" (if).

2. **The main clause:** This clause expresses the consequence or result of the condition.

Types of Conditional Sentences:

1. **Conditionnel présent:** This type expresses a possible or probable condition and its likely result.

   - **Example:** *Si tu étudies, tu réussiras.* (If you study, you will succeed.)

2. **Conditionnel passé:** This type expresses an unlikely or impossible condition and its hypothetical result.

   - **Example:** *Si j'avais eu le temps, je serais allé au cinéma.* (If I had had the time, I would have gone to the cinema.)

3. **Conditionnel futur:** This type expresses a future condition and its potential result.

   - **Example:** *Si il pleut demain, nous resterons à la maison.* (If it rains tomorrow, we will stay at home.)

Verb Tenses Used:

- **If clause:**

   - **Conditionnel présent:** Present tense

   - **Conditionnel passé:** Past tense (imparfait or passé composé)

   - **Conditionnel futur:** Future tense

- **Main clause:**

   - **Conditionnel présent:** Conditionnel simple

   - **Conditionnel passé:** Conditionnel passé

   - **Conditionnel futur:** Future simple

Examples:

- **Conditionnel présent:** *Si tu as faim, je te donnerai un sandwich.* (If you are hungry, I will give you a sandwich.)

- **Conditionnel passé:** *Si j'avais eu l'argent, j'aurais acheté une nouvelle voiture.* (If I had had the money, I would have bought a new car.)

- **Conditionnel futur:** *Si il pleut demain, nous annulerons le pique-nique.* (If it rains tomorrow, we will cancel the picnic.)

Expressing Certainty, Doubt, and Uncertainty

Expressing Certainty

- **Using "être sûr" or "être certain":**
    - *Je suis sûr qu'il viendra.* (I'm sure he will come.)
    - *Nous sommes certains d'avoir raison.* (We are certain to be right.)
- **Using adverbs of certainty:**
    - *Certainement, il va gagner.* (Certainly, he will win.)
    - *Indubitablement, c'est vrai.* (Undoubtedly, it's true.)

Expressing Doubt

- **Using "douter" or "être incertain":**
    - *Je doute qu'il soit arrivé.* (I doubt that he has arrived.)
    - *Nous sommes incertains de la décision.* (We are uncertain about the decision.)
- **Using adverbs of doubt:**
    - *Probablement, il ne viendra pas.* (Probably, he won't come.)
    - *Peut-être, il a oublié.* (Maybe he forgot.)

Expressing Uncertainty

- **Using "peut-être" or "il se peut que":**
    - *Peut-être qu'il viendra demain.* (Maybe he will come tomorrow.)
    - *Il se peut qu'elle soit malade.* (It's possible that she is sick.)
- **Using "je ne sais pas" or "je suis indécis":**
    - *Je ne sais pas s'il va venir.* (I don't know if he will come.)
    - *Je suis indécis sur ce que faire.* (I am undecided about what to do.)

Expression Type	French Expression	English Translation	Mood Used
Certainty	Il est certain que...	It is certain that...	Indicative
	Je suis sûr(e) que...	I am sure that...	Indicative

	Il est évident que...	It is obvious that...	Indicative
	Je sais que...	I know that...	Indicative
	Je crois que...	I believe that...	Indicative
	Je pense que...	I think that...	Indicative
Doubt	Je doute que...	I doubt that...	Subjunctive
	Il est douteux que...	It is doubtful that...	Subjunctive
	Il est improbable que...	It is unlikely that...	Subjunctive
	Je ne suis pas sûr(e) que...	I am not sure that...	Subjunctive
	Il est peu probable que...	It is not very likely that...	Subjunctive
Uncertainty	Il se peut que...	It may be that...	Subjunctive
	Il est incertain que...	It is uncertain that...	Subjunctive
	Je ne crois pas que...	I do not believe that...	Subjunctive
	Je ne pense pas que...	I do not think that...	Subjunctive
	Il n'est pas certain que...	It is not certain that...	Subjunctive

Exercises

1. **Which is the correct conditional present conjugation of the verb "avoir" for the pronoun "nous?"**

    a) aurions

    b) serions

    c) aurais

    d) aurait

2. **What is the conditional present conjugation of the verb "être" for the pronoun "il/elle/on?"**

    a) aurais

    b) serais

    c) aurait

    d) serait

3. **The Conditionnel Passé is formed using:**

    a) the present tense of avoir or être and the past participle of the main verb

    b) the future tense of avoir or être and the present participle of the main verb

    c) the imperfect tense of avoir or être and the past participle of the main verb

    d) the subjunctive tense of avoir or être and the present participle of the main verb

4. **When using "être" as the auxiliary verb in the Conditionnel Passé, the past participle must agree in:**

    a) gender only

    b) number only

    c) gender and number with the subject

    d) tense with the subject

5. **The Conditionnel Passé is primarily used to express:**

    a) future actions

    b) past actions that actually happened

    c) hypothetical or conditional actions in the past

    d) present actions

6. **Which of the following is NOT a common use of the Conditionnel Passé?**

    a) Expressing regret

    b) Giving advice

    c) Expressing politeness

d) Expressing speculation

7. **A conditional sentence in French typically consists of:**

   a) a main clause only

   b) an if clause and a main clause

   c) a past tense clause and a future tense clause

   d) a subjunctive clause and an indicative clause

8. **In a conditional sentence, the if clause is introduced by the conjunction:**

   a) que

   b) si

   c) parce que

   d) mais

9. **To express certainty in French, you can use the verb:**

   a) avoir

   b) être

   c) vouloir

   d) pouvoir

10. **Which adverb is commonly used to express doubt in French?**
    a) certainement
    b) probablement
    c) toujours
    d) jamais

Answer Key

1. a) aurions

2. d) serait

3. a) the present tense of avoir or être and the past participle of the main verb

4. c) gender and number with the subject

5. c) hypothetical or conditional actions in the past

6. b) Giving advice

7. b) an if clause and a main clause

8. b) si

9. b) être

10. b) probablement

Chapter 6: Nothing Personal

"Il est impossible de se soustraire au jugement des autres, mais il est possible de construire son propre jugement."

- Jean-Paul Sartre

In this chapter, we will explore sentences that omit or conceal the subject, or shift the focus to another part of the sentence, making the subject appear less accountable.

Impersonal Constructions

Impersonal constructions are grammatical structures that do not refer to a specific subject.

Common Impersonal Verbs

- **Il faut:** This is the most common impersonal construction in French, meaning "it is necessary."
    - *Exemple:* Il faut étudier pour réussir. (It is necessary to study to succeed.)
- **Il y a:** This means "there is" or "there are."
    - *Exemple:* Il y a un livre sur la table. (There is a book on the table.)
- **Il semble:** This means "it seems."
    - *Exemple:* Il semble qu'il pleut. (It seems like it's raining.)
- **Il fait:** This can mean "it's" (referring to weather) or "it does" (referring to actions).
    - *Exemple:* Il fait chaud. (It's hot.)
    - *Exemple:* Il fait nuit. (It's night.)

Other Impersonal Constructions

- **Ce n'est pas la peine de:** This means "it's not worth."
    - *Exemple:* Ce n'est pas la peine de s'inquiéter. (It's not worth worrying.)
- **Il est inutile de:** This means "it's useless to."
    - *Exemple:* Il est inutile de se plaindre. (It's useless to complain.)

- **Il est dommage que:** This means "it's a pity that."
  - *Exemple:* Il est dommage qu'il ne soit pas venu. (It's a pity that he didn't come.)

Examples of Impersonal Constructions in Context

- **Weather:** Il fait beau aujourd'hui. (It's nice today.)
- **Time:** Il est tard. (It's late.)
- **Opinion:** Il me semble que tu as raison. (It seems to me that you're right.)
- **Necessity:** Il faut manger sainement. (It's necessary to eat healthily.)
- **Existence:** Il y a un nouveau restaurant dans le quartier. (There's a new restaurant in the neighborhood.)

Verbs in the third-person singular/plural

Third-Person Singular

The third-person singular refers to **he**, **she**, or **it**. It's used to talk about a single person or thing.

Regular Verbs:

- **-er verbs:** Add **-e** for masculine or **-e** for feminine.
  - *Exemple:* parler - il parle (to speak - he speaks), elle parle (to speak - she speaks)
- **-ir verbs:** Add **-it** for masculine or **-it** for feminine.
  - *Exemple:* finir - il finit (to finish - he finishes), elle finit (to finish - she finishes)
- **-re verbs:** The endings vary depending on the stem.
  - **-re:** Add **-t** for masculine or **-t** for feminine. (Example: vendre - il vend, elle vend)
  - **-dre:** Add **-t** for masculine or **-t** for feminine. (Example: attendre - il attend, elle attend)
  - **-ivre:** Add **-t** for masculine or **-t** for feminine. (Example: vivre - il vit, elle vit)
  - **-oir:** Add **-t** for masculine or **-t** for feminine. (Example: devoir - il doit, elle doit)

Irregular Verbs: Many verbs have irregular third-person singular forms. Some common examples include:

- **avoir:** il a (to have - he has), elle a (to have - she has)
- **être:** il est (to be - he is), elle est (to be - she is)
- **aller:** il va (to go - he goes), elle va (to go - she goes)
- **faire:** il fait (to do - he does), elle fait (to do - she does)
- **voir:** il voit (to see - he sees), elle voit (to see - she sees)

Third-Person Plural

The third-person plural refers to **they** (masculine or feminine). It's used to talk about a group of people or things.

Regular Verbs:

- **-er verbs:** Add **-ent**.
  - *Exemple:* parler - ils parlent (to speak - they speak)
- **-ir verbs:** Add **-issent**.
  - *Exemple:* finir - ils finissent (to finish - they finish)
- **-re verbs:** The endings vary depending on the stem.
  - **-re:** Add **-ent**. (Example: vendre - ils vendent)
  - **-dre:** Add **-ent**. (Example: attendre - ils attendent)
  - **-ivre:** Add **-ent**. (Example: vivre - ils vivent)
  - **-oir:** Add **-oivent**. (Example: devoir - ils doivent)

Irregular Verbs: Many verbs have irregular third-person plural forms. Some common examples include:

- **avoir:** ils ont (to have - they have)
- **être:** ils sont (to be - they are)
- **aller:** ils vont (to go - they go)
- **faire:** ils font (to do - they do)
- **voir:** ils voient (to see - they see)

Agreement with Adjectives

Adjectives must agree in gender and number with the noun they modify. This also applies to the third-person singular and plural.

- *Exemple:* Le livre est intéressant. (The book is interesting.)
- *Exemple:* La fille est gentille. (The girl is kind.)
- *Exemple:* Les livres sont intéressants. (The books are interesting.)
- *Exemple:* Les filles sont gentilles. (The girls are kind.)

Remember that mixed groups of masculine and feminine default to the masculine gender agreement.

Examples

- Il parle français. (He speaks French.)
- Elle aime la musique. (She likes music.)
- Ils parlent français. (They speak French.)
- Elles aiment la musique. (They like music.)

French Expression	Usage Context	Example in French	English Translation
Il est interdit de...	Verbs in the infinitive	Il est interdit de fumer ici.	It is forbidden to smoke here.
Il est permis de...	Verbs in the infinitive	Il est permis de marcher sur l'herbe.	It is allowed to walk on the grass.
Est interdit...	Singular nouns (masc./fem.)	L'accès est interdit aux animaux.	Access is forbidden to animals.
Est permis...	Singular nouns (masc./fem.)	L'accès est permis aux visiteurs.	Access is allowed to visitors.
Sont interdits/interdites...	Plural nouns (masc./fem.)	Les voitures sont interdites dans le parc.	Cars are forbidden in the park.
Sont permis/permis(es)...	Plural nouns (masc./fem.)	Les animaux sont permis dans certaines zones.	Animals are allowed in certain areas.

To form impersonal sentences, the verb "être" is used in the third-person singular (il est) combined with an infinitive verb.

Adjectives should remain in the masculine form to agree with the infinitive verb. For example, "Il est obligatoire de faire tous les devoirs" ("Doing all the assignments is compulsory"). Other adjectives commonly used in this structure include:

Adjective in French	Pronunciation	Translation	Example in French	English Translation
normal	nohr-MAL	normal	Il est normal de suivre les règles.	It is normal to follow the rules.

habituel	ah-bee-too-AHL	usual	Il est habituel de saluer en arrivant.	It is usual to greet upon arrival.
fréquent	freh-kahn	frequent	Il est fréquent de voir des touristes ici.	It is frequent to see tourists here.
rare	rrarr	rare	Il est rare de trouver ce livre.	It is rare to find this book.
convenable	kawn-vuh-nah-bluh	convenient	Il est convenable de prendre le train.	It is convenient to take the train.
recommandé	rruh-kaw-muhn-day	advisable	Il est recommandé de boire de l'eau.	It is advisable to drink water.
meilleur	meh-yur	better	Il est meilleur de rester calme.	It is better to stay calm.
pire	peer	worse	Il est pire de ne rien faire.	It is worse to do nothing.
facile	fah-seel	easy	Il est facile de comprendre cette règle.	It is easy to understand this rule.
difficile	dee-fee-seel	hard	Il est difficile de résoudre ce problème.	It is hard to solve this problem.
utile	oo-teel	useful	Il est utile de connaître plusieurs langues.	It is useful to know several languages.

inutile	ee-noo-teel	unuseful	Il est inutile de s'inquiéter pour cela.	It is unuseful to worry about that.
important	an-pohr-tahn	important	Il est important de faire ses devoirs.	It is important to do one's homework.

Verb in the second-person singular

The second-person singular in French refers to **you** (singular, informal).

Regular Verbs

- **-er verbs:** Add **-es**.
  - *Exemple:* parler - tu parles (to speak - you speak)
- **-ir verbs:** Add **-is**.
  - *Exemple:* finir - tu finis (to finish - you finish)
- **-re verbs:** The endings vary depending on the stem.
  - **-re:** Add **-s**. (Example: vendre - tu vends)
  - **-dre:** Add **-s**. (Example: attendre - tu attends)
  - **-ivre:** Add **-s**. (Example: vivre - tu vis)
  - **-oir:** Add **-s**. (Example: devoir - tu dois)

Irregular Verbs

Many verbs have irregular second-person singular forms. Some common examples include:

- **avoir:** tu as (to have - you have)
- **être:** tu es (to be - you are)
- **aller:** tu vas (to go - you go)
- **faire:** tu fais (to do - you do)
- **voir:** tu vois (to see - you see)

Agreement with Adjectives

Adjectives must agree in gender and number with the noun they modify. Since "tu" is a singular pronoun, adjectives must be singular.

- *Exemple:* Tu es intelligent. (You are intelligent.)
- *Exemple:* Tu as une belle robe. (You have a beautiful dress.)

Examples

- Tu parles français. (You speak French.)
- Tu es étudiant. (You are a student.)
- Tu vas au cinéma. (You are going to the cinema.)

Use of the pronoun se

The pronoun "se" in French serves several functions:

1. Reflexive Pronoun:

- **Direct object:** When used as a direct object, "se" refers back to the subject of the sentence.
  - *Example:* Il se lave. (He washes himself.)
- **Indirect object:** When used as an indirect object, "se" refers to the subject of the sentence as the beneficiary of the action.
  - *Example:* Elle s'achète un nouveau livre. (She buys herself a new book.)

2. Impersonal Pronoun:

- In impersonal constructions, "se" represents a general or unspecified subject.
  - *Example:* Il se dit que… (It is said that…)
  - *Example:* On se demande… (One wonders…)

3. Passive Voice:

- "Se" can be used to form the passive voice in French.
  - *Example:* La maison se construit. (The house is being built.)

4. Middle Voice:

- In some cases, "se" can be used to express a middle voice, where the subject both performs and is affected by the action.
  - *Example:* Le livre se lit facilement. (The book is easy to read.)

5. Reciprocal Pronoun:

- "Se" can be used to indicate a reciprocal action between two or more people.
  - *Example:* Ils se parlent. (They talk to each other.)

Examples of "se" in Different Contexts:

- **Reflexive:** Je me lave les mains. (I wash my hands.)
- **Impersonal:** On se dit que la vie est belle. (It is said that life is beautiful.)
- **Passive:** Le film se termine. (The movie is ending.)
- **Middle Voice:** La porte s'ouvre. (The door opens.)
- **Reciprocal:** Nous nous connaissons depuis longtemps. (We have known each other for a long time.)

Passive voice

The passive voice in French is used to emphasize the action rather than the subject performing it. It's often used to:

- **Highlight the action:** "The book was written by a famous author."
- **De-emphasize the subject:** "The car was stolen."
- **Avoid naming the subject:** "It is said that..."

Formation of the Passive Voice in French

1. **Use the auxiliary verb *être* (to be).**
2. **Conjugate *être* according to the subject and tense.**
3. **Add the past participle of the main verb.**

Example:

- **Active:** *Je mange une pomme.* (I eat an apple.)
- **Passive:** *La pomme est mangée.* (The apple is eaten.)

Example:

- **Future:** *Le livre sera écrit par un auteur célèbre.* (The book will be written by a famous author.)
- **Past:** *La maison a été construite en 1950.* (The house was built in 1950.)

Exercises

1. **What is the correct third-person plural conjugation of the verb "parler" (to speak)?**

   a) parle

   b) parlent

   c) parlons

   d) parlez

2. **Which verb has an irregular third-person plural form?**

   a) finir

   b) vendre

   c) vivre

   d) être

3. **How do you form the third-person plural conjugation of a regular -ir verb?**

   a) Add -ent to the stem.

   b) Add -issent to the stem.

   c) Add -it to the stem.

   d) Add -ent or -ent, depending on the stem.

4. **In the sentence "Ils aiment la musique," what does "ils" refer to?**

   a) He

   b) She

   c) It

   d) They

5. **What is the correct third-person plural conjugation of the verb "avoir" (to have)?**

   a) avons

b) avez

c) ont

d) ont

6. **How do you form the third-person singular conjugation of a regular -er verb for a feminine subject?**

a) Add -e to the stem.

b) Add -es to the stem.

c) Add -ent to the stem.

d) Add -it to the stem.

7. **Which verb has an irregular third-person singular form for a masculine subject?**

a) finir

b) vendre

c) être

d) vivre

8. **In the sentence "Elle parle français," what does "elle" refer to?**

a) He

b) She

c) It

d) They

9. **What is the correct third-person singular conjugation of the verb "aller" (to go) for a feminine subject?**

a) va

b) vas

c) vont

d) allez

10. **In the sentence "Il est étudiant," what does "il" refer to?**

    a) He

    b) She

    c) It

    d) They

Answer Key

1. b) parlent
2. d) être
3. b) Add -issent to the stem.
4. d) They
5. c) ont
6. a) Add -e to the stem.
7. c) être
8. b) She
9. a) va
10. a) He

Chapter 7: That's an Order!

"Si tu veux comprendre le mot bonheur, il faut l'entendre comme récompense et non comme but."

- Antoine de Saint-Exupéry

The imperative is used to give commands, offer advice, make recommendations, or request something directly.

Uses of the Imperative

The imperative mood in French is used to give commands, orders, or requests. It's a direct and forceful way of expressing a wish or instruction. Here are some common uses:

Giving Orders or Commands

- **Direct commands:**
  - **Ne mange pas!** (Don't eat!)
  - **Sortez!** (Get out!)
- **Military commands:**
  - **Marchez!** (March!)
  - **Tournez à gauche!** (Turn left!)

Making Requests

- **Polite requests:**
  - **Fermez la porte, s'il vous plaît.** (Close the door, please.)
  - **Pouvez-vous me donner un verre d'eau?** (Can you give me a glass of water?)
- **Informal requests:**
  - **Passe-moi le sel.** (Pass me the salt.)
  - **Attends-moi!** (Wait for me!)

Expressing Wishes or Desires

- **Expressing hopes:**
  - **Sois heureux!** (Be happy!)

- ○ **Ayez du courage!** (Be courageous!)
- **Offering advice:**
  - ○ **Mange moins.** (Eat less.)
  - ○ **Écoute-moi.** (Listen to me.)

Creating Slogans or Catchphrases

- **Advertising slogans:**
  - ○ **Achetez maintenant!** (Buy now!)
  - ○ **Essayez-nous!** (Try us!)
- **Motivational phrases:**
  - ○ **Ne jamais abandonner!** (Never give up!)
  - ○ **Croyez en vous!** (Believe in yourself!)

Affirmative and Negative Imperative

Affirmative imperative

The French affirmative imperative is used to give commands or orders.

Formation

1. **Remove the subject pronoun:** The subject pronoun (e.g., "tu," "vous") is usually omitted in the imperative.
2. **Use the verb stem:** The imperative form is simply the verb stem.

Examples:

- **Parle!** (Speak!)
- **Mange!** (Eat!)
- **Écoute!** (Listen!)

Formal and Informal Imperatives

French differentiates between formal and informal commands based on the relationship between the speaker and the listener.

- **Informal imperative:** Used to address friends, family, or people younger than you.
  - ○ **Tu + verb stem**
- **Formal imperative:** Used to address strangers, superiors, or people you respect.

○ **Vous + verb stem**

Examples:

- **Informal:** Tu parles français. (You speak French.)
- **Formal:** Vous parlez français. (You speak French.)

Verb in French	Singular (tu)	Singular (vous - formal)	Plural (vous)	Translation
Chanter (to sing)	Chante	Chantez	Chantez	Sing!
Manger (to eat)	Mange	Mangez	Mangez	Eat!
Vivre (to live)	Vis	Vivez	Vivez	Live!

Irregular Imperatives

Some verbs have irregular imperative forms. Common examples include:

- **Avoir:** Aie (have)
- **Être:** Sois (be)
- **Aller:** Va (go)
- **Faire:** Fais (do)
- **Voir:** Vois (see)

Negative imperative

The negative imperative in French is used to tell someone not to do something.

Formation

1. **Use "ne" before the verb stem.**
2. **Use "pas" after the verb stem.**

Example:

- **Ne mange pas!** (Don't eat!)

Common Uses of the Negative Imperative

- **Prohibiting actions:** Ne fume pas ici. (Don't smoke here.)
- **Giving orders:** Ne touchez pas à ça. (Don't touch that.)
- **Expressing warnings:** Ne vous inquiétez pas. (Don't worry.)

Formal and Informal Negative Imperatives

As with the affirmative imperative, the negative imperative also has formal and informal forms.

- **Informal: Ne + verb stem + pas**
- **Formal: Ne + vous + verb stem + pas**

Example:

- **Informal:** Ne parle pas! (Don't speak!)
- **Formal:** Ne vous parlez pas! (Don't speak!)

Verb in French	Singular (tu)	Singular (vous - formal)	Plural (vous)	Translation
Chanter (to sing)	Ne chante pas	Ne chantez pas	Ne chantez pas	Do not sing!
Manger (to eat)	Ne mange pas	Ne mangez pas	Ne mangez pas	Do not eat!
Vivre (to live)	Ne vis pas	Ne vivez pas	Ne vivez pas	Do not live!

Irregular Negative Imperatives

Some verbs have irregular negative imperative forms. Here are a few examples:

- **Avoir:** N'aie pas (don't have)
- **Être:** Ne sois pas (don't be)
- **Aller:** Ne va pas (don't go)
- **Faire:** Ne fais pas (don't do)
- **Voir:** Ne vois pas (don't see)

Verb in French	Singular (tu)	Singular (vous - formal)	Plural (vous)	Translation
Mettre (to put)	Ne mets pas	Ne mettez pas	Ne mettez pas	Do not put!
Faire (to do)	Ne fais pas	Ne faites pas	Ne faites pas	Do not do/make!
Avoir (to have)	N'aie pas	N'ayez pas	N'ayez pas	Do not have!
Aller (to go)	Ne va pas	N'allez pas	N'allez pas	Do not go!
Dire (to say)	Ne dis pas	Ne dites pas	Ne dites pas	Do not say!

Reflexive verbs

With reflexive verbs in French, the affirmative imperative is formed by attaching the reflexive pronoun directly to the Verb. In the negative imperative, instead, , the reflexive pronoun is placed between "ne" and the verb.

Verb in French	Affirmative	Negative	Affirmative	Negative
Se lever (to get up)	lève-toi	ne te lève pas	habille-toi	ne t'habille pas
	levez-vous	ne vous levez pas	habillez-vous	ne vous habillez pas
	levez-vous	ne vous levez pas	habillez-vous	ne vous habillez pas
	levons-nous	ne nous levons pas	habillons-nous	ne nous habillons pas

Imperative with Direct and Indirect Objects

When using the imperative with direct and indirect objects in French, the order of the objects can sometimes differ.

General Rule: Indirect Object Before Direct Object

Typically, the indirect object (who or what benefits from the action) comes before the direct object (the thing affected by the action).

Example:

- **Donne-moi le livre.** (Give me the book.)

    ○ "Moi" is the indirect object (to me).

    ○ "Le livre" is the direct object (the book)

Exceptions:

1. **When the direct object is a pronoun:** If the direct object is a pronoun (me, te, nous, vous, le, la, l', les), it usually comes before the indirect object.

Examples:

- **Donne-le-moi.** (Give it to me.)
- **Achete-nous des bonbons.** (Buy us some candy.)

2. **When the indirect object is "y" or "en":** These pronouns, which refer to a place or a quantity, always come before the direct object.

Examples:

- **Va-y.** (Go there.)
- **Mange-en.** (Eat some.)

Placement of "y" and "en":

- **"Y"** refers to a place or an abstract concept.

    ○ **Va-y.** (Go there.)

    ○ **Pense-y.** (Think about it.)

- **"En"** refers to a quantity or something previously mentioned.

    ○ **Mange-en.** (Eat some.)

    ○ **Parle-en.** (Talk about it.)

Exercises

1. **What is the imperative form of the verb "parler" (to speak)?**

   a) parle

   b) parles

   c) parlons

   d) parlez

2. **Which verb has an irregular imperative form?**

   a) manger

   b) vendre

   c) être

   d) vivre

3. **How do you form the formal imperative of the verb "chanter" (to sing)?**

   a) chante

   b) chantes

   c) chantez

   d) chantez

4. **In the sentence "Mange!," what is the imperative form of the verb "manger" (to eat)?**

   a) mange

   b) manges

   c) mangons

   d) mangez

5. **What is the informal imperative form of the verb "avoir" (to have)?**

   a) ayez

b) avons

c) avez

d) aie

6. **How do you form the negative imperative of the verb "aller" (to go)?**

   a) ne vas pas

   b) ne va pas

   c) ne va pas

   d) ne allez pas

7. **Which verb has an irregular negative imperative form?**

   a) finir

   b) vendre

   c) être

   d) vivre

8. **In the sentence "Ne mange pas!," what is the negative imperative form of the verb "manger" (to eat)?**

   a) ne mange pas

   b) ne manges pas

   c) ne mangons pas

   d) ne mangez pas

9. **How do you form the formal negative imperative of the verb "parler" (to speak)?**

   a) ne parlez pas

   b) ne parles pas

   c) ne parlons pas

   d) ne parlez pas

10. **What is the informal negative imperative form of the verb "avoir" (to have)?**

   a) n'ayez pas

   b) n'avons pas

   c) n'avez pas

   d) n'aie pas

Answer Key

1. a) parle
2. c) être
3. c) chantez
4. a) mange
5. d) aie
6. b) ne va pas
7. c) être
8. a) ne mange pas
9. a) ne parlez pas
10. d) n'aie pas

Chapter 8: Step into the Future

"Le futur appartient à ceux qui croient à la beauté de leurs rêves."

- Victor Hugo

An interesting aspect of the French language is that we can use the present indicative to refer to future events. For example:

"Ne t'inquiète pas. Demain, je lui dirai."

As we explored in Chapter 5, the simple future tense can also be used to make assumptions about the present:

"Marie doit être en train de dîner, c'est pourquoi elle ne répond pas au téléphone."

Let's keep exploring French's interesting ways of talking about the future.

Forms of the Future

Présent de l'indicatif

Présent de l'indicatif is the present tense in French. It's used to express actions happening now, habits, and general truths. However, it's also used to discuss future plans.

Formation

Here's a refresher on how to form the present indicative tense:

Regular Verbs:

- **-er verbs:** Add the following endings to the verb stem:
    - **Je:** -e
    - **Tu:** -es
    - **Il/Elle/On:** -e
    - **Nous:** -ons
    - **Vous:** -ez
    - **Ils/Elles:** -ent

- **-ir verbs:** Add the following endings:
  - **Je:** -is
  - **Tu:** -is
  - **Il/Elle/On:** -it
  - **Nous:** -issons
  - **Vous:** -issez
  - **Ils/Elles:** -issent
- **-re verbs:** The endings vary depending on the verb stem.

Aller + infinitif (ou futur périphrastique)

Subject	Aller (conjugated)	Infinitive	Example in French	English Translation
Je	vais	manger	Je vais manger.	I am going to eat.
Tu	vas	étudier	Tu vas étudier.	You are going to study.
Il/Elle	va	partir	Il/Elle va partir.	He/She is going to leave.
Nous	allons	regarder	Nous allons regarder un film.	We are going to watch a movie.
Vous	allez	voyager	Vous allez voyager en France.	You are going to travel to France.
Ils/Elles	vont	visiter	Ils/Elles vont visiter leurs amis.	They are going to visit their friends.

Futur simple

The future simple tense, or *futur simple*, is used to express actions or events that will happen in the future.

Formation

Regular verbs:

- **Group 1:** Add the endings *ai, as, a, ons, ez, ont*.
  - Example: *parler* (to speak) becomes *parlerai, parleras, parlera, parlerons, parlerez, parleront*.
- **Group 2:** Add the endings *irai, iras, ira, irons, irez, iront*.
  - Example: *finir* (to finish) becomes *finirai, finiras, finira, finirons, finirez, finiront*.
- **Group 3:** Add the endings *ai, as, a, ons, ez, ont*.
  - Example: *rendre* (to return) becomes *rendrai, rendras, rendra, rendrons, rendrez, rendront*.

Irregular verbs:

Some verbs have irregular future simple forms. These verbs must be memorized. Examples include:

- *avoir* (to have): *aurai, auras, aura, aurons, aurez, auront*
- *être* (to be): *serai, seras, sera, serons, serez, seront*
- *aller* (to go): *irai, iras, ira, irons, irez, iront*

Usage

The *futur simple* is used for:

- **Predictions:** *Il pleuvra demain.* (It will rain tomorrow.)
- **Promises:** *Je t'aiderai.* (I will help you.)
- **Commands:** *Tu finiras tes devoirs.* (You will finish your homework.)
- **Hypothetical situations:** *Si tu étudies, tu réussiras.* (If you study, you will succeed.)

Futur antérieur

The future anterior tense, also known as the *futur antérieur*, is used to express actions or events that will have been completed before a specific time in the future.

Formation

1. **Use the future simple tense of the auxiliary verb *avoir* or *être*.** The choice of auxiliary depends on the main verb:
   - ***Avoir:*** Most verbs use *avoir*.
   - ***Être:*** Verbs that indicate movement, change of state, or reflexive verbs use *être*.

2. **Add the past participle of the main verb.**

Example:

- *Avoir*: *Je aurai fini mes devoirs.* (I will have finished my homework.)
- *Être*: *Il sera parti avant midi.* (He will have left before noon.)

Usage

The *futur antérieur* is often used to:

- **Express an action that will be completed before another future action:** *Avant de partir, j'aurai mangé.* (Before leaving, I will have eaten.)

- **Describe a future event that will have a result in the present or future:** *Demain, il aura plu toute la nuit.* (Tomorrow, it will have rained all night.)

- **Express a future action that is considered certain or inevitable:** *D'ici la fin de l'année, nous aurons déménagé.* (By the end of the year, we will have moved.)

Note: The *futur antérieur* can sometimes be replaced by the *passé composé* (past compound) in informal speech, especially when the context is clear.

Subject	Auxiliary Verb (Future Tense)	Past Participle	Example in French	English Translation
Je (I)	aurai	mangé	J'aurai mangé.	I will have eaten.
Tu (You, singular)	auras	terminé	Tu auras terminé.	You will have finished.
Il / Elle / On (He / She / One)	aura	parti(e)	Il/Elle aura parti(e).	He/She will have left.
Nous (We)	aurons	travaillé	Nous aurons travaillé.	We will have worked.
Vous (You, plural/formal)	aurez	étudié	Vous aurez étudié.	You will have studied.
Ils / Elles (They)	auront	vu	Ils/Elles auront vu.	They will have seen.

Time markers for the future

Here are some common time markers used with the future tense:

General Time Markers

- **Demain:** Tomorrow
- **Après-demain:** The day after tomorrow
- **La semaine prochaine:** Next week
- **Le mois prochain:** Next month
- **L'année prochaine:** Next year
- **Dans une heure:** In an hour
- **Dans deux jours:** In two days
- **Dans un mois:** In a month

Specific Time Markers

- **À huit heures:** At eight o'clock
- **À midi:** At noon
- **Le soir:** In the evening
- **La nuit:** At night
- **En janvier:** In January
- **Au printemps:** In spring
- **À Noël:** At Christmas

Time Markers Indicating Certainty or Uncertainty

- **Sûrement:** Surely
- **Probablement:** Probably
- **Peut-être:** Maybe
- **Certainement:** Certainly
- **Indubitablement:** Undoubtedly

Example sentences:

- **Demain**, il fera beau. (Tomorrow, it will be nice.)
- **Dans deux semaines**, nous partirons en vacances. (In two weeks, we will go on vacation.)

- **À midi**, je mangerai au restaurant. (At noon, I will eat at the restaurant.)
- **Peut-être** que je viendrai à la fête. (Maybe I will come to the party.)

How to make hypotheses about the future

Word/Expression in French	Pronunciation	Translation
certainement	sehr-tay-ne-mahn	very likely
probablement	proh-ba-bleh-mahn	probably
possiblement	poh-see-bleh-mahn	possibly
sûrement	syur-mahn	surely
je suppose que	zhuh soo-pohz kuh	I suppose

Expressing conditions

Conditional clauses in French are used to express situations that are dependent on certain conditions.

Conditional I (Present Condition and Future Result)

- **Structure:** *Si + present tense, future tense*
- **Usage:** This conditional is used to express a possible or probable condition and its corresponding result.
- **Example:** *Si tu étudies, tu réussiras.* (If you study, you will succeed.)

Conditional II (Hypothetical Condition and Past Result)

- **Structure:** *Si + imperfect tense, conditional tense*
- **Usage:** This conditional is used to express an unlikely or impossible condition and its hypothetical result.
- **Example:** *Si j'avais eu le temps, je serais allé au cinéma.* (If I had had the time, I would have gone to the cinema.)

Conditional III (Hypothetical Past Condition and Past Result)

- **Structure:** *Si + pluperfect tense, pluperfect conditional tense*

- **Usage:** This conditional is used to express a hypothetical past condition and its hypothetical past result.

- **Example:** *Si tu avais étudié, tu aurais réussi.* (If you had studied, you would have succeeded.)

Other Conditional Structures

- **The *il est possible que* construction:** This can be used to express a possible or probable condition.

  - Example: *Il est possible que je sois en retard.* (It's possible that I'll be late.)

- **The *à condition que* construction:** This can be used to express a necessary condition.

  - Example: *Je viendrai à condition que tu m'aides.* (I'll come if you help me.)

Exercises

1. **Which of the following is NOT a use of the present tense in French?**

   a) Expressing current actions

   b) Describing habits or routines

   c) Talking about past events

   d) Expressing future plans

2. **How is the verb "parler" (to speak) conjugated in the present tense for the "nous" form?**

   a) parlons

   b) parlez

   c) parlent

   d) parler

3. **Which verb is irregular in the present tense?**

   a) manger (to eat)

   b) finir (to finish)

   c) être (to be)

   d) vendre (to sell)

4. **What is the future periphrastic used for in French?**

   a) Expressing past actions

   b) Expressing future actions

   c) Describing habits

   d) Giving commands

5. **How would you say "I am going to eat" in French using the future periphrastic?**

   a) Je mange

b) Je vais manger

c) Je mangerais

d) J'ai mangé

6. **Which tense is used to express actions or events that will happen in the future?**

a) Présent de l'indicatif

b) Futur simple

c) Passé composé

d) Imparfait

7. **How is the verb "avoir" (to have) conjugated in the future simple for the "je" form?**

a) aurai

b) auras

c) aura

d) avons

8. **Which of the following is NOT a typical use of the futur simple?**

a) Making predictions

b) Giving orders

c) Describing past events

d) Expressing promises

9. **What tense is used to express actions or events that will have been completed before a specific time in the future?**

a) Futur simple

b) Futur antérieur

c) Passé composé

d) Imparfait

10. **How would you say "I will have finished my homework" in French using the future anterior?**

a) J'ai fini mes devoirs

b) Je finirai mes devoirs

c) J'aurai fini mes devoirs

d) Je finissais mes devoirs

Answer Key

1. c) Talking about past events

2. a) parlons

3. c) être (to be)

4. b) Expressing future actions

5. b) Je vais manger

6. b) Futur simple

7. a) aurai

8. c) Describing past events

9. b) Futur antérieur

10. c) J'aurai fini mes devoirs

Cultural Annex

Here's a list of French songs for additional practice:

1. "Le Temps des Cerises" – Written by Jean-Baptiste Clément (lyrics) and Antoine Renard (music).

2. "Avec le Temps" – Written and performed by Léo Ferré.

3. "Le Temps Qui Court" – Written by Jean-Michel Rivat and Alain Boublil, performed by Alain Chamfort.

4. "Le Temps Ne Fait Rien à l'Affaire" – Written and performed by Georges Brassens.

5. "Le Temps de Vivre" – Written by Georges Moustaki.

6. "Au Fil du Temps" – Written by Jean-Louis Murat.

7. "Le Temps Est Bon" – Written by Jean-Pierre Ferland.

8. "Il Est Cinq Heures, Paris S'éveille" – Written by Jacques Dutronc, Jacques Lanzmann, and Anne Ségalen.

Conclusion

Throughout this section, we've covered a wide variety of topics, some of which are challenging even to native French speakers! Félicitations!

BOOK 5

Practice French with Short Stories for Adults

Shortcut Your French Fluency!
(Fun & Easy Reads)

Explore to Win

Book 5 Description

Are you ready to start reading French at a more intermediate level? We have the perfect solution for you: Practice French with Short Stories for Adults.

These high-quality short stories are exactly what you need to elevate your French skills to the next level. You'll gain a rich vocabulary and the confidence needed to practice your French with real French speakers.

In Practice French with Short Stories for Adults, you will discover:

- Captivating stories.

- Rich vocabulary and practical everyday phrases.

- Stories structured to challenge your French comprehension.

- Helpful glossaries.

- A summary for each story.

- Exercises to test your skills.

Don't worry if you don't understand the stories the first few times you read them. Just focus on understanding what you can and use our helpful glossaries and English summaries for assistance until you're able to read fluidly on your own.

Chapter 1: L'anniversaire de Thomas – Thomas' birthday.

"Chaque homme dans sa nuit s'en va vers sa lumière."

- Victor Hugo

Tomás se réveille avec un terrible mal de tête, toute la pièce tourne autour de lui. L'horloge indique 14 heures et il ne se souvient pas de grand-chose de ce qui s'est passé la nuit précédente. Tomás porte encore les vêtements d'hier soir, deux de ses amis dorment sur des matelas par terre dans sa chambre. Luis se réveille, tout aussi désorienté que lui, et lui demande quelle heure il est.

- Tu te souviens de quelque chose d'hier soir? – demande Tomás.

- Bien sûr, pourquoi? Et toi?

- Pas vraiment, pour être honnête.

Luis commence à lui raconter ce qui s'est passé la nuit dernière. Leurs amis sont venus chez lui vers 22 heures et ils ont pris un verre. Luis a apporté une bouteille de rhum, un autre ami a apporté de la vodka. Personne ne savait préparer de cocktails compliqués, alors ils ont bu de la vodka avec du jus d'orange et du rhum avec de la soda. Ils ont bu et discuté pendant environ trois heures, puis ils ont pris deux taxis pour se rendre à la discothèque Blue, à environ trente minutes de route. L'entrée de la discothèque coûtait 200 pesos, mais Tomás est entré gratuitement car c'était son anniversaire. On lui a aussi offert un cocktail en cadeau. Le DJ passait principalement les chansons pop les plus populaires du moment, et tout le monde dans la foule chantait en dansant.

Les lumières tournantes illuminaient l'endroit au rythme de la musique. Il y avait de très jolies filles, et en peu de temps les garçons avaient trouvé avec qui danser. Tomás a rencontré une fille nommée Valentina, elle avait les cheveux blonds et courts et un très beau sourire. Elle l'a félicité pour son anniversaire et lui a offert un verre. Après avoir dansé un moment, Tomás s'est assis avec Valentina et ils ont discuté de plusieurs choses. Ils étaient tous deux tellement concentrés sur la conversation qu'ils ont à peine remarqué l'agitation sur la piste de danse, et quand Tomás s'en est rendu compte, Luis était en train de se disputer avec un des gardes de sécurité.

Tomás est allé demander ce qui se passait, et à sa surprise, les gardes de sécurité ont expulsé lui et ses amis du lieu. Tomás était furieux, non seulement parce qu'il était un peu ivre, mais aussi parce qu'il ne comprenait rien à ce qui se passait. Luis était tout aussi furieux et lui a expliqué que quelqu'un avait sorti son téléphone de sa poche et qu'il pensait que c'était l'un des gardes qui était sur la piste de danse.

Quand il l'a confronté, l'homme a tout nié et a dit aux autres gardes de les faire sortir parce qu'ils faisaient une scène. Tomás lui a demandé s'il était vraiment sûr que le garde lui avait volé son téléphone, et il a répondu que non, car il faisait très sombre. Malgré ce qui s'était passé, et même si Tomás était frustré de ne pas avoir eu le temps de demander à Valentina son numéro, les garçons ne voulaient pas encore rentrer chez eux, alors ils sont allés dans une autre discothèque appelée Caribe, où la musique était de la salsa, du merengue et du reggaeton. Il y avait un open bar jusqu'à 4 heures du matin, alors ils en ont profité pour boire autant qu'ils pouvaient.

Tomás a trop bu et a dû aller aux toilettes parce qu'il pensait qu'il allait vomir, mais heureusement ce n'était qu'une fausse alerte. À 2 heures du matin, il y a eu un spectacle de drag queens, et finalement les garçons se sont rendu compte qu'ils étaient dans une discothèque gay. Ils se sentaient stupides d'être aussi distraits, mais ils ont quand même rencontré des filles qui pensaient qu'ils étaient ouverts d'esprit parce qu'ils étaient dans un endroit comme celui-ci et elles les ont invités à danser. Ils ont passé un bon moment le reste de la nuit, jusqu'à la fermeture de la discothèque. Ensuite, tout le monde est rentré en taxi chez Tomás.

- Maintenant, tu te souviens? – demande Luis.

- Plus ou moins.

Le téléphone de Tomás vibre, c'est un message d'un numéro inconnu. – Salut, c'est Rebeca, la fille de la discothèque d'hier soir, voici mon numéro.

Résumé

Tomás se réveille avec un terrible mal de tête sans se souvenir de grand-chose de ce qui s'est passé la nuit précédente. Luis lui raconte qu'ils ont célébré son anniversaire en prenant un verre chez lui, puis en allant dans une discothèque où Tomás a rencontré une fille nommée Valentina. Il y a eu un problème avec l'un des gardes de sécurité du lieu, et Tomás et ses amis ont été expulsés de la discothèque, mais comme ils ne voulaient pas encore rentrer chez eux, ils sont allés au Caribe, où ils ont beaucoup bu et dansé avec des filles. C'était une nuit folle qu'ils se souviendront sans aucun doute pendant de nombreuses années.

Summary

Tomás wakes up with a throbbing headache without remembering much of what happened the previous night. Luis tells him that they celebrated Tomás' birthday by drinking a bit at his house and then going to a club where Tomás met a girl namedValentina. There was a problem with one of the security guards of the place and Tomás and his friends got kicked out of the club, but since they didn't want to go home yet, they went to Caribe, where they drank a lot and danced with some girls. It was a crazy night that they will definitely remember for many years.

Glossaire – Glossary

- **La pièce tourne:** The room spins

- **Ce qui s'est passé:** what happened

- **Matelas:** mattresses

- **Désorienté:** disoriented

- **Tu te souviens?:** Do you remember?

- **Honnêtement:** Honestly

- **Il commence à lui dire:** He starts telling him

- **Ce qui est arrivé:** What happened

- **Ils ont bu un peu:** They drank a bit

- **Il a apporté:** He brought

- **Une bouteille de rhum:** A bottle of rum

- **Aucun d'eux ne savait préparer de cocktails compliqués:** None of them knew how to make complicated cocktails

- **Soda:** Soda

- **Ils ont bu:** They were drinking

- **Pendant environ trois heures:** For about three hours

- **Discothèque:** Night club

- **Ça coûtait:** It cost

- **Il est entré gratuitement:** He entered for free

- **Ils lui ont offert un cocktail en cadeau:** They gave him a cocktail as a gift

- **Le DJ passait:** The DJ played

- **Principalement:** Mostly

- **La foule:** The crowd

- **Ils chantaient en dansant:** They were singing while dancing

- **Les lumières tournantes illuminaient:** The rotating lights lit up

- **Au rythme de la musiquE:** To the rhythm of the music

- **Ils avaient trouvé:** They had found

- **Avec qui danser:** Who to dance with

- **Il a rencontré:** He met

- **Une fille nommée:** A girl called

- **Elle l'a félicité pour son anniversaire:** She said happy birthday to him

- **Elle lui a offert un verre:** She bought him a drink

- **Il s'est assiS:** He sat

- **Ils ont discuté:** They talked

- **Ils étaient tellement concentrés sur la conversation:** They were so focused on the conversation

- **Ils ont remarqué:** They noticed

- **La piste de danse:** The dance floor

- **Il s'est rendu compte:** He noticed

- **Il se disputait avec:** He was arguing with

- **Les gardes de sécurité:** Security guards

- **Il est allé demander ce qui se passait:** He went to ask what was happening

- **À sa surprise:** To his surprise

- **Ils les ont expulsés:** They kicked them out

- **Enragé:** Enraged

- **Il ne comprenait pas:** He didn't understand

- **Il lui a expliqué:** He explained

- **Quelqu'un avait pris son téléphone de sa poche:** Someone had grabbed his phone from his pocket

- **Il pensait que c'était:** He thought that it had been

- **Il l'a confronté:** He confronted him

- **Il a nié:** He denied it

- **Ils faisaient une scène:** They were making a scene

- **Si le garde lui avait volé son téléphone:** If the guard had stolen his phone

- **Ce qui s'était passé:** What had happened

- **Il n'a pas eu le temps de demander à Valentina son numéro:** He didn't have time to ask Valentina for her number

- **Ils ne voulaient pas encore rentrer chez eux:** They didn't want to go back home yet

- **Ils sont allés:** They went

- **Il y avait un open bar:** There was an open bar

- **Ils en ont profité pour boire autant qu'ils pouvaient:** They took advantage of the situation to drink as much as they could

- **Il a dû aller:** He had to go

- **Il pensait qu'il allait vomir:** He thought he was going to throw up

- **C'était une fausse alerte:** It was a false alarm

- **Ils se sentaient stupides:** They felt stupid

- **D'être aussi distraits:** For being so absent-minded

- **Ouverts d'esprit:** Open-minded

- **Ils les ont invités à danser:** They asked them to dance

- **Ça a fermé:** It closed

- **Ils sont revenus:** They went back

- **Tu te souviens maintenant?:** Do you remember now?

- **Ça vibre:** It vibrates

- **Un numéro inconnu:** An unknown number

Exercice 1

Répondez aux questions suivantes– Answer the following questions

1- À quelle heure Tomás se réveille-t-il? (What time does Tomás wake up?)

_____

2- Qu'est-ce qu'ils ont bu chez Tomás? (What did they drink in Tomás' house?)

_____

3- Combien Tomás a-t-il payé pour entrer dans la discothèque?
(How much did Tomás pay to enter the club?)

_____

4- À quoi ressemblait Valentina? (What did Valentina look like?)

_____

5- Avec qui Luis se disputait-il? (Who was Luis arguing with?)

_____

6- Qu'est-il arrivé à Luis? (What happened to Luis?)

_____

Exercice 2

Choisissez entre "vrai" ou "faux" – choose "true" or "false

1- Tomás se réveille chez Luis. (Tomás wakes up at Luis' house.)

_____

2- Luis a apporté une bouteille de rhum. (Luis brought a bottle of rum.)

3- L'entrée de la discothèque coûtait 300 pesos. (The entry to the club was 300 pesos.)

_____

4- Valentina avait les cheveux noirs. (Valentina had black hair.)

_____

5- Luis s'est battu avec quelqu'un. (Luis had a fight with someone.)

_____

6- Tomás a demandé le numéro de Valentina. (Tomás asked Valentina for her phone number.)

_____

Réponses – Answers

Exercice 1

1- Tomás se réveille à 14 heures.

2- Chez Tomás, ils ont bu de la vodka avec du jus d'orange et du rhum avec du soda.

3- Tomás n'a pas payé pour entrer, l'entrée était gratuite parce qu'il fêtait son anniversaire.

4- Valentina avait les cheveux blonds et courts et un joli sourire.

5- Luis se disputait avec l'un des gardes de sécurité de la discothèque.

6- Quelqu'un a pris le téléphone de Luis dans sa poche.

Exercice 2

1- Faux

2- Vrai

3- Faux

4- Faux

5- Faux

6- Faux

Chapter 2: Mon enfance – My childhood

"Toutes les grandes personnes ont d'abord été des enfants, mais peu d'entre elles s'en souviennent."

- Antoine de Saint-Exupéry

Quand Tomás était petit, il passait habituellement les vacances d'été chez ses grands-parents à la campagne. Il ne pouvait pas attendre que les vacances arrivent. Il se comportait toujours bien le mois précédant les vacances pour que ses parents le laissent aller à la campagne. La maison des grands-parents de Tomás était immense, ils avaient un grand terrain où il y avait beaucoup de plantes et ils cultivaient des tomates et des pommes de terre, ainsi que des noix de coco et des bananes. Ils avaient aussi plus de dix chiens, et le chien préféré de Tomás était Girasol, une golden retriever très espiègle qui devenait très joyeuse chaque fois qu'elle voyait Tomás. Ils avaient également d'autres animaux comme des chevaux, des canards et des poules. Il n'y avait jamais de silence dans la maison.

Pendant ces jours de vacances, Tomás se levait à 8 heures du matin et aidait sa grand-mère à préparer les œufs pour le petit-déjeuner, puis il regardait des dessins animés en mangeant. Après un moment, il sortait jouer avec les chiens ou regarder ses cousins plus âgés monter à cheval. On ne lui permettait pas de monter à cheval parce qu'il était trop petit, mais parfois son cousin Juan le laissait monter à cheval avec lui, et ils ne le disaient pas à la grand-mère pour qu'elle ne se fâche pas. Tomás aimait aussi se baigner dans la piscine tous les jours, même quand il pleuvait. Parfois, Girasol entrait dans la piscine avec lui et ils jouaient un moment dans l'eau. Les nuits à la campagne étaient un peu fraîches, donc la grand-mère ne laissait pas Tomás rester dans la piscine pour qu'il ne prenne pas froid. Une nuit, Tomás n'a pas écouté sa grand-mère et a attrapé un rhume si fort qu'il a même eu de la fièvre, cette fois-là il a appris sa leçon. Le soir, Tomás jouait normalement à des jeux de société avec ses cousins, dessinait dans sa chambre ou regardait les nouvelles avec son grand-père.

Tomás était un petit-fils très gâté. Ses cousins devaient généralement partager une chambre, mais lui avait une chambre pour lui tout seul, c'était peut-être parce qu'il était le plus jeune, mais il pense que c'était ainsi parce qu'il était le seul petit-fils qui passait tous les étés chez ses grands-parents.

Ses cousins voyageaient parfois dans d'autres endroits, mais Tomás demandait à ses parents de l'emmener chez ses grands-parents tous les ans parce qu'il adorait ça.

La seule chose que Tomás n'aimait pas, c'était quand son oncle Manuel les emmenait tous à la chasse. Il aimait passer du temps avec ses cousins dans les champs, mais chaque fois qu'il voyait des animaux mourir, Tomás se mettait à pleurer. Une fois, même, son oncle s'est fâché contre lui parce que Tomás a refusé de manger le lapin qu'ils avaient chassé, ils pensaient que Tomás faisait des caprices et ils l'ont même puni. Ils lui ont dit que cette nuit-là, il ne mangerait rien et qu'il irait se coucher le ventre vide, mais sa grand-mère, en cachette, lui a donné un bon morceau de tarte aux pommes. Jusqu'à ce jour, personne ne sait que cela est arrivé. Depuis cette nuit-là, Tomás a décidé qu'il ne mangerait plus de viande, et même si personne ne le comprenait au début, avec le temps, ils ont compris et l'ont respecté.

Depuis, chaque fois que Tomás allait chez ses grands-parents, la grand-mère lui préparait quelque chose de spécial avec des légumes. Avec Tomás, la grand-mère a planté des concombres, des poivrons et des avocats, puis l'une des activités préférées de Tomás était de prendre soin des plantes et de récolter les fruits qu'elles produisaient. Malgré quelques moments pas si bons, Tomás se souvient de son enfance avec beaucoup de joie et souhaiterait souvent revivre ces moments.

Résumé

Quand Tomás était petit, il passait chaque été chez ses grands-parents à la campagne. Il aimait jouer avec les animaux et passer du temps avec ses cousins, en plus de nager dans la piscine. Un jour en particulier, il a eu un problème avec son oncle Manuel et a été puni pour avoir refusé de manger la viande d'un animal qu'ils avaient chassé, alors Tomás a décidé qu'il ne mangerait plus jamais de viande. Malgré quelques moments pas si bons, Tomás était très heureux à la campagne avec ses grands-parents et se souvient de ces jours avec beaucoup d'affection.

Summary

When Tomás was little, he used to spend every summer in his grandparents' house in the countryside. He liked playing with the animals and spending time with his cousins, as well as swimming in the pool. One day in particular he had a problem with his uncle Manuel and they grounded him for refusing to eat the meat of an animal they had hunted, then Tomás decided he would never eat meat again. Despite some not so great moments, Tomás was really happy in the country with his grandparents and he remembers those days fondly.

Glossaire – Glossary

- **Il avait l'habitude de:** He used to
- **A la campagne:** In the countryside
- **Il ne pouvait pas attendre que les vacances arrivent:** He couldn't wait for vacations to arrive
- **Il se comportait bien:** He would behave well
- **Pour que ses parents le laissent partir:** So that his parents would let him go
- **Terrain étendu:** Extensive land
- **Il y avait:** There was/there were
- **Ils plantaient:** They would plant
- **Noix de coco:** Coconut
- **Espiègle:** Mischievous

- **Qui se réjouissait:** Who would get happy
- **Chaque fois qu'elle voyait Tomás:** Every time she saw Tomás
- **Chevaux, canards et poules:** Horses, ducks and hens
- **Il n'y avait jamais de silence**: There was never silence
- **Il se levait:** He would get up
- **Il aidait:** He would help
- **Il regardait des dessins animés:** He would watch cartoons
- **Il sortait jouer:** He would go out to play
- **Monter à cheval:** To ride a horse
- **Ils ne le laissaient pas:** They wouldn't let him
- **Ils ne disaient pas:** They wouldn't tell
- **Pour qu'elle ne se fâche pas:** So that she wouldn't get mad
- **Il aimait entrer dans la piscine:** He used to like getting in the pool
- **Même quand il pleuvait:** Even when it was raining
- **Elle entrait:** She would get in
- **Ils jouaient un moment dans l'eau:** They would play for a while in the water
- **Elle ne le laissait pas être dans la piscine:** She wouldn't let him be in the pool.
- **Pour qu'il ne prenne pas froid:** So that he wouldn't catch a cold
- **Il n'a pas écouté sa grand-mère:** He didn't listen to his grandmother
- **Il a attrapé un rhume:** He caught a cold
- **A tel point qu'il a même eu de la fièvre:** It was so strong that he even had fever
- **Il a appris sa leçon:** He learned his lesson
- **Jeux de société:** Board games
- **Les nouvelles:** The news
- **Il était un petit-fils très gâté:** He was a very spoiled grandson
- **Ils devaient partager une chambre:** They had to share a room
- **Il avait une chambre pour lui tout seul:** He had a room just for him
- **Il était le seul petit-fils qui passait tous les étés:** He was the only grandson that would spend every summer
- **Ils voyageaient:** They would travel
- **Il demandait à ses parents de l'emmener:** He would ask his parents to take him
- **Il les emmenait tous à la chasse:** He would take them all hunting
- **Il voyait les animaux mourir:** He would watch the animals die
- **Il commençait à pleurer:** He would start crying

- **Il a refusé de manger:** He refused to eat
- **Le lapin qu'ils avaient chassé:** The rabbit they had hunted
- **Il faisait des caprices:** He was being a brat
- **Ils l'ont puni:** They grounded him
- **Il irait se coucher le ventre vide:** He would go to bed with an empty stomach
- **En cachette:** Behind their backs
- **Elle lui a donné un bon morceau de tarte aux pommes:** She gave him a generous piece of apple pie
- **Jusqu'à ce jour:** To this day
- **Personne ne sait que cela est arrivé:** No one knows that that happened
- **Il ne mangerait plus de viande:** He wouldn't eat meat anymore
- **Personne ne le comprenait au début:** No one understood it at first
- **Avec le temps:** With time
- **Ils l'ont respecté:** They respected it
- **Depuis lors:** Since then
- **Il allait:** He would go
- **Elle a planté des concombres, des poivrons et des avocats:** She planted cucumber, pepper and avocado
- **S'occuper des plantes:** To take care of the plants
- **Récolter les fruits:** To reap the fruits
- **Pas si bons:** Not so good
- **Son enfance:** His childhood
- **Il souhaiterait revivre:** He wishes he could relive

Exercice 1

Répondez aux questions suivantes – Answer the following questions

1- Pourquoi Tomás se comportait-il bien? (Why did Tomás use to behave well?)

_____

2- Comment était Girasol? (How was Girasol like?)

_____

3- Quels autres animaux y avait-il? (What other animals were there?)

_____

4- Pourquoi ne le laissaient-ils pas monter à cheval? (Why wouldn't they let him ride a horse?)

_____

5- Que faisait son cousin Juan? (What would his cousin Juan do?)

_____

6- Qu'est-il arrivé à Tomás quand il n'a pas écouté sa grand-mère? (What happened to Tomás when he didn't listen to his grandma?)

_____

Exercice 2

Choisissez "vrai" ou "faux" – Choose "true" or "false"

1- Les grands-parents de Tomás plantaient des fruits. (Tomás' grandparents would plant fruits.)

_____

2- Ils avaient aussi des chats. (They also had cats.)

3- Tomás préparait le café pour tout le monde le matin. (Tomás would make coffee for everybody in the morning.)

_____

4- Ils ne laissaient pas Tomás nourrir les chevaux. (They wouldn't let Tomás feed the horses.)

_____

5- Les nuits étaient froides. (The nights were cold.)

_____

6- Tomás partageait une chambre avec Juan. (Tomás shared a room with Juan.)

_____

Réponses – Answers

Exercice 1

1- Tomás se comportait bien pour que ses parents le laissent aller chez ses grands-parents à la campagne.

2- Girasol était une golden retriever très espiègle.

3- À la campagne, il y avait aussi des chevaux, des canards et des poules.

4- On ne laissait pas Tomás monter à cheval parce qu'il était très petit.

5- Son cousin Juan le laissait monter à cheval avec lui.

6- Quand Tomás n'a pas écouté sa grand-mère, il a attrapé un rhume si fort qu'il a même eu de la fièvre.

Exercice 2

1- Vrai

2- Faux

3- Faux

4- Faux

5- Vrai

6- Faux

Chapter 3: Le voyage de Cristina – Cristina's trip

"Le véritable voyage de découverte ne consiste pas à chercher de nouveaux paysages, mais à avoir de nouveaux yeux."

- Marcel Proust

Cette année, Cristina a très bien réussi au travail. Elle travaille plus d'heures que jamais, mais grâce à cela, elle a pu économiser beaucoup d'argent. Son petit ami lui a demandé ce qu'elle comptait faire de tout cet argent, et elle n'avait pas de réponse à ce moment-là. Puis, après y avoir longuement réfléchi, elle s'est rappelée que l'un de ses rêves avait toujours été de voyager à travers le monde. Elle a pensé à la France, à l'Italie et au Portugal, des pays riches en histoire qui lui paraissaient fascinants.

Ainsi, Cristina a passé les trois dernières semaines en voyage ; demain sera son dernier jour au Portugal, et elle en repartira avec des souvenirs inoubliables. Elle a enfin pu voir ces châteaux anciens où la royauté vivait il y a des siècles, avec une architecture hors du commun. Sur les photos qu'elle a prises, il est presque impossible de distinguer les gens ; tous semblent de petits insectes à côté des majestueux châteaux. Pendant un instant, elle a vécu ce fantasme qu'elle avait étant enfant ; elle s'est sentie comme une princesse de contes de fées, avec ces colliers et bagues en or extravagants. Lors de son voyage à Lisbonne, Cristina a également pu goûter des plats délicieux de fruits de mer. Cristina n'a pas l'habitude de manger des choses aussi exotiques, mais elle a décidé de le faire car elle savait qu'elle le regretterait si elle ne le faisait pas. Elle a goûté des crevettes, des poulpes et des palourdes dans plusieurs restaurants de la région. Si elle devait choisir son préféré, elle opterait pour le restaurant qui se trouve à deux pâtés de maisons de l'endroit où elle loge, un lieu très accueillant tenu par une dame âgée très douce qui rappelle à Cristina sa grand-mère.

Bien qu'au début, le plan était que le petit ami de Cristina l'accompagne, il n'a finalement pas pu le faire car il devait travailler, alors Cristina a entrepris ce voyage seule. Malgré cela, elle ne regrette pas. Elle a eu l'occasion de rencontrer des personnes très intéressantes, comme des filles d'Allemagne qui parlaient un peu espagnol. L'une d'elles était une fille très grande qui était venue à Lisbonne pour chercher l'inspiration pour un roman qu'elle écrivait. Cristina a passé trois jours avec elles, et l'écrivaine lui posait toutes sortes de questions, semblant fascinée par tout ce que Cristina avait à dire. Elle a également rencontré un couple de jeunes mariés qui étaient au Portugal pour leur lune de miel. Les circonstances de leur rencontre étaient assez inhabituelles ; le jeune homme a parlé à Cristina parce qu'il pensait que c'était sa sœur, ce qui a semblé étrange à Cristina, et pendant un moment, elle a pensé que c'était une stratégie pour la voler ou quelque chose du genre. Mais le garçon a montré des photos à Cristina, et en effet, la sœur du garçon lui ressemblait beaucoup. Après cet étrange incident, Cristina a déjeuné avec eux, mais il était difficile de communiquer car les jeunes mariés ne parlaient pas espagnol, seulement un peu d'anglais.

Malheureusement, tout n'a pas été rose lors de ce voyage. Cristina a séjourné dans sept endroits différents tout au long de son voyage au Portugal, et le seul endroit où elle a eu des problèmes était un hôtel qui, en vérité, était un peu coûteux. Lors de son deuxième jour de séjour à l'hôtel, Cristina a perdu son sèche-cheveux et quelques euros qu'elle avait dans sa valise. Elle a signalé cela aux responsables de l'hôtel, mais ils n'ont rien fait, se contentant de dire qu'ils ne seraient pas responsables de ses pertes. Cristina suppose que la responsable était la femme de ménage qui était entrée pour nettoyer sa chambre lorsqu'elle n'était pas à l'hôtel. Mais en dehors de cela, l'expérience a été très enrichissante pour Cristina, et elle pense continuer à voyager autant qu'elle le pourra.

Résumé

Le rêve de Cristina a toujours été de voyager à travers le monde, et maintenant qu'elle travaille dans une entreprise où elle a un bon salaire, elle peut se permettre de le faire. Elle choisit le Portugal comme première destination et y passe de très bons moments, notamment à Lisbonne, où elle visite quelques châteaux majestueux et rencontre plusieurs personnes intéressantes. Tout n'a pas été parfait dans cette aventure, mais ce fut une expérience très enrichissante.

Summary

Cristina's dream has always been to travel around the world and now that she works at a company where she has a good salary, she can do that. She chooses Portugal as her first destination and has had a great time there, especially in Lisbon, where she visits some majestic castles and meets several interesting people. Not everything was perfect in this adventure, but it was a very rewarding experience.

Glossaire – Glossary

- **Elle a très bien réussi au travail:** Things have been going great for her at work

- **Plus d'heures que jamais:** More hours than ever

- **Grâce à cela:** Thanks to that

- **Elle a pu économiser beaucoup d'argent:** She has been able to save a lot of money

- **Il lui a demandé ce qu'elle comptait faire:** He asked her what she was planning to do

- **A quoi elle n'avait pas de réponse:** To which she had no answer

- **l'un de ses rêves avait toujours été de voyager autour du monde:** One of her dreams had always been to travel around the world

- **Qu'elle trouvait très fascinants:** Which she found so fascinating

- **Demain sera son dernier jour au Portugal:** Tomorrow will be her last day in Portugal

- **Elle repartira avec des souvenirs inoubliables:** She's taking unforgettable memories with her

- **Elle a pu voir ces châteaux anciens:** She has been able to see those old castles

- **Où la royauté vivait il y a des siècles:** Where the royalty lived centuries ago

- Hors de ce monde: Out of this world

- **Il est presque impossible de distinguer les gens:** It's almost impossible to distinguish the people

- **Ce fantasme qu'elle avait étant petite:** That fantasy she had as a little girl

- **Une princesse de contes de fées:** A princess from fairy tales

- **Ces colliers et bagues en or extravagants:** Those extravagant gold necklaces and rings

- **Elle a pu goûter toutes sortes de plats de fruits de mer:** She has been able to try all kinds of seafood dishes

- **Elle n'est pas habituée à manger des choses aussi exotiques:** She's not used to eating exotic things

- **Parce qu'elle savait qu'elle le regretterait si elle ne le faisait pas**: Because she knew she would regret it if she didn't

- **Crevettes, poulpes et palourdes:** Shrimp, octopus, and clam

- **Si elle devait choisir:** If she had to choose

- **Elle choisirait:** She would pick

- **A deux pâtés de maisons de l'endroit où elle loge:** Two blocks away from the place she's staying

- **Accueillant:** cozy

- **Qui est tenu par une vieille dame très douce:** Which is run by a sweet old lady

- **Qui rappelle à Cristina sa grand-mère:** Who reminds Cristina of her grandmother

- **Le plan était que le petit ami de Cristina l'accompagne:** The plan was for Cristina's boyfriend to go with her

- **Il n'a pas pu:** He couldn't

- **Il devait travailler:** He had to work

- **Cristina a entrepris ce voyage seule:** Cristina embarked on this trip alone

- **Elle a eu l'occasion de rencontrer:** She has had the opportunity to meet

- **Des filles d'Allemagne qui parlaient un peu espagnol:** Girls from Germany who spoke a little Spanish

- **Qui était venue à Lisbonne:** Who had come to Lisbon

- **Pour chercher l'inspiration pour le roman qu'elle écrivait:** To search for inspiration for the novel she was writing

- **Elle lui posait toutes sortes de questions:** She made her all kinds of questions

- **Fascinée par tout ce que Cristina avait à dire:** Fascinated with everything Cristina had to say

- **Un couple de jeunes mariés:** A couple of newlyweds

- **Lune de miel:** Honeymoon

- **Les circonstances de leur rencontre:** The circumstances of how they met

- **Cristina a trouvé cela étrange:** Cristina found it strange

- **Une stratégie pour la voler:** Some strategy to rob her

- **Quelque chose comme ça:** Something like that

- **Il lui a montré quelques photos:** He showed her some pictures

- **La sœur du garçon lui ressemblait:** The guy's sister looked like her

- **Elle a déjeuné avec eux:** She had lunch with them

- **Tout n'a pas été rose:** It hasn't all been peaches and cream

- **Elle est restée:** She has stayed

- **Tout au long de son voyage:** Throughout her journey

- **Sèche-cheveux:** Hairdryer

- **Valise:** Suitcase

- **Qu'elle a signalé aux responsables de l'hôtel:** Which she reported to the hotel managers

- **Ils ne seraient pas responsables de ses pertes:** They wouldn't take responsibility for her lost item

- **Elle suppose que la responsable était la femme de ménage:** She assumes the responsible was the housekeeper

- **Quand elle n'était pas à l'hôtel:** When she wasn't in the hotel

- **En mettant cela de côté:** Leaving that aside

- **L'expérience a été enrichissante:** The experience has been rewarding

Exercice 1

Répondez aux questions suivantes – Answer the following questions

1- Qu'a-t-elle pu faire grâce à son travail? (What has she been able to do thanks to her job?)

_____

2- Depuis combien de temps est-elle en voyage? (How long has she been on her trip?)

_____

3- Dans quelle partie du Portugal est-elle allée? (What part of Portugal did she go to?)

_____

4- Quelle nourriture a-t-elle essayée au Portugal? (What food has she tried in Portugal?)

_____

5- Comment était la personne qui tenait le restaurant? (What was the person who ran the restaurant like?)

_____

6- Pourquoi la fille allemande est-elle venue au Portugal? (What did the German girl come to Portugal to do?)

_____

Exercice 2

Choisissez "vrai" ou "faux" – choose "true" or "false"

1- Elle pense que le Portugal est fascinant. (She thinks Portugal is fascinating.)

_____

2- Elle mange toujours des choses exotiques. (She always eats exotic food.)

3- Le restaurant est à 1 kilomètre. (The restaurant is 1 kilometer away.)

4- Cristina a voyagé seule. (Cristina traveled by herself.)

5- Elle a rencontré deux filles russes. (She met two Russian girls.)

6- La fille était enseignante. (The girl was a teacher.)

Réponses – Answers

Exercice 1

1- Cristina a pu économiser beaucoup d'argent avec son nouveau travail et grâce à cela, elle peut voyager.

2- Cristina est en voyage depuis trois semaines.

3- Cristina est allée à Lisbonne.

4- Cristina a goûté des fruits de mer comme des crevettes, du poulpe et des palourdes.

5- La personne qui tenait le restaurant était une vieille dame très douce qui rappelait à Cristina sa grand-mère.

6- La fille allemande est venue au Portugal pour chercher l'inspiration pour le roman qu'elle est en train d'écrire.

Exercice 2

1- Vrai

2- Faux

3- Faux

4- Vrai

5- Faux

6- Faux

Chapter 4: Mes objectifs – My goals

"Pour ce qui est de l'avenir, il ne s'agit pas de le prévoir, mais de le rendre possible."

- Antoine de Saint-Exupéry

Marisol travaille comme rédactrice dans un magazine appelé *"La Mirada"* depuis l'année 2007. Elle aime travailler là-bas, elle s'entend très bien avec tout le monde et a beaucoup appris dans ce poste toutes ces années, mais dernièrement, elle se sent insatisfaite et se sent un peu stupide pour cela. Elle a un emploi stable qui lui permet de subvenir à ses besoins et, ce qui est encore plus important, à ceux de ses enfants, ce qui est beaucoup plus que ce que d'autres personnes ont.

Mais après 15 ans dans la même entreprise, à faire le même travail tous les jours, Marisol a l'impression qu'il n'y a plus rien à apprendre chez *"La Mirada."* Son rêve à l'université était de devenir rédactrice en chef un jour, mais elle sait que c'est impossible dans ce magazine, car ce poste est occupé par sa chef Jasmine, la fille du propriétaire de l'entreprise. Elle ne gagnera pas non plus plus d'argent dans son poste actuel ; à ce rythme, les choses resteront les mêmes pour le reste de sa vie, chaque jour sera identique et Marisol se sentira de plus en plus mal.

Mardi, Marisol a rendez-vous chez son dentiste, et l'après-midi, elle retrouve sa sœur pour prendre un café et lui explique sa situation.

- Tu te sens ennuyée ou quoi? – demande sa sœur.

- C'est plus que ça, je sens que je n'ai pas d'opportunité de grandir là-bas.

- Mais tu as eu beaucoup de mal à avoir un emploi stable en tant que rédactrice, non?

- Oui, mais ça ne me comble plus, je veux un plus grand défi.

- As-tu parlé avec ta chef?

- Oui, et elle m'a dit qu'elle était contente de mon travail, mais que c'était en gros tout ce que je pouvais faire dans l'entreprise. Et je sais que c'est un travail stable et que j'aime bien.

- Mais tu veux devenir rédactrice en chef, n'est-ce pas? As-tu pensé à travailler ailleurs?

- Oui.

Le 10 août, Marisol aura un entretien d'embauche dans l'un des magazines les plus importants du pays. Cela fait de nombreuses années qu'elle n'a pas eu d'entretien d'embauche, alors elle est très nerveuse, mais elle a confiance en ses compétences et son expérience, donc elle sait que tout se passera bien. De toute façon, Marisol se préparera pour l'entretien, elle étudiera le marché du travail actuel et combien elle pourrait demander comme salaire.

Si les choses se passent comme Marisol le souhaite, tout changera chez elle, car elle devra travailler plus d'heures et ne pourra pas être à la maison avec ses enfants tout le temps. Marisol devra engager une nounou pour rester avec ses enfants jusqu'à ce qu'elle rentre à la maison, même si, en attendant, elle sait qu'elle peut compter sur sa sœur pour s'occuper de ses enfants. Marisol devra faire quelques sacrifices, mais elle est prête à le faire, non seulement pour elle-même mais aussi pour ses enfants. Si Marisol obtient le poste de rédactrice en chef, elle gagnera beaucoup plus d'argent, ce qui signifie qu'elle pourra investir plus d'argent dans l'éducation de ses enfants, elle pourra les inscrire dans une école privée avec de meilleurs professeurs. Elle pourra aussi les emmener en voyage plus souvent. Elle est sûre que ses enfants adorent voyager, mais ils ne lui disent rien parce qu'ils savent qu'en ce moment elle n'a pas l'argent pour ces luxes. Ce soir, Marisol allumera une bougie à la Vierge et priera pour qu'elle l'éclaire et que tout se passe bien alors qu'elle entre dans cette nouvelle étape de sa vie.

Résumé

Marisol se sent insatisfaite à ce stade de sa vie ; elle pense à toutes les années passées à travailler comme rédactrice dans le magazine *"La Mirada"* et au fait qu'elle n'a aucune opportunité d'évoluer davantage dans l'entreprise. Son rêve a toujours été de devenir rédactrice en chef, mais ce n'est pas possible dans l'entreprise où elle travaille actuellement. Après avoir parlé avec sa sœur et mis les choses en perspective, Marisol décide de chercher un emploi ailleurs où elle pourra exploiter tout son potentiel.

Summary

Marisol feels dissatisfied at this point in her life. She thinks about all the years she has been working as a writer in the magazine *"La Mirada,"* and the fact that she has no opportunity to grow more in the company. Her dream has always been to bc an cditor, but that's not possible in the company she currently works at. After talking to her sister and putting things into perspective, Marisol decides to look for a job in a place where she can explore her full potential.

Glossaire – Glossary

- **Depuis:** since

- **Elle s'entend bien avec tout le monde:** She gets along well with everybody

- **Elle a appris:** She has learned

- **Ce poste:** That position

- **Toutes ces années:** All these years

- **Elle s'est sentie insatisfaite:** She has been feeling dissatisfied

- **Un peu bête:** Somewhat silly

- **Stable:** stable
- **Avec lequel elle peut subvenir à ses besoins:** With which she can support herself
- **En faisant le même travail:** Doing the same work
- **Elle n'a plus rien à apprendre:** She has nothing else to learn
- **Un jour:** Some day
- **Ce poste est occupé par sa chef:** That position belongs to her boss
- **Le propriétaire de l'entreprise:** The owner of the company
- **Elle ne gagnera pas plus d'argent non plus:** She's not going to earn more money either
- **A ce rythme:** At this rate
- **Les choses resteront les mêmes:** Things will stay the same
- **Le reste de sa vie:** The rest of her life
- **Chaque jour sera le même:** Every day will be the same
- **Elle se sentira de plus en plus mal:** She will feel worse as time goes on
- **Elle rencontre:** She meets with
- **Tu te sens ennuyée ou quoi?:** Do you feel bored or what?
- **Je n'ai pas d'opportunité de grandir:** I don't have the opportunity to grow
- **Il t'a été difficile d'avoir:** It was hard for you to have
- **Ca ne me comble plus:** It's not fulfilling for me anymore
- **Un défi:** A challenge
- **Elle était contente de mon travail:** She was happy with my work
- **As-tu pensé à travailler...?:** Have you thought about working...?
- **Le 10 août:** On August 10th
- **Elle aura un entretien d'embauche:** She's going to have a job interview
- **Il y a de nombreuses années qu'elle n'a pas eu d'entretien d'embauche:** It has been many years since she last had a job interview
- **Elle a confiance:** She trusts
- **Elle sait que tout se passera bien:** She knows everything will go well
- **Elle se préparera:** She will prepare herself

- **Elle fera des recherches sur le marché du travail:** She will do research about the labor market

- **Combien elle pourrait demander comme salaire:** How much she could ask as salary

- **Si les choses se passent comme Marisol le souhaite:** If things go the way Marisol wants

- **Tout changera:** Everything will change

- **Elle devra travailler:** She will have to work

- **En attendant:** In the meantime

- **Elle sait qu'elle peut compter sur sa sœur pour s'occuper de ses enfants:** She knows she can count on her sister to take care of her kids

- **Elle devra engager une nounou pour garder ses enfants jusqu'à ce qu'elle rentre à la maison:** She will have to hire a nanny to stay with her kids until she gets home

- **Quelques sacrifices:** Some sacrifices

- **Elle est prête à le faire:** She is willing to do it

- **Pas seulement pour elle mais pour ses enfants:** Not only for her but for her kids

- **Si Marisol obtient le poste:** If Marisol gets the job

- **Elle gagnera:** She will earn

- **Ce qui signifie qu'elle pourra investir:** Which means she will be able to invest

- **L'éducation de ses enfants:** Her kids' education

- **Elle pourra les inscrire dans une école privée:** She will be able to enroll them in a private school

- **Elle pourra les emmener en voyage:** She will be able to take them on trips

- **Elle est sûre:** She is sure

- **Ils ne lui disent rien:** They don't say anything to her

- **Des luxes:** Luxuries

- **Elle allumera une bougie à la Vierge:** She will light a candle in the Virgin's name

- **Elle priera pour qu'elle l'éclaire:** She will pray for her to shine her light upon her

- **Que tout se passe bien:** Everything goes well

- **Cette nouvelle étape de sa vie:** This new stage of her life

Exercice 1

Répondez aux questions suivantes – Answer the following questions.

1- Depuis quelle année Marisol travaille-t-elle à La Mirada? (Since what year has Marisol been working at La Mirada?)

_____

2- Comment s'est-elle sentie dernièrement? (How has she been feeling lately?)

_____

3- Quel était son rêve à l'université? (What was her dream at college?)

_____

4- Qui est Jasmine? (Who is Jasmine?)

_____

5- Que fait Marisol mardi? (What does Marisol do on Tuesday?)

_____

6- Quand est son entretien d'embauche? (When's her job interview?)

_____

Exercice 2

Choisissez "vrai" ou "faux" – choose "true" or "false"

1- Elle s'entend bien avec ses collègues. (She gets along well with her coworkers.)

_____

2- Son travail actuel est instable. (Her current job is unstable.)

_____

3- Elle craint que tous ses jours soient les mêmes pour le reste de sa vie. (She fears that all her days will be the same for the rest of her life.)

_____

4- Sa sœur lui a dit de ne pas démissionner. (Her sister told her not to quit.)

_____

5- Elle a un entretien dans un journal important. (She has an interview with an important newspaper.)

_____

6- Elle sent que tout va mal se passer. (She feels like everything will go wrong.)

_____

Réponses – Answers

Exercice 1

1- Marisol travaille à La Mirada depuis l'année 2007.

2- Marisol s'est sentie insatisfaite dernièrement.

3- Son rêve à l'université était de devenir rédactrice en chef un jour.

4- Jasmine est sa chef, la rédactrice en chef du magazine et la fille du propriétaire de l'entreprise.

5- Mardi, Marisol a rendez-vous chez le dentiste et l'après-midi, elle retrouve sa sœur pour prendre un café.

6- L'entretien de Marisol est le 10 août.

Exercice 2

1- Vrai

2- Faux

3- Vrai

4- Faux

5- Faux

6- Faux

Conclusion

By reading all these stories and completing all the exercises, you've absorbed so much grammar that you probably didn't even realize. Add all that to the vocabulary you now have, and you're ready to go out into the world and have richer and more meaningful conversations in French.

BOOK 6

Learn Advanced French for Adults Workbook

Explore to Win

Book 6 Description

You know that "aha" moment when everything you've been learning suddenly makes sense? That's exactly what you'll experience with this workbook!

In Learn Advanced French for Adults Workbook you will find:

- Clear and simple explanations of complex grammatical structures

- Common phrases

- Specialized vocabulary on diverse topic

- Practical exercises and answer keys on every topic covered

- And much more!

Even if you're already enrolled in a French course or have a solid understanding of the language, this workbook is an excellent tool to keep your skills sharp and fresh!

Chapter 1: I Am What I Am

"Chaque homme dans sa nuit s'en va vers sa lumière."

- Victor Hugo

Illnesses and Pains

Illnesses (Maladies)

- **Maladie** (disease, illness)
- **Grippe** (flu)
- **Rhume** (cold)
- **Toux** (cough)
- **Mal de tête** (headache)
- **Mal de gorge** (sore throat)
- **Mal de dents** (toothache)
- **Fièvre** (fever)
- **Diarrhée** (diarrhea)
- **Vomissement** (vomiting)
- **Allergie** (allergy)
- **Asthme** (asthma)
- **Cancer** (cancer)

Pains (Douleurs)

- **Douleur** (pain)
- **Mal** (ache, pain)
- **Douleur aiguë** (acute pain)
- **Douleur chronique** (chronic pain)

- **Douleur lancinante** (throbbing pain)
- **Douleur brûlante** (burning pain)
- **Douleur sourde** (dull pain)

Other Related Terms
- **Symptôme** (symptom)
- **Traitement** (treatment)
- **Médecin** (doctor)
- **Hôpital** (hospital)
- **Pharmacie** (pharmacy)

Adjective (French)	Adjective (English)	Sentence in French	Sentence in English
Fatigué(e)	Tired	Il est fatigué après une longue journée de fièvre.	He is tired after a long day of fever.
Malade	Sick	Elle est malade et reste au lit aujourd'hui.	She is sick and staying in bed today.
Fiévreux(se)	Feverish	Il se sent fiévreux depuis ce matin.	He has felt feverish since this morning.
Enrhumé(e)	Having a cold	Je suis enrhumé et j'ai le nez qui coule.	I have a cold, and my nose is running.
Nauséeux(se)	Nauseous	Elle se sent nauséeuse après avoir mangé.	She feels nauseous after eating.
Épuisé(e)	Exhausted	Il est épuisé après sa maladie.	He is exhausted after his illness.
Congestionné(e)	Congested	Mon nez est congestionné à cause du rhume.	My nose is congested because of the cold.

Migraineux(se)	Having a migraine	Elle est migraineuse aujourd'hui.	She has a migraine today.
Faible	Weak	Il se sent très faible après l'opération.	He feels very weak after the operation.
Étourdi(e)	Dizzy	Je me sens étourdi quand je me lève trop vite.	I feel dizzy when I stand up too quickly.
Tremblant(e)	Shaky	Elle est tremblante à cause de la fièvre.	She is shaky because of the fever.
Douleur(eux/se)	In pain	Il est douloureux après l'accident.	He is in pain after the accident.
Déprimé(e)	Depressed	Elle se sent déprimée à cause de sa maladie.	She feels depressed because of her illness.
Grippé(e)	Having the flu	Je suis grippé et je ne peux pas travailler.	I have the flu and cannot work.
Constipé(e)	Constipated	Il est constipé et doit voir un médecin.	He is constipated and needs to see a doctor.
Anxieux(se)	Anxious	Elle est anxieuse à cause de son état de santé.	She is anxious because of her health condition.

Describing People

Adjectives to Describe People

Adjective (French)	Adjective (English)	Sentence in French	Sentence in English
Aimable	Friendly	Elle est très aimable avec tout le monde.	She is very friendly with everyone.

Courageux(se)	Courageous	Il est courageux face aux défis.	He is courageous in the face of challenges.
Gentil(le)	Kind	Elle est toujours gentille avec ses voisins.	She is always kind to her neighbors.
Intelligent(e)	Intelligent	Il est intelligent et comprend vite.	He is intelligent and understands quickly.
Joyeux(se)	Joyful	Elle est joyeuse et apporte de la bonne humeur.|	She is joyful and brings good cheer.
Travailleu(r/se)	Hardworking	Il est très travailleur et dédié à son travail.	He is very hardworking and dedicated to his job.
Timide	Shy	Elle est timide et parle peu en public.	She is shy and speaks little in public.
Généreux(se)	Generous	Il est généreux et aime aider les autres.	He is generous and likes to help others.
Sincère	Sincere	Elle est sincère dans ses paroles.	She is sincere in her words.
Drôle	Funny	Il est très drôle et fait rire tout le monde.	He is very funny and makes everyone laugh.
Ambitieux(se)	Ambitious	Elle est ambitieuse et veut réussir dans sa carrière.	She is ambitious and wants to succeed in her career.
Calme	Calm	Il est calme même dans les situations difficiles.	He is calm even in difficult situations.

Optimiste	Optimistic	Elle est toujours optimiste, même quand c'est dur.	She is always optimistic, even when it's tough.
Poli(e)	Polite	Il est poli avec tout le monde qu'il rencontre.	He is polite with everyone he meets.
Créatif(ve)	Creative	Elle est très créative dans son travail d'artiste.	She is very creative in her work as an artist.
Séduisant(e)	Attractive	Il est séduisant et attire beaucoup d'attention.	He is attractive and gets a lot of attention.

Refléter/Montrer la personnalité

In French, the phrases "refléter la personnalité" (to reflect the personality) and "montrer la personnalité" (to show the personality) are both used to describe how someone's character or inner qualities are expressed.

Refléter la personnalité (To Reflect the Personality)

1. Meaning and Usage:

- The verb "refléter" in French means "to reflect." So this phrase often implies that visual aspects such as behavior, clothing, language, art, actions, or facial expressions provide insight into a person's inner self.

2. Examples:

- Sa manière de parler reflète sa personnalité.
- ("The way he/she speaks reflects his/her personality.")
- Les choix de décoration de sa maison reflètent sa personnalité créative.
- ("The decoration choices of his/her house reflect his/her creative personality.")

Montrer la personnalité (To Show the Personality)

1. Meaning and Usage:

- The verb "montrer" means "to show" or "to display." When using the phrase "montrer la personnalité," it implies an active and deliberate demonstration or presentation of one's personality traits through their behavior, speech, or actions.

2. Examples:

- Il montre sa personnalité généreuse en aidant toujours les autres.

- ("He shows his generous personality by always helping others.")

- Elle montre sa personnalité courageuse en prenant des risques dans sa carrière.

- ("She shows her courageous personality by taking risks in her career.")

Key Differences Between "Refléter" and "Montrer" in this Context

- "Refléter la personnalité" suggests an indirect or passive expression, where the personality is revealed through actions, choices, or external elements that may not be consciously controlled.

- "Montrer la personnalité" implies a more direct or active demonstration, where the person consciously or deliberately expresses certain traits.

Propre à/Typique de

"Propre à" and "Typique de" are two expressions in French that help to describe the characteristics, traits, or behaviors of a specific person, group, thing, or situation.

1. Propre à (Characteristic of / Specific to)

Meaning and Usage:

- The phrase "propre à" means "characteristic of" or "specific to." It is used to describe something that is inherently and distinctively associated with a particular entity.

- It often conveys a sense of exclusivity or uniqueness, suggesting that the quality or characteristic in question isn't common elsewhere.

Examples:

- Cette manière de parler est propre à cette région.

- ("This way of speaking is characteristic of this region.")

- Le calme est une qualité propre à cette personne.

- ("Calmness is a quality specific to this person.")

- Les coutumes sont propres à chaque culture.

- ("Customs are unique to each culture.")

2. Typique de (Typical of)

Meaning and Usage:

- The phrase "typique de" translates to "typical of." It is used to indicate that a particular characteristic, behavior, or trait is commonly associated with and emblematic of a person, group, place, or thing, without necessarily implying exclusivity.

Examples:
- C'est typique de sa manière de réagir.

- ("That's typical of his/her way of reacting.")

- La chaleur est typique du climat méditerranéen.

- ("Heat is typical of the Mediterranean climate.")

- Les croissants sont typiques de la cuisine française.

- ("Croissants are typical of French cuisine.")

Key Differences Between "Propre à" and "Typique de"

Exclusivity vs. Commonality:

- "Propre à" emphasizes exclusivity or uniqueness. For example, "Une habitude propre à cette famille" ("A habit specific to this family") suggests that this habit is unique to that family.

- "Typique de" describes something that is generally representative or expected within a certain context.

For example, "Un comportement typique des adolescents" ("A behavior typical of teenagers") suggests a behavior that is common among all teenagers, not unique to one person or group.

Context of Use:

- "Propre à" is often used in formal, academic, or descriptive writing to highlight distinctiveness or to point out what makes something or someone unique.

- "Typique de" is more versatile and can be used in both formal and informal contexts to describe general trends, patterns, or common characteristics.

Exercises

1. Which of the following French terms means "fever?"

    A. Mal de tête
    B. Fièvre
    C. Diarrhée
    D. Rhume

2. What is the French word for "toothache?"

    A. Mal de dents
    B. Mal de gorge
    C. Mal de tête
    D. Grippe

3. Which French adjective means "tired?"

    A. Fatigué(e)
    B. Malade
    C. Fiévreux(se)
    D. Enrhumé(e)

4. What is the French word for "asthma?"

    A. Allergie
    B. Asthme
    C. Cancer
    D. Diarrhée

5. Which French phrase means "to have a cold?"

    A. Avoir la grippe
    B. Avoir mal de tête
    C. Être enrhumé(e)
    D. Être fatigué(e)

6. What is the French word for "hospital?"

    A. Médecin
    B. Pharmacie
    C. Hôpital
    D. Traitement

7. Which French adjective means "depressed?"

    A. Déprimé(e)
    B. Douleur(eux/se)
    C. Étourdi(e)
    D. Tremblant(e)

8. What is the French word for "constipated?"

    A. Constipé(e)
    B. Grippé(e)
    C. Anxieux(se)
    D. Épuisé(e)

9. Which French adjective means "creative?"

    A. Aimable
    B. Courageux(se)
    C. Créatif(ve)
    D. Séduisant(e)

10. What is the French word for "shy?"

    A. Timide
    B. Généreux(se)
    C. Sincère
    D. Drôle

Answer Key

1. B. Fièvre est le mot français pour "fièvre."

2. A. Mal de dents signifie "mal de dents" en français.

3. A. Fatigué(e) est l'adjectif français pour "fatigué."

4. B. Asthme est le mot français pour "asthme."

5. C. Être enrhumé(e) signifie "avoir un rhume" en français.

6. C. Hôpital est le mot français pour "hôpital."

7. A. Déprimé(e) est l'adjectif français pour "déprimé."

8. A. Constipé(e) signifie "constipé" en français.

9. C. Créatif(ve) est l'adjectif français pour "créatif."

10. A. Timide est le mot français pour "timide."

Chapter 2: Careers

"Il n'y a pas de honte à préférer le bonheur."

- Albert Camus

In this next section, we will explore careers and professions in greater detail.

Vocabulary to talk about careers

French	English
J'ai étudié	I studied
à...	at...
jusqu'à...	until...
Je suis	I am
licencié(e)	licensed/degree holder
diplômé(e)	graduated
diplômé(e)	diploma holder
en...	in...
Je me suis licencié(e)	I got my degree
Je me suis diplômé(e)	I graduated
Je me suis diplômé(e)	I earned my diploma

J'ai de l'expérience	I have experience
dans...	in...
avec...	with...
comme...	as...
J'aspire à...	I aspire to...
Je suis spécialisé(e) en...	I am specialized in...
Mes réussites sont...	My achievements are...
ont été...	have been...

Expressing beginnings, development, progress, and endings

Beginning

- Commencer à + infinitif
- Se mettre à + infinitif
- Commencer par + infinitif

These expressions are used to indicate the beginning of an action:

- J'ai commencé à étudier le français il y a trois ans. ("I started studying French three years ago.")

- Je me suis mis à pratiquer la conversation parce que je visiterai bientôt la France. ("I started practicing conversation because I'm visiting France soon.")

Note: Se mettre à + infinitif it conveys a sudden start, often without a transition, and is usually applied to a subject who has control over the action.

- En raison de la crise, l'entreprise a commencé à perdre des clients. ("Because of the crisis, the company started losing clients") — but not En raison de la crise, l'entreprise s'est mise à perdre des clients.

Development

- Continuer à + infinitif and continuer sans + infinitif

We use continuer à + infinitif to express the continuation of an action:

- Clara continue à travailler dans le restaurant de ses parents. ("Clara is still working in her parents' restaurant.")

In its negative form, continuer sans + infinitif, it indicates that an action has not been completed:

- Clara continue sans trouver un autre emploi. ("Clara still can't find another job; she's been searching for a while but hasn't found one.")

- Aller + gérondif

This expression is used to indicate that an event unfolds gradually, in different stages, towards a final result:

- Elle lui parlait des changements au fur et à mesure qu'ils se produisaient. ("She told him about the changes as they were happening.")

- Je récupère de l'énergie au fur et à mesure que j'avance. ("I recover energy as I go forward.")

In certain contexts, it indicates the beginning of an action that develops gradually:

- L'examen est dans deux semaines, commencez à lire le matériel. ("The exam is in two weeks; you should start reading the material.")

- Ne m'attendez pas, commencez à manger. ("Don't wait for me, start eating.")

- Venir de + infinitif

We use venir de + infinitif to indicate that a process develops in stages from a prior moment, usually accompanied by a time reference that marks the start or end:

- Clara vient de travailler au restaurant depuis un certain temps. ("Clara has been working at the restaurant for a while.")

- Que penses-tu de ce que je viens de faire jusqu'à présent? ("What do you think of what I've been doing so far?")

- Elle vient de penser à ce sujet depuis quelques semaines. ("She's been thinking about the issue for a few weeks.")

Interruption

- Cesser de + infinitif

This expression is used to indicate that an action has been interrupted:

- Clara a cessé de travailler dans le restaurant de ses parents. ("Clara has stopped working in her parents' restaurant." She no longer works there.)

Note: We use cesser de + infinitif when we want to emphasize that the action did not reach its natural or intended conclusion but was interrupted. It's also used to show the breaking of a habit. :

- Les ouvriers ont cessé de travailler. ("The laborers stopped working.")

- As-tu cessé de fumer? ("Have you quit smoking?")

In its negative form, ne pas cesser de + infinitif, it conveys that an action continues despite expectations to the contrary:

- Clara n'a pas cessé de travailler dans le restaurant. ("Clara has not stopped working in the restaurant." She continues to work there, even if it might be unexpected.)

Ending

- Finir par + infinitif

We use this expression to indicate that an action occurs at the end of a series of actions or events. It often carries a judgment about the series of events as a whole:

- Après des années dans le restaurant de ses parents, Clara a fini par travailler à l'endroit où elle voulait. ("After years working at her parents' restaurant, Clara ended up working at the place she wanted.")

- Clara n'a pas eu de chance. Elle réussissait bien à l'université, mais elle a eu du mal à trouver un emploi et a fini par travailler dans le restaurant de ses parents, ce qui n'était pas ce qu'elle voulait. ("Clara was unlucky. She was doing well at school, but had trouble finding a job and ended up working in her parents' restaurant, which wasn't what she wanted.")

Note: It is important to differentiate this from finir de + infinitif, which is used to indicate that an action has been completed:

- J'ai fini de nettoyer la maison. ("I've finished cleaning the house.")

- J'ai fini par nettoyer la maison. ("I ended up cleaning the house," even though it wasn't part of my plans.)

Making a comparison

Read these phrases about education in France, where comparisons are made:

Les revenus restent beaucoup plus élevés pour ceux qui ont un diplôme universitaire ou même un diplôme de niveau supérieur par rapport à ceux qui se sont arrêtés après le lycée.

("Income is still much higher for those who have a university degree or even a tertiary degree compared to those who stopped their studies after high school.")

En France, on investit 7 % du PIB dans l'éducation, tandis que la moyenne de l'OCDE n'est que de 3 %.

("In France, 7% of GDP is invested in education, while the OECD average is only 3%.")

Here are some more expressions that can be used to make comparisons:

Bien que: although

Comparé à: compared to, with

Alors que: whereas

En comparaison avec: in comparison with

Pendant, tandis que

Pendant and tandis que are both used to make comparisons or express simultaneity. However, their usage is slightly different:

Pendant que je mets la table, tu peux finir de préparer le dîner.

("While I set the table, you can finish making dinner.")

Tandis que je mets la table, tu peux finir de préparer le dîner.

("While I set the table, you can finish making dinner.")

A Manolo, il aime les mathématiques, tandis que Marco préfère l'histoire.

("Manolo likes math, while Marco prefers history.")

While both terms are used to make comparisons, tandis que is most often used when making contrasts between two or more things. On the other hand, pendant que is the only correct way to express simultaneous actions or events.

Avant que, avant de

To express a preference when comparing two elements, avant que and avant de are commonly used:

Avant que de le voir ruiné, je préfère lui prêter de l'argent.

("Before seeing him ruined, I'd rather lend him money.")

Avant de finir, je veux te poser une question importante.

("Before we finish, I want to ask you something important.")

To indicate that one option is preferred over another, use avant que. To show that something occurs before another in time, use avant de.

Plus de, moins de, plus que, moins que

Next, we'll look at some examples involving quantities and comparisons. Pay attention to the use of plus de, moins de, plus que, and moins que. Below, there is a chart with the usage rules:

En France, on investit plus dans l'éducation que dans la moyenne des pays de l'OCDE, il y a plus d'heures d'enseignement et le ratio enseignant-élève est plus faible que dans d'autres pays.

("In France, there is more investment in education than in the average OECD countries, there are more teaching hours, and the teacher-student ratio is lower than in other countries.")

Pour résoudre le problème, il faut plus que des mots, il faut agir.

("To solve the problem, we need more than words; we have to act.")

Il existe une différence de salaire importante entre les hommes et les femmes: dans des postes similaires, les femmes ont tendance à gagner moins que les hommes.

("There is a significant pay gap between men and women: in similar positions, women tend to earn less than men.")

Le salaire minimum en France est un peu plus de sept cents euros par mois.

("The minimum wage in France is just over seven hundred euros per month.")

La crise a fait plus qu'augmenter le chômage: elle a brisé la vie de beaucoup de personnes.

("The crisis has done more than increase unemployment: it has shattered the lives of many.")

Plus... moins.../Moins... moins...

We use these constructions to express that a change (increase or decrease) in one thing leads to a change in another:

Plus elle lit, moins elle comprend.

("The more she reads, the less she understands.")

Plus je grandis, plus je ressemble à mon frère.

("The older I get, the more I look like my brother.")

Plus de fruits tu manges, mieux tu te sens.

("The more fruit you eat, the better you feel.")

Plus il vit près, plus il arrive tard.

("The closer he lives, the later he arrives.")

Sentences with plus or moins are typically constructed in the present or imparfait past tenses of the indicative mood (to express current or past habits) or in the present subjunctive (to express potential future events):

Plus j'étudie, mieux je réussis.

("The more I study, the better I do.")

Plus j'étudiais, mieux je réussissais.

("The more I studied, the better I did.")

Plus j'étudierai, mieux je réussirai.

("The more I study, the better I'll do.")

Exercises

1. Which of the following expressions indicates the beginning of an action in French?

   a) Continuer à + infinitif
   b) Finir par + infinitif
   c) Commencer à + infinitif
   d) Cesser de + infinitif

2. What does "se mettre à + infinitif" typically convey in French?

   a) A gradual continuation of an action
   b) A sudden start of an action
   c) The end of a series of actions
   d) An interrupted action

3. How is "aller + gérondif" used in French?

   a) To express an action that has been interrupted
   b) To indicate an action that develops gradually
   c) To show a comparison between two actions
   d) To express a preferred action

4. Which expression is used to indicate an interrupted action in French?

   a) Finir de + infinitif
   b) Cesser de + infinitif
   c) Continuer à + infinitif
   d) Venir de + infinitif

5. How would you express the continuation of an action in French, even when the result is contrary to expectations?

   a) Continuer sans + infinitif
   b) Ne pas cesser de + infinitif
   c) Finir par + infinitif
   d) Se mettre à + infinitif

6. What is the difference between "avant que" and "avant de" in French?

   a) "Avant que" is used before a noun, "avant de" before a verb
   b) "Avant que" indicates preference, "avant de" indicates time
   c) "Avant de" indicates a preference, "avant que" indicates a past action
   d) "Avant de" indicates future action, "avant que" indicates present action

7. When is "finir par + infinitif" used in French?

   a) To indicate a completed action

b) To indicate an action that begins suddenly
c) To indicate an action occurring at the end of a sequence
d) To indicate a continuous action

8. In which context would you use "plus... moins..." in French?

a) To express the continuation of an action
b) To show that an increase in one thing leads to a decrease in another
c) To indicate a completed action
d) To express simultaneity

9. What does "venir de + infinitif" indicate in French?

a) A future action that is planned
b) A process developing in stages from a prior moment
c) An action that has been completed
d) A simultaneous action

10. To express that an action has not reached its intended end but has been interrupted, which expression is correct in French?

a) Commencer par + infinitif
b) Continuer sans + infinitif
c) Cesser de + infinitif
d) Finir par + infinitif

Answer Key

1. c) Commencer à + infinitif

2. b) A sudden start of an action

3. b) To indicate an action that develops gradually

4. b) Cesser de + infinitif

5. b) Ne pas cesser de + infinitif

6. b) "Avant que" indicates preference, "avant de" indicates time

7. c) To indicate an action occurring at the end of a sequence

8. b) To show that an increase in one thing leads to a decrease in another

9. b) A process developing in stages from a prior moment

10. c) Cesser de + infinitif

Chapter 3: Anecdotes and Gossip

"Le bruit ne fait pas de bien, et le bien ne fait pas de bruit."

- Victor Hugo

In this chapter, we'll learn how to tell captivating stories and engage in gossip with French locals.. Ready to dive in?

Direct and Indirect Speech

Speaking verbs

While in spoken conversation, we might end up using the French verb "dire" often, there are a number of other speaking and narration verbs that can make conversations more enriching and natural:

- *Exclamer*: to exclaim

- *Demander*: to ask (for something)

- *Nier*: to deny

- *Ordonner*: to order

- *Rappeler*: to remind

- *Clarifier*: to clarify

- *Répéter*: to repeat

- *Assurer*: to ensure

- *Suggérer*: to suggest

- *Préciser*: to specify

- *Raconter*: to tell

- *Proposer*: to propose

- *Expliquer*: to explain

Direct Speech

Direct speech is the simplest way of conveying what other people have said. To use it, you simply need a verb to indicate speech (properly conjugated), followed by a colon, and the direct quote in quotation marks.

Paola a affirmé fermement : "Personne n'entrera dans cette pièce." ("Paola asserted emphatically: 'Nobody will enter this room.'")

Facundo m'a dit : "Je ne veux plus te voir." ("Facundo told me: 'I don't want to see you anymore.'")

Hier, j'ai parlé à Mariana, et elle m'a demandé : "Où fais-tu tes ongles?" ("Yesterday, I talked to Mariana, and she asked me: 'Where do you get your nails done?'")

Facundo lui a dit à Anabel : "Je ne veux plus te voir." ("Facundo told Anabel: 'I don't want to see you anymore.'")

Lucas et Marie ont parlé à François, et il leur a demandé : "Quel ordinateur utilisez-vous?" ("Yesterday, Lucas and Marie talked to François, and he asked them: 'What computer do you use?'")

Indirect Speech

In indirect speech, you don't have to worry about quoting what someone said exactly, so there's no need to use colons or quotation marks. Simply use the verb indicating speech in its proper conjugation::

Paola a affirmé fermement que personne n'entrerait dans cette pièce. ("Paola asserted strongly that nobody would enter that room.")

Facundo a dit qu'il ne voulait plus le voir. ("Facundo said that he didn't want to see him anymore.")

Hier, j'ai parlé à Mariana, et elle m'a demandé où je faisais mes ongles. ("Yesterday I talked to Mariana, and she asked me where I got my nails done.")

As we've seen, after the verb of saying, we add que, which introduces the subordinate clause containing the message. Since this message forms a subordinate clause, it must be like any other sentence, with at least a subject (which can sometimes be implied) and a verb.

In most cases, the paraphrased text is introduced by the word "que." However, in the case of most questions that ask where, when, why, what, and how, we use an interrogative adverb. In the case of yes/no questions, we instead use "si" (if).

Indirect speech has a few particulars to keep in mind as well:

Deictic words and expressions are those that refer to the time, place, or situation the speaker is in while speaking. We cannot use these terms in indirect speech unless we are in the same context as when the speaker originally said them.

Here are some examples comparing direct and indirect speech:

Caroline a dit : "Aujourd'hui, je ne veux pas dîner." ("Caroline said: 'I don't want to have dinner today.'")

Caroline a dit qu'elle ne voulait pas dîner ce jour-là. ("Caroline said that she didn't want to have dinner that day.")

Quand nous étions à la plage, Gérard s'est exclamé : "Je ne veux pas partir d'ici !" ("When we were at the beach, Gerard exclaimed: 'I don't want to leave this place!'")

Quand nous étions à la plage, Gérard a dit qu'il ne voulait pas partir de là. ("When we were at the beach, Gerard said that he didn't want to leave that place.")

Verb tenses also change in indirect speech because we are talking about something that has already occurred.

Discours Direct	Discours Indirect
Présent de l'indicatif Elle a dit : "Je ne mange pas de riz."	Imparfait de l'indicatif Elle a dit qu'elle ne mangeait pas de riz.
Passé composé Elle a dit : "Je n'ai pas mangé de riz depuis des années."	Plus-que-parfait Elle a dit qu'elle n'avait pas mangé de riz depuis des années.
Imparfait de l'indicatif Elle a dit : "Je ne mangeais pas de riz quand j'étais petite."	Imparfait de l'indicatif Elle a dit qu'elle ne mangeait pas de riz quand elle était petite.
Passé simple Elle a dit : "Je n'ai pas mangé de riz hier."	Plus-que-parfait Elle a dit qu'elle n'avait pas mangé de riz la veille.
Plus-que-parfait Elle a dit : "Je n'avais pas mangé de riz depuis des années."	Plus-que-parfait Elle a dit qu'elle n'avait pas mangé de riz depuis des années.
Futur Elle a dit : "Je ne mangerai pas de riz."	Conditionnel présent Elle a dit qu'elle ne mangerait pas de riz.

Conditionnel présent Elle a dit : "Je ne mangerais pas de riz si on ne m'y obligeait pas."	Conditionnel présent Elle a dit qu'elle ne mangerait pas de riz si on ne l'y obligeait pas.
Présent du subjonctif Elle a dit : "Je ne veux pas que tu manges du riz."	Imparfait du subjonctif Elle a dit qu'elle ne voulait pas que je mange du riz.
Imparfait du subjonctif Elle a dit : "Je ne voulais pas que tu manges du riz."	Imparfait du subjonctif Elle a dit qu'elle ne voulait pas que je mange du riz.
Impératif Elle a dit : "Ne mange pas de riz, mange des pommes de terre."	Imparfait du subjonctif Elle m'a dit de ne pas manger de riz, mais de manger des pommes de terre.

Indirect speech is most often used to add commentary to what someone has said or to provide a sense of detachment.

Relative Constructions with *lo*

Relative constructions with expressions like ce qui and ce que are another useful tool for gossiping in French. They're used to refer to a topic that is or might be familiar to those in the conversation. Let's look at a few examples:

- Tu as entendu ce qui est arrivé à Catherine ? ("Have you heard what happened to Catherine?")

- Non, quoi? ("No, what?")

- Eh bien, elle a eu un accident. ("Well, she has had an accident.")

- Je n'en reviens pas ! ("I can't believe it!")

- Hier, François a raconté ce qui est arrivé à Catherine. ("Yesterday, François told what happened to Catherine.")

- Oui, j'en ai entendu parler. C'est terrible, mais je suis content qu'elle aille bien. ("Yes, I've heard. It's awful, but I'm glad she's fine.")

- Ce qui m'est arrivé avec cet accident me semble horrible. ("What happened to me with that accident seems horrible.")

We use ce qui or ce que to introduce both nouns and verbs. We use ce qui with a subject or verb in the infinitive, and ce que with conjugated verbs.

You can also use le fait que or le fait de with entire sentences in the indicative or subjunctive. Here are some examples:

- Est-ce vrai le fait que Monique va vivre en Italie? ("Is it true that Monique is going to live in Italy?")

- Oui, c'est vrai! ("Yes, it's true!")

- Le fait que tu manges plus de légumes me semble une bonne idée. ("That you eat more vegetables seems like a good idea.")

- Merci, moi aussi! ("Thanks, I think so too!")

Asserting and Hedging

Use phrases such as sans aucun doute, sans doute, avec certitude, and selon toute probabilité to add assertion to what you're saying: "Sans aucun doute, il pleuvra demain" ("Without a doubt, it will rain tomorrow"). You can also emphasize the truth or certainty of our statement by using the present indicative tense.

To soften statements or express uncertainty, use phrases like apparemment, d'une certaine manière, en quelque sorte, and selon toute apparence: "En quelque sorte, je pense que cette voiture est meilleure que la précédente" ("In a sense, I think this car is better than the previous one").

You can also use the conditional tense, which creates a supposition, hypothesis, or bit of gossip: "Le comportement de Bruno refléterait qu'il traverse une période difficile" ("Bruno's behavior would reflect that he's going through a tough time").

Consecutive Conjunctions and Connectors

To express consequence, use conjunctions or connectors.

Consecutive conjunctions introduce subordinate clauses, and are separated from the main sentence by a comma or semicolon. Here are some examples of consecutive conjunctions:

- de sorte que: "so"

Je n'étais pas de bonne humeur, de sorte que j'ai regardé un film et je suis resté à la maison. ("I wasn't in a good mood, so I watched a movie and stayed at home.")

- c'est pourquoi: "so"

Je n'avais pas faim, c'est pourquoi je n'ai pas mangé. ("I wasn't hungry, so I didn't eat.")

- donc: "so"

Il faisait froid, donc j'ai mis une veste. ("It was cold, so I put on a jacket.")

- d'où: "hence," "which is why"

Note: This expression is typically followed by a subjunctive when the consequence is a known fact.

- Elle était malade, d'où qu'elle n'ait pas assisté aux cours. ("She was sick, which is why she didn't attend class.")

- Elle était malade, d'où mon absence. ("She was sick, hence my absence.")

Consecutive connectors can be placed at the beginning, in the middle, or at the end of a sentence, separated from the rest of the elements by a comma:

- c'est pourquoi: "which is why," "for that reason"

Mes chats sont très espiègles. C'est pourquoi je leur achète des jouets pour qu'ils ne cassent pas mes affaires. ("My cats are very playful. For that reason, I buy them toys so they don't break my things.")

- par conséquent: "therefore"

Ma sœur a cinq ans, elle s'intéresse à la musique, par conséquent, elle apprend à jouer du violon. ("My sister is five, she is interested in music, therefore, she is learning to play the violin.")

- en conséquence: "consequently"

J'étais malade et, en conséquence, mon frère est tombé malade aussi. ("I was sick, and, consequently, my brother got sick too.")

- par suite: "as a result"

J'étais très occupé et j'ai oublié de chercher mon fils à l'école, par suite. ("I was really busy and forgot to pick up my son from school, as a result.")

- ainsi donc: "therefore"

Avec mes revenus, je ne pouvais plus entretenir la voiture, ainsi donc, je l'ai vendue. ("With my income, I could no longer maintain the car, therefore, I sold it.")

- car: "thus"

Note: When placed at the beginning of the clause, it expresses cause; when it is in the middle or at the end of the sentence, it expresses consequence.

Il n'a pas pu venir en classe, car son père était malade. ("He couldn't come to class because his father was sick.") → cause

Son père était malade, il ne pouvait donc pas venir en classe. ("His father was sick; he couldn't, therefore, come to class.") → consequence

Exercises

1. Which of the following verbs is most commonly used to express "to say" in French?

A) dire

B) parler

C) raconter

D) répéter

2. What is the correct way to introduce direct speech in French?

A) With a comma followed by the speaker's name
B) With a colon followed by quotation marks
C) With a question mark followed by the speaker's name
D) With a semicolon followed by quotation marks

3. When converting direct speech to indirect speech, which of the following elements should be adjusted?

A) Verb tenses
B) Pronouns
C) Deictic words
D) All of the above

4. Which verb is typically used to introduce indirect speech in French?

A) dire
B) parler
C) raconter
D) répéter

5. In indirect speech, how are yes/no questions introduced?

A) With the word "si" (if)
B) With the word "oui" (yes)
C) With the word "non" (no)
D) With the word "que" (that)

6. Which of the following is a consecutive conjunction used to express consequence in French?

A) parce que (because)
B) donc (therefore)
C) mais (but)
D) ou (or)

7. When using relative constructions with "lo" to refer to a familiar topic, which word is used with a subject or verb in the infinitive?

A) ce qui

B) ce que

C) le fait que

D) le fait de

8. To express uncertainty in French, which of the following techniques can be used?

A) Using the conditional tense

B) Using phrases like "apparemment" (apparently)

C) Using hedging expressions

D) All of the above

9. Which verb is used to express "to order" in French?

A) commander

B) ordonner

C) demander

D) suggérer

10. When recounting a past event in indirect speech, which tense is typically used for the verb in the main clause?

A) Present tense

B) Past simple

C) Past continuous

D) Present perfect

Answer Key

1. A) dire
2. B) With a colon followed by quotation marks
3. D) All of the above
4. A) dire
5. A) With the word "si" (if)
6. B) donc (therefore)
7. A) ce qui
8. D) All of the above
9. B) ordonner
10. A) Present tense

Chapter 4: Protecting the Environment

"Nous n'héritons pas de la terre de nos ancêtres, nous l'empruntons à nos enfants."

- Antoine de Saint-Exupéry

In this chapter, we'll provide you with tools for discussing the environment.

How to Talk About Nature and Landscapes

Adjectives and expressions to talk about la terre ("the land"):

- Riche: rich
- Fertile: fertile
- Stérile: barren

Adjectives and expressions to talk about la région ("the area"):

- Sismique: seismic
- Dangereuse: dangerous
- Protégée: protected
- Maritime: maritime
- Boisée: wooded
- Alpine: Alpine

Adjectives and expressions to talk about le ciel ("the sky"):

- Clair: clear
- Nuageux: cloudy
- Dégagé: cloudless
- Orageux: stormy

Adjectives and expressions to talk about la catastrophe ("the catastrophe"):

- Imminente: impending
- Irréparable: irréparable
- Humanitaire: humanitarian
- Climatique: climate

Adjectives and expressions to talk about le climat ("the weather"):

- Humide: humid
- Accablant: scorching
- Instable: unsteady
- Pluvieux: rainy
- Sec: dry
- Clément: favorable

Vocabulary Related to Pollution and the Environment

- Heure de pointe: rush hour

- Embouteillage: traffic jam

- Matières particulaires en suspension: suspended particulate matter

- Nuage de smog: smog cloud

- Tomber malade: to get/fall sick

- Voies respiratoires: respiratory tracts

- Qualité de l'air: air quality

- Pollution atmosphérique: air pollution

- Véhicules anciens: old vehicles

- Compensation financière: economic compensation

- Véhicule plus écologique: greener vehicle

- Camions: trucks

- Gaz à effet de serre: greenhouse gas

- Sans émissions / Émissions zéro: zero emission

- Amélioration de la qualité de l'air: improvement in air quality

- Substances toxiques: toxic substances

- Gestion environnementale: environmental management

- Réduire: to reduce

Concessive clauses

Bien que

Concessive sentences in French usually have two parts. The subordinate clause is introduced by a concessive conjunction, such as bien que or même si, which presents an unfavorable circumstance or obstacle to the main clause. Let's look at some examples:

Bien que cela ne fasse pas de différence, je continuerai à recycler les déchets. ("Even if it doesn't make any difference, I'll continue to recycle.")

Bien que vous l'ayez peut-être déjà mentionné, que pensez-vous des incendies dans la forêt amazonienne? ("Although you may have already said it, what do you think of the fires in the Amazon rainforest?")

Même si vous faites déjà partie d'une ONG, voici un dépliant pour vous montrer ce que nous faisons à Greenpeace. ("Although you may already take part in an NGO, here's a leaflet for you to see what we do in Greenpeace.")

Choosing tense and mood

- When using the structure bien que + present indicative, the concession in the subordinate clause is presented as a real situation:

Bien que le gouvernement dit qu'il fera quelque chose pour éviter la déforestation illégale, je ne les crois pas. ("Despite the government saying they'll do something to prevent illegal logging, I don't believe them." — The government is actually saying it.)

- We use the structure bien que + present subjunctive when we cannot confirm whether the concession is real, or when it is presented as something assumed or known:

Bien que le gouvernement dise qu'il fera quelque chose, je ne les crois pas. ("Even though the government says they'll do something, I don't believe them." — I don't know or it's not relevant whether the government says it or not.)

- We use bien que + imperfect subjunctive to present the concession as an unlikely situation in the future, or something unreal in the present:

Bien que le gouvernement dît quelque chose, je ne les croirais pas. ("Even if the government said something, I wouldn't believe them." — I don't believe the government is going to say anything.)

- We use bien que + pluperfect subjunctive to talk about unreal past concessions:

Bien que le gouvernement eût dit quelque chose, je ne les aurais pas cru. ("Even if the government had said something, I wouldn't have believed them." — The government didn't say anything.)

Uses of Prepositions *par and pour*

In French. "Par" and "pour" have similar meanings, but they are applied in different contexts.

Referring to location

Par + location indicates an approximate place.

Mon frère est par Paris. ("My brother is around Paris.")

Par + location also indicates the path or route of a real or figurative movement.

La porte était bloquée, donc nous avons dû sortir par la fenêtre. ("The door was stuck, so we had to leave through the window.")

Pour + location expresses direction.

Mon frère part pour Paris demain. ("My brother is leaving for Paris tomorrow.")

Referring to time

Par + part of the day is used to situate an event at a specific time of day.

Demain par l'après-midi, ils manifesteront contre la pollution. ("Tomorrow afternoon, they will demonstrate against pollution.")

Pour + moment is used to express the intended or appropriate time for something.

Ils préparent des banderoles pour demain. ("They are making banners for tomorrow.")

Referring to cause

Parce que/par + infinitive/noun/pronoun is used to express cause.

L'entreprise ne respecte pas les normes environnementales. C'est pourquoi ils vont manifester demain. ("The company does not comply with environmental standards. That's why they are protesting tomorrow.")

Ils vont manifester demain parce que l'entreprise ne respecte pas les normes environnementales. ("They are protesting tomorrow because the company does not comply with environmental standards.")

Pour + que/infinitive/noun/pronoun is used to express motive: a subsequent situation we want to achieve through an action.

Le gouvernement devait décider quoi faire concernant la marée noire. Pour cela, ils ont consulté des experts. ("The government had to decide what to do about the oil spill. That's why they consulted experts.")

Le gouvernement a consulté des experts pour décider quoi faire concernant la marée noire. ("The government consulted the experts to decide what to do about the oil spill.")

Pour + noun/infinitive, main clause is used to express a concession to what's being stated in the main sentence.

Pour avoir fait campagne avec les écologistes, le parti au pouvoir a fait peu pour l'environnement. ("Despite having run the campaign with the ecologists, the ruling party has done little for the environment.")

Referring to people

Par + noun of a person is used to indicate the person performing the action.

Les incendies ont été causés par les propriétaires des champs. ("The fires were started by the owners of the fields.")

Par + personal pronoun is used to express how an action affects us.

Par lui, toute la région peut prendre feu. Cela ne lui importe pas du tout. ("As far as he's concerned, the whole region can catch fire. He couldn't care less.")

Faire quelque chose pour quelqu'un expresses that someone does something on behalf of someone else.

Les ONG font le travail ingrat pour le gouvernement. ("NGOs are doing the government's dirty job.")

Pour + noun of a person is used to indicate the recipient of an action.

Ces lois ont été rédigées pour les PDG. ("Those laws were written for the CEOs.")

Pour + personal pronoun is used to introduce an opinion.

Pour moi, ce qui se passe en Amazonie est la plus grande catastrophe environnementale du siècle dernier. ("For me, what's happening in the Amazon rainforest is the biggest environmental disaster of the last century.")

Referring to objects

Nom + par + infinitive is used to indicate that the action of the infinitive (to be performed on the object) is still pending.

Il y a encore beaucoup de choses par faire en ce qui concerne l'environnement. ("There's still a lot to be done regarding the environment.")

Nom + pour + infinitive expresses that the object is intended for the action of the infinitive.

Ils ont acheté des camions de pompiers pour combattre les incendies. ("They bought fire trucks to fight the fires.")

Talking About Rights and Responsibilities

Se conformer à + les tâches, les instructions et exigences, les attentes ("To comply with + the tasks, instructions and requirements, demands, expectations").

Garantir + l'exercice des droits, l'application de la loi, les services de base ("To guarantee + the exercise of rights, law enforcement, basic services").

Accéder à + les données, l'information, le dossier ("To access + the data, information, file").

Veiller à + l'observation des règles, la sécurité des citoyens, les droits des consommateurs ("To ensure + the observance of norms, the safety of citizens, consumer rights").

Demander + la révision de l'accord ("To request + the revision of the agreement").

Respecter + l'accord signé, le contrat, les droits ("To respect + the signed agreement, the deal, rights").

Déposer + une plainte, une demande, une requête, une réclamation ("To file + a report, a demand, a request, a complaint").

Traiter + une demande, une requête ("To process + a request, an application").

Exercises

1: Which adjective would you use to describe a region that is prone to earthquakes?

    A) Maritime

    B) Boisée

    C) Sismique

    D) Alpine

2: What is the French word for "air pollution?"

    A) Pollution atmosphérique

    B) Qualité de l'air

    C) Matières particulaires en suspension

    D) Heure de pointe

3: Which concessive conjunction is used to introduce a subordinate clause that presents an unfavorable circumstance or obstacle?

    A) Parce que

    B) Bien que

    C) Si

    D) Mais

4: When using the structure "bien que + present subjunctive," the concession is presented as:

    A) A real situation

    B) An unlikely situation in the future

    C) An unreal situation in the present

    D) An assumed or known situation

5: The preposition "par" is used to indicate:

    A) Direction

    B) Time

    C) Cause

    D) All of the above

6: Which expression would you use to say "to comply with the law?"

    A) Se conformer à la loi

    B) Respecter la loi

    C) Garantir la loi

    D) Veiller à la loi

7: What is the French word for "greenhouse gas?"

A) Gaz à effet de serre

B) Substances toxiques

C) Matières particulaires en suspension

D) Nuage de smog

8: Which preposition would you use to express the motive for an action?

A) Par

B) Pour

C) Avec

D) Depuis

9: The word "catastrophe" can be described as:

A) Imminente

B) Irréparable

C) Humanitaire

D) All of the above

10: Which verb would you use to express "to guarantee the exercise of rights?"

A) Garantir

B) Respecter

C) Veiller

D) Demander

Answer Key

1. C) Sismique

2. A) Pollution atmosphérique

3. B) Bien que

4. D) An assumed or known situation

5. D) All of the above

6. A) Se conformer à la loi

7. A) Gaz à effet de serre

8. B) Pour

9. D) All of the above

10. A) Garantir

Chapter 5: Online and Offline Relationships

"Ne marche pas devant moi, je pourrais ne pas suivre. Ne marche pas derrière moi, je pourrais ne pas guider. Marche juste à côté de moi et sois mon ami."

- Albert Camus

In this chapter, we'll explore both online and offline relationships.

Vocabulary About Social Media and the Internet

- *Les réseaux sociaux:* social media

- *La publication:* post

- *Le profil:* profile

- *Les abonnés:* followers

- *Abonnements:* following

- *Les souscripteurs:* subscribers

- *Le "j'aime":* like

- *Le sujet tendance:* trending topic

- *Le tweet:* tweet

- *La chaîne:* channel

- *Le hashtag:* tag/hashtag

- *La demande d'ami:* friend request

- *Le commentaire:* comment

- *Le message direct:* direct message

- *La boîte de réception:* inbox

- *Le fil d'actualités:* feed

- *Le courrier indésirable:* spam

- *Le filtre:* filter
- *La caméra frontale:* front camera

Here are some verbs and expressions related to social media and key:

- *Suivre:* to follow
- *Partager:* to share
- *S'abonner:* to subscribe
- *Ajouter:* to add
- *Publier:* to post
- *Taguer:* to tag
- *Tweeter:* to tweet
- *Mettre un "j'aime":* to like
- *Être tendance:* to be a trending topic
- *Avoir des abonnés:* to have followers
- *Bloquer:* to block
- *Signaler:* to report
- *Envoyer un message:* to send a message
- *Laisser un commentaire:* to leave a comment
- *Modifier le profil:* to edit profile

As you might have noticed, French has adopted some English social media terms.

Adjectives commonly used on social media:

Viral: viral

- Publication virale / viral post
- Même viral / viral meme
- Influenceur viral / viral influencer

Enviado: sent

- Message envoyé / sent message
- Courrier envoyé / sent mail

- Tweet envoyé / sent tweet

Recibido: received

- Message reçu / received message

- Courrier reçu / received mail

- Visto: seen

- Message vu / seen message

Suscrito: subscribed

- Abonné / subscribed

- Guardado/a: saved

- Publication sauvegardée / saved post

Verbs Used to Talk About Relationships

- mettre mal à l'aise (quelqu'un) / to make (someone) uncomfortable

- présenter (quelqu'un) / to introduce (someone)

- agresser/insulter (quelqu'un) / to attack/insult (someone)

- offenser (quelqu'un) / to offend (someone)

- tomber amoureux(se) de... / to fall in love (with...)

- s'attacher à... / to get attached (to...), to be fond (of...)

- quitter (quelqu'un) / to leave (someone)

- aimer (quelqu'un) / to like (someone)

- ne pas s'intéresser à (quelqu'un), mépriser (quelqu'un) / to not have interest (in someone), despise (someone)

- séduire (quelqu'un) / to seduce (someone)

- fasciner / to fascinate

- attirer (quelqu'un) / to attract (someone)

- conquérir (quelqu'un) / to win over (someone)

- tromper (quelqu'un) / to cheat (on someone)

- persuader (quelqu'un) / to persuade (someone)

- éblouir (quelqu'un) / to dazzle (someone)

- traiter (quelqu'un) (+ adverbe) / to treat (someone) (+ adverb)

- bien traiter (quelqu'un) / to treat someone well

- mal traiter (quelqu'un) / to treat someone badly

- traiter d'égal à égal (quelqu'un) / to treat someone as an equal

- traiter avec cordialité (quelqu'un) / to treat someone cordially

- traiter avec amabilité (quelqu'un) / to treat someone kindly

- traiter avec froideur (quelqu'un) / to treat someone coldly

- être distant avec (quelqu'un) / to be distant (with someone)

Expressions with "avoir":

- avoir beaucoup/peu de relations (avec…) / to interact (a lot/little) (with…)

- avoir une relation (+ adjectif) / to have a (+ adjective) relationship

- avoir du respect pour… / to have respect for

- avoir de l'affection pour… / to be fond of

- envier (quelqu'un) / to envy someone

- avoir peur de… / to be afraid of

- être jaloux de… / to be jealous of

- avoir de la patience avec… / to have patience with

- avoir confiance en… / to confide in

Expressions with "s'entendre"

- s'entendre bien (avec…) / to get on well (with…)

- s'entendre à merveille (avec…) / to get on great (with…)

- s'entendre mal (avec…) / to get on badly (with…)

- s'entendre très mal (avec…) / to get on awfully (with…)

- s'entendre comme chien et chat (avec…) / to fight like cats and dogs (with…)

Referring to People

De ceux-là / De celles-là and De ceux-ci / De celles-ci

In French, de ceux-là/celles-là and de ceux-ci/celles-ci are used to diminish the importance or prestige of people or things.. :

- Elle a publié un de ces articles qui parlent d'un restaurant à la mode. ("She uploaded one of those articles that talk about a trendy restaurant.")

- C'est une de ces personnes qui disent tout ce qu'elles pensent. ("He's one of those people who say everything they think.")

As you can see, the choice between ceux-là/celles-là and ceux-ci/celles-ci depends on the gender of the noun being referred to. In these examples, the number remains plural (ceux/celles) because these expressions are used to generalize or speak in broad terms.

Un/une tel(le)

In French, the demonstrative "tel/telle" refers to people we do not know much about. It conveys a certain vagueness or unfamiliarity.:

- Ma nouvelle collègue est une telle Alejandra Ríos, tu la connais? ("My new partner is somebody named Alejandra Ríos, do you know her?")

- Un tel André est venu te chercher. ("Someone named André came looking for you.")

The indefinite article (un/une) changes according to the gender of the person being referred to, but the demonstrative "tel/telle" itself does not change. Plural forms (des tels/des telles) are less common in French.

Ce que... le plus/Ce que... le moins

In romantic and non-romantic relationships, use "ce que... le plus" and "ce que... le moins" to discuss what you like most or least about someone.:

Ce que j'aime le moins chez Lorenzo, c'est son désordre. ("What I like the least about Lorenzo is his disorganization.")

Start with "ce que... le plus" or "ce que... le moins," followed by a verb. If referring to someone, add the preposition chez before the name or pronoun of the person being discussed.:

- Ce que j'apprécie le plus chez mes enfants, c'est de passer du temps avec eux. ("What I enjoy the most about my children is spending time with them.")

- Ce que je déteste le plus chez Guillaume, c'est son manque de ponctualité. ("What I hate the most about Guillaume is his lack of punctuality.")

- Ce que je veux le plus dans cette vie, c'est que Léon m'épouse. ("What I want the most in this life is for Léon to marry me.")

Comme si + imparfait/plus-que-parfait du subjonctif

In French, we use "comme si + imparfait/plus-que-parfait" to describe a situation by comparing it to another hypothetical or imagined scenario.

Imparfait de l'indicatif:

Verb	French Equivalent (Imparfait de l'indicatif)
	je
chanter	chantais
manger	mangeais
vivre	vivais
	tu
chanter	chantais
manger	mangeais
vivre	vivais
	il / elle / on
chanter	chantait
manger	mangeait
vivre	vivait
	nous
chanter	chantions

manger	mangions
vivre	vivions
	vous
chanter	chantiez
manger	mangiez

Plus-que-parfait de l'indicatif

French Equivalent	Participle
j'avais	chanté (chanter), mangé (manger), vécu (vivre)
avais	
tu avais	chanté (chanter), mangé (manger), vécu (vivre)
avais	
il / elle avait	chanté (chanter), mangé (manger), vécu (vivre)
avait	
nous avions	chanté (chanter), mangé (manger), vécu (vivre)
avions	
vous aviez	chanté (chanter), mangé (manger), vécu (vivre)
aviez	
ils / elles avaient	chanté (chanter), mangé (manger), vécu (vivre)

avaient	

Certain expressions describe ongoing or incomplete situations. For example: "Maintenant, mon petit ami me traite comme si j'étais une princesse" ("Now my boyfriend treats me like a princess"), or "À ce moment-là, mon petit ami m'a traité comme si j'étais une princesse" ("At that time, my boyfriend treated me like a princess").

Alternatively, use the plus-que-parfait to refer to situations that have already ended: "Mon petit ami me traite comme si j'avais fait quelque chose de mal" ("My boyfriend treats me as if I had done something wrong").

Note: This form can also be used independently to respond to something perceived as inappropriate:

"Remets tout pour demain." ("Hand in everything by tomorrow.")

"Comme si tu étais le patron!" ("As if you were the boss!").

Exercises

1. Which of the following is NOT a common French social media noun?

    A. Hashtag

    B. Inbox

    C. Filter

    D. Relationship

2. What is the French equivalent of "to like" on social media?

    A. Suivre

    B. Partager

    C. Mettre un "j'aime"

    D. Tweeter

3. Which verb is used to describe the act of sending a message on social media?

    A. Envoyer un message

    B. Publier

    C. Taguer

    D. Bloquer

4. What is the French expression for "to fall in love (with someone)?"

    A. Aimer (quelqu'un)

    B. Tomber amoureux(se) de...

    C. S'attacher à...

    D. Quitter (quelqu'un)

5. Which verb is used to express the idea of "to get on well (with someone)?"

    A. S'entendre mal

    B. S'entendre bien

    C. Avoir peur de

    D. Être jaloux de

6. The phrase "de ceux-là/celles-là" is used to:

    A. Express admiration

    B. Diminish the importance of something

    C. Show great enthusiasm

    D. Indicate a strong connection

7. The structure "comme si + imparfait/plus-que-parfait du subjonctif" is used to:

A. Express a wish or desire

B. Compare a situation to a hypothetical scenario

C. Give advice or recommendations

D. Describe a past event in detail

8. Which of the following is an example of a French verb adapted from an English word?

A. Suivre

B. Partager

C. Taguer

D. Aimer

9. What is the French equivalent of "to be a trending topic?"

A. Être populaire

B. Être tendance

C. Avoir du succès

D. Être connu

10. Which phrase is used to express "to treat someone badly" in French?

A. Traiter bien (quelqu'un)

B. Mal traiter (quelqu'un)

C. Traiter avec amabilité (quelqu'un)

D. Traiter d'égal à égal (quelqu'un)

Answer Key

1. D. Relationship
2. C. Mettre un "j'aime"
3. A. Envoyer un message
4. B. Tomber amoureux(se) de...
5. B. S'entendre bien
6. B. Diminish the importance of something
7. B. Compare a situation to a hypothetical scenario
8. C. Taguer
9. B. Être tendance
10. B. Mal traiter (quelqu'un)

Cultural Annex

Here are some French songs to inspire your learning:

1. "Parle à ma main" by Fatal Bazooka (featuring Yelle)

2. "Je t'aime moi non plus" by Serge Gainsbourg (featuring Jane Birkin)

3. "Elle me dit" by Mika

4. "Dis-moi" by BB Brunes

5. "Ma Philosophie" by Amel Bent

6. "Marcia Baïla" by Les Rita Mitsouko

7. "Virtuel" by Eddy de Pretto

Conclusion

Congratulations!

This book was packed with vocabulary, grammar, examples, exercises, and reading materials on a wide range of topics, and you have successfully worked your way through it all, emerging stronger and more knowledgeable!

BOOK 7

Learn French with Short Stories for Adults

Engaging Stories to Shortcut Your French Fluency!
(Fun & Easy Reads)

Explore to Win

Book 7 Description

Are you ready to practice your French skills? Look no further! "Learn French with Short Stories for Adults" is exactly what you need to elevate your language skills to the next level!

Our carefully crafted short stories are captivating and easy to follow, yet designed to challenge and enhance your skills.

In "Learn French with Short Stories for Adults," you will find:

- Engaging stories

- Rich vocabulary and practical everyday phrases

- Tips and techniques for making the most of these stories

- Helpful glossaries to clarify new terms

- Summaries of each story for easy comprehension

- Exercises and answer keys to test your reading skills

Chapter 1: Les voleurs – The thieves

"Les voleurs ne volent jamais que ce qui est riche; c'est pourquoi ils ont plus de délicatesse que les grands seigneurs."

- Victor Hugo

Daniela était assise dans la salle d'attente du commissariat de police lorsque sa tante arriva. Elle et sa colocataire étaient là depuis près d'une heure, pratiquement immobiles, le regard perdu. Daniela serra sa tante dans ses bras pendant quelques minutes, ses mains tremblaient encore, sans aucun doute elle était toujours effrayée.

- Dis-moi ce qui s'est passé, dit la tante de Daniela.

Daniela prit une profonde inspiration et commença à raconter l'histoire. Il y a quelques heures, elle était rentrée chez elle à la même heure que d'habitude. Elle avait passé la majeure partie de la journée debout, et ses pieds lui faisaient terriblement mal ; tout ce qu'elle souhaitait, c'était enlever ses talons et se détendre un peu sur le canapé. Alors qu'elle sortait ses clés pour ouvrir la porte, elle remarqua que la poignée était cassée, il y avait des morceaux de métal sur le sol. La porte était complètement ouverte. Pendant un instant, elle ne comprenait pas ce qu'elle voyait, elle pensa que peut-être elle ou sa colocataire avaient laissé la porte ouverte.

Ensuite, toutes les possibilités de ce qui aurait pu se passer la paralysèrent, la peur l'empêchait de penser clairement. Il était fort probable que quelqu'un était entré pour cambrioler son appartement, mais comment pouvait-elle savoir s'ils étaient vraiment partis? Et si les voleurs étaient encore à l'intérieur? Que lui feraient-ils s'ils la voyaient? Elle panique et décida de demander de l'aide à son voisin. L'homme ne comprenait d'abord pas ce qu'elle lui disait parce qu'elle parlait trop vite et semblait très agitée. Il lui donna un verre d'eau et lui demanda de lui expliquer la situation avec un peu plus de calme. Il prit une batte de baseball et se rendit à l'appartement de Daniela tandis qu'elle appelait la police. Après quelques minutes, son voisin revint et lui dit qu'il n'avait vu personne, qu'elle pouvait se sentir un peu plus tranquille. Le chat de Daniela se faufila par la porte et sauta sur les jambes de Daniela, et elle se mit à pleurer.

Elle était soulagée parce qu'il n'était rien arrivé à son chat, et aussi parce que les voleurs n'étaient plus là ; et bien qu'elle ne sache pas encorc cxactcmcnt ce qui s'était passé, cela ne semblait pas aussi grave que tout ce qu'elle s'était imaginé il y a quelques minutes.

Parmi les choses que les voleurs avaient volées, il y avait le petit téléviseur qui se trouvait dans le placard de Daniela, ce qui, d'une certaine manière, l'amusa parce que ce téléviseur ne fonctionnait pas. Ils avaient également emporté son ordinateur portable et quelques économies qu'elle avait gardées dans la table de nuit, un peu moins de 500 dollars. Ce qui lui faisait le plus mal, c'était de perdre son ordinateur portable, non seulement parce qu'il était coûteux, mais aussi parce qu'elle n'en avait pas d'autre, et elle ne savait pas comment elle allait faire pour travailler maintenant. Malgré tout, elle se sentait reconnaissante d'être arrivée après le départ des voleurs, car elle n'imaginait pas ce qui se serait passé s'ils l'avaient vue. L'auraient-ils blessée? L'auraient-ils attachée à une chaise comme dans les films? Rien que d'y penser, cela lui faisait peur.

Sa tante insista pour qu'elle reste avec elle quelques jours et Daniela accepta, ne voulant pas passer la nuit seule. Elle et sa colocataire se rendirent à l'appartement pour chercher quelques affaires, et avant de fermer la porte, Daniela regarda vers le salon, se demandant quand elle se sentirait de nouveau en sécurité ici.

Résumé

Daniela se trouve au commissariat de police après que quelqu'un soit entré dans son appartement pour y voler quelques heures auparavant. Sa tante vient la soutenir, et Daniela lui raconte ce qui s'est passé, les objets qui ont été volés, comment elle se sentait à ce moment-là et comment elle se sent maintenant. Daniela accepte l'offre de sa tante et décide de rester chez elle quelques jours, car elle ne se sent pas en sécurité dans son appartement et se demande si elle s'y sentira un jour de nouveau en sécurité.

Summary

Daniela finds herself in the police station after someone broke into and robbed her apartment a few hours ago. Her aunt comes to offer her support, and Daniela tells her what happened, the things they stole, how she felt in the moment, and how she feels now. Daniela accepts her aunt's offer and decides to stay with her for a few days because she doesn't feel safe in her apartment, and she wonders if she will ever feel safe again there.

Glossaire – Glossary

- **Elle était assise dans la salle d'attente:** She was sitting in the waiting room

- **Le commissariat de police:** The police station

- **Ils étaient là depuis presque une heure:** They had been there for almost an hour

- **Pratiquement immobiles:** Practically motionless

- **Le regard perdu:** Looking vacantly

- **Ses mains tremblaient encore:** Her hands were still shaking

- **Il n'y avait aucun doute qu'elle avait encore peur:** There was no doubt she was still scared

- **Dis-moi ce qui s'est passé:** Tell me what happened

- **Elle prit une profonde inspiration:** She took a deep breath

- **Elle commença à raconter l'histoire:** She began to tell the story

- **Il y a quelques heures:** Some hours ago

- **À la même heure que d'habitude:** At the same time she's used to

- **Elle avait passé la majeure partie de la journée debout:** She had spent most of the day on her feet

- **Ses pieds lui faisaient terriblement mal:** Her feet hurt terribly

- **Ce qu'elle désirait le plus, c'était enlever ses talons:** What she wished with all her might was to take off her high heels

- **Elle sortait ses clés pour ouvrir la porte:** She was taking out her keys to open the door

- **Elle remarqua que la poignée était cassée:** She noticed the door handle was broken

- **Il y avait des morceaux de métal:** There were pieces of metal

- **Ils avaient laissé la porte ouverte:** They had left their door open

- **Les possibilités de ce qui s'était passé la paralysèrent:** The possibilities of what had happened paralyzed her

- **La peur l'empêchait de penser clairement:** The fear wouldn't let her think clearly

- **Quelqu'un était entré pour cambrioler:** Someone had gotten into rob

- **Comment pouvait-elle savoir qu'ils étaient vraiment partis?:** How could she know they had really left?

- **Et si les voleurs étaient encore à l'intérieur?:** What if the thieves were still inside?

- **Que lui feraient-ils s'ils la voyaient?:** What would they do to her if they saw her?

- **Elle panique:** She panicked

- **Elle décida de demander de l'aide à son voisin:**

  She decided to ask her neighbor for help

- **Il ne comprenait pas ce qu'elle lui disait:** He couldn't understand what she was saying

- **Exaltée:** Frenzied

- **Il lui dit de lui expliquer la situation:** He told her to explain the situation

- **Pendant qu'elle appelait:** While she was calling

- **Il lui dit qu'il n'avait vu personne:** He told her that he hadn't seen anybody

- **Qu'elle pouvait être:** That she could be

- **Il s'est faufilé:** He sneaked in

- **Il sauta sur les jambes de Daniela:** He jumped on Daniela's lap

- **Elle se mit à pleurer:** She started crying

- **Soulagée:** Relieved

- **Rien n'était arrivé à son chat:** Nothing had happened to her cat

- **Ils n'étaient plus là:** They were gone

- **Elle ne savait pas encore exactement ce qui s'était passé:** She still didn't know in full detail what had happened

- **Cela ne semblait pas aussi grave que tout ce qu'elle avait imaginé:** It didn't seem as bad as everything she had imagined

- **Ils avaient volé:** She had stolen

- **Ce qui, d'une certaine manière, l'amusa:** Which in a way amused her

- **Il ne fonctionnait pas:** It didn't work

- **Quelques économies qu'elle gardait dans la table de nuit:** Some savings she was keeping in her nightstand

- **Un peu moins de:** A bit under

- **Ce qui lui faisait le plus mal, c'était de perdre:** What hurt her the most was losing

- **Non seulement parce que:** Not only because

- **Mais elle n'en avait pas d'autre:** But she didn't have another one

- **Elle ne savait pas comment elle allait faire pour travailler maintenant:** She didn't know how she was going to manage to work now

- **Malgré tout:** Still

- **Elle se sentait reconnaissante d'être arrivée après que les voleurs étaient partis:** She was grateful she had arrived after the thieves were gone

- **Elle n'imaginait pas ce qui se serait passé s'ils l'avaient vue:** She couldn't imagine what would have happened if they had seen her

- **Lui auraient-ils fait du mal?:** Would they have hurt her?

- **L'auraient-ils attachée à la chaise comme dans les films?:** Would they have tied her to a chair like in the movies?

- **Rien que d'y penser, cela lui faisait peur:** Just thinking about it fueled her fear

- **Elle insista pour qu'elle reste avec elle:** She insisted Daniela should stay with her

- **Elle ne voulait pas passer la nuit seule:** She didn't want to spend the night alone

- **Elles sont allées chercher quelques affaires à l'appartement:** They went to the apartment to pick up some things

- **Avant de fermer:** Before closing

- **Pensant au moment où elle se sentirait de nouveau en sécurité là-bas:** Thinking about when she would feel safe there again

Exercice 1

Contestez aux questions suivantes– Answer the following questions

1. Où Daniela a-t-elle rencontré sa tante? – Where did Daniela meet her aunt?

_____

2. Que voulait-elle faire le plus en rentrant chez elle? – What did she want to do the most when she got home?

_____

3. Qu'a-t-elle vu sur le sol? – What did she see on the floor?

_____

4. Comment se sentait-elle? – How did she feel?

_____

5. À qui a-t-elle demandé de l'aide? – Who did she ask for help?

_____

6. Qu'a fait son voisin? – What did her neighbor do?

_____

Exercice 2

Choisissez entre "vrai" ou "faux"– Choose "true" or "false"

1. Daniela était dans la salle d'attente avec son petit ami. – Daniela was in the waiting room with her boyfriend.

_____

2. Elle avait mal aux pieds parce qu'elle avait fait de l'exercice. – Her feet hurt because she had been working out.

_____

3. Sa colocataire était dans l'appartement. – Her roommate was in the apartment.

_____

4. Son voisin a appelé la police. – His neighbor called the police.

5. Il n'y avait personne dans l'appartement. – There was no one in the apartment.

6. Son chat allait bien. – Her cat was fine.

Réponses – Answers

Exercice 1

1- Daniela a rencontré sa tante au commissariat de police.

2- Ce que Daniela voulait le plus faire en rentrant chez elle, c'était enlever ses talons et se détendre un peu sur le canapé.

3- Il y avait des morceaux de métal sur le sol.

4- Elle avait très peur, elle ne pouvait pas penser clairement.

5- Daniela a demandé de l'aide à son voisin.

6- Le voisin de Daniela a pris une batte de baseball et est allé à l'appartement de Daniela pendant qu'elle appelait la police.

Exercice 2

1- Faux

2- Faux

3- Faux

4- Faux

5- Vrai

6- Vrai

Chapter 2: La compétition – The competition

"Il n'y a pas de réussite facile ni d'échecs définitifs."

- André Gide

Il y a trois mois, Marisol a quitté son ancien travail d'écrivain pour devenir éditrice dans l'un des magazines les plus importants de la ville, "L'autre mirage." Le changement a été radical, peut-être plus qu'elle ne l'imaginait. Avant, elle n'avait qu'à se soucier d'écrire de bons articles, ce qui n'avait jamais été un problème pour elle, mais maintenant, elle est responsable du travail de dizaines d'écrivains, ce qui implique non seulement de s'assurer que chacun écrive un nombre minimum d'articles par semaine, mais aussi que ces articles soient pratiquement parfaits.

Il n'y a pas de marge pour les erreurs. Elle doit lire chaque mot, chaque signe de ponctuation avant d'approuver les articles. Parfois, c'est beaucoup de pression. Cependant, l'ambiance au travail rend les choses plus faciles. Tout le monde la traite avec respect, personne ne remet en question son autorité, ce qui est un soulagement, car elle était un peu nerveuse étant donné qu'on lui avait dit qu'elle serait la première femme éditrice du magazine ; elle imaginait donc qu'ils ne respecteraient peut-être pas son autorité ou qu'ils lui manqueraient de respect parce qu'elle est une femme. Heureusement, ce ne fut pas le cas.

À la maison, les choses ont été un peu difficiles. Elle a engagé une nounou de confiance, une voisine, qui s'occupe de ses enfants lorsqu'elle n'est pas là. Certains jours, la nounou reste avec eux parce que Marisol doit travailler tard et ne veut pas que ses enfants soient seuls. Le temps de qualité avec ses enfants est une lutte constante dans son esprit, car parfois elle a l'impression de le sacrifier pour atteindre d'autres objectifs. Et peut-être qu'elle n'est pas la seule à le penser. Sa fille aînée, Anabel, passe beaucoup de temps dans sa chambre ces derniers temps, et lorsque Marisol veut lui parler ou faire quelque chose ensemble, elle lui dit qu'elle n'en a pas envie, elle l'évite. Marisol pense que sa fille se sent peut-être abandonnée, qu'elle ne lui prête pas l'attention dont elle a besoin.

C'est pourquoi, lorsque Marisol a appris que le groupe de chant auquel appartient sa fille participerait à une compétition, elle savait qu'elle devait être là, que ce jour serait très important pour sa fille. Si elle manquait cet événement, il se pourrait que sa fille ne lui pardonne pas. Elle doit être présente, quoi qu'il arrive.

La compétition a lieu à l'école d'Anabel. À l'entrée de l'école, de nombreux parents et proches des enfants se réunissent, discutent, prennent des photos. Anabel semble heureuse de voir sa mère. Son sourire illumine son visage. Tout le monde entre dans une grande salle où il y a une multitude de chaises orientées vers la scène ; une femme prend le micro et souhaite la bienvenue à tous, leur demande de s'asseoir parce que la compétition va bientôt commencer. Cinq groupes vont participer, et celui d'Anabel sera le deuxième à monter sur scène. Marisol voit sa fille de loin et lui fait signe de la main, elle essaie de lui dire de ne pas s'inquiéter, que tout ira bien. Elle veut juste que sa fille s'amuse, qu'elle fasse ce qu'elle aime, peu importe le résultat.

Quand vient le tour du groupe de sa fille, Marisol applaudit avec beaucoup d'enthousiasme. Elle enregistre une vidéo pour en garder un souvenir et pouvoir la montrer à la famille, afin que tous disent à Anabel combien ils sont fiers d'elle. Anabel se tient droite, chante chaque note à la perfection. On sent l'effort qu'elle a mis chaque jour à pratiquer la chanson, un chant de Noël que Marisol n'avait pas entendu depuis des années.

Pendant quelques secondes, tout le monde reste silencieux, la lumière du projecteur et toute l'attention se concentrent sur Anabel. C'est le moment de son solo. Anabel ferme les yeux et chante de tout son cœur. À un moment donné, elle chante un peu faux, mais elle ne laisse pas cela l'arrêter, elle continue avec la même confiance. Marisol est très émue, elle a les larmes aux yeux. La voix de sa fille lui rappelle celle de sa grand-mère, décédée avant la naissance d'Anabel. C'est quelque chose de magique, comme si elle était sur scène. Anabel rouvre les yeux quand la chanson se termine. Tout le monde applaudit.

- Est-ce que ça se voyait que j'étais nerveuse? — demande Anabel.

- Non, mon amour, ne t'inquiète pas, dit Marisol. Regarde comme tu es belle sur la vidéo.

La compétition est terminée. En ce moment, les juges prennent la décision de savoir quel sera le groupe gagnant. Tout le monde est très anxieux en attendant le résultat. Anabel, contrairement à ses camarades, semble tranquille. Elle dit à sa mère que peut-être que son groupe gagnera la compétition, ou peut-être qu'il perdra, mais que cela ne lui importe pas.

- Tu es ici avec moi, dit Anabel. J'ai déjà gagné.

Résumé

Le nouveau travail de Marisol a apporté beaucoup de changements dans sa vie. Elle gagne plus d'argent, et avec cela viennent de nouvelles responsabilités, ce qui explique pourquoi elle ne peut pas passer autant de temps avec ses enfants. Celle qui en souffre le plus est Anabel. C'est pourquoi Marisol fait tout son possible pour assister à la compétition de chant à laquelle sa fille participera. Qu'elle gagne ou non, Marisol veut être là pour lui montrer son soutien et son amour, afin que sa fille sache qu'elle sera toujours là pour elle.

Summary

Marisol's new job has brought lots of changes to her life. She earns more money, and along with it come new responsibilities, the reason why she can't spend as much time with her kids. Anabel is the most affected by it. That's why Marisol does everything she can to go to the singing competition her daughter will be participating in. Whether she wins or not, Marisol just wants to be there to show her support and love so that her daughter knows she will always be there for her.

Glossaire – Glossary

- **Il y a trois mois, Marisol a quitté son ancien travail:** Three months ago, Marisol left her old job

- **Pour devenir:** To become

- **Peut-être plus que ce qu'elle attendait:** Perhaps more than what she expected

- **Elle devait se soucier d'écrire:** She had to worry about writing

- **Elle est responsable de:** She's in charge of

- **Ce qui signifie non seulement s'assurer que tout le monde écrit:** Which means not only having to make sure they all write

- **Mais aussi que les articles soient parfaits:** But also that the articles are perfect

- **Il n'y a pas de marge pour les erreurs:** There's no margin for errors

- **Signe de ponctuation:** Punctuation

- **Cela rend les choses plus faciles:** It makes things easier

- **Ils ne remettent pas en question son autorité:** They don't question her authority

- **Ils lui ont dit qu'elle serait la première:** They told her she would be the first

- **Elle pensait qu'ils ne respecteraient peut-être pas son autorité:** She thought they perhaps wouldn't respect her authority

- **Ils lui manqueraient de respect parce qu'elle est une femme:** They would disrespect her for being a woman

- **Les choses à la maison ont été un peu difficiles:** Things at home have been a little difficult

- **Elle s'occupe de ses enfants quand elle n'est pas là:** She takes care of her kids when she's not there

- **Elle ne veut pas que ses enfants soient seuls:** She doesn't want her kids to be alone

- **Temps de qualité:** Quality time

- **C'est une lutte constante dans son esprit:** It's a constant struggle in her mind

- **Elle pense parfois qu'elle le sacrifie pour atteindre ses objectifs:** She sometimes feels like she's sacrificing it so that she can achieve her goals

- **Peut-être qu'elle n'est pas la seule à le penser:** She might not be the only one who thinks that

- **Elle n'en a pas envie:** She doesn't want to

- **Elle l'évite:** She avoids her

- **Peut-être que sa fille se sent:** Her daughter might feel

- **Elle ne lui accorde pas l'attention dont elle a besoin:** She doesn't give her the attention she needs

- **Quand Marisol a appris:** When Marisol found out

- **Le groupe de chant auquel appartient sa fille participerait:** The singing group her daughter belongs to would participate

- **Elle savait qu'elle devait être là:** She knew she had to be there

- **Ce jour-là serait:** That day would be

- **Si elle manque cet événement, sa fille pourrait ne pas lui pardonner:** If she misses it, her daughter might not forgive her

- **Ils se rassemblent:** They gather

- **Ils prennent des photos:** They take pictures

- **Elle semble heureuse de voir:** She seems happy to see

- **Son sourire illumine son visage:** Her smile lights up her face

- **Regardant:** Facing

- **Elle souhaite la bienvenue à tous:** She welcomes everybody

- **Elle leur demande de s'asseoir:** She asks them to take a seat

- **Cela commencera bientôt:** It will start soon

- **Ils participeront:** They will participate

- **Ce sera le deuxième à monter sur scène:** It will be the second one to get on the stage

- **Elle essaie de lui dire de ne pas s'inquiéter:** She tries to tell her not to worry

- **Sûrement tout ira bien:** Surely everything will be fine

- **Elle veut que sa fille s'amuse:** She wants her daughter to have fun

- **Qu'elle fasse ce qu'elle aime, peu importe le résultat:** That she does what she likes no matter the result

- **Pour le garder en souvenir et pouvoir le montrer:** To keep it as a souvenir and so that she can show it to

- **Que tout le monde lui dise:** So that they all tell her

- **Elle se tient droite:** She stands up straight

- **Elle chante chaque note à la perfection:** She sings every note to perfection

- **On voit l'effort qu'elle a mis:** You can see the effort she put in

- **Un chant de Noël que Marisol n'avait pas entendu depuis des années:** A Christmas carol Marisol hadn't heard in years

- **Tout le monde se tait:** They all fall silent

- **Projecteur:** Spotlight

- **Elle chante de tout son cœur:** She sings with everything in her

- **Elle chante faux:** She is off pitch

- **Elle ne laisse pas cela l'arrêter:** She doesn't let that stop her

- **Cela l'émeut beaucoup:** It moves her

- **Cela lui rappelle sa grand-mère qui est décédée avant la naissance d'Anabel:** It reminds her of her grandmother who died before Anabel was born

- **Comme si elle était:** As if she was

- **Est-ce que tu as remarqué que j'étais nerveuse?**: Could you tell I was nervous?

- **Regarde comme tu es belle sur la vidéo:** Look how pretty you look in the video

- **C'est terminé:** It ended

- **Ils sont en train de décider quel sera le groupe gagnant:** They're making the decision of who will be the winning group

- **Contrairement à:** Unlike

- **Peut-être que son groupe gagnera:** Her group might win

- **Peut-être qu'il perdra:** It might lose

- **Elle s'en fiche:** She doesn't care about that

- **J'ai déjà gagné:** I already won

Exercice 1

Répondez aux questions suivantes – Answer the following questions

1. Quel était son ancien travail? – What was her old job?

_____

2. Quelles sont ses nouvelles responsabilités? – What are her new responsibilities?

_____

3. Comment est l'ambiance de travail? – What's the working environment like?

_____

4. Pourquoi était-elle nerveuse? – Why was she nervous?

_____

5. Quelle est la lutte constante dans son esprit? – What's the constant struggle in her mind?

_____

6. Pourquoi est-il si important qu'elle aille à la compétition de sa fille? – Why is it so important that she goes to her daughter's competition?

_____

Exercice 2

Choisissez entre "vrai" ou "faux" – choose "true" or "false"

1. Elle est la PDG du magazine. – She is the CEO of the magazine.

_____

2. Elle ressent beaucoup de pression dans son travail. – She feels a lot of pressure in her job.

_____

3. Ils lui manquent de respect parce qu'elle est une femme. – They disrespect her for being a woman.

_____

4. Elle laisse toujours ses enfants seuls. – She always leaves her kids alone.

_____

5. Anabel l'évite parfois. – Anabel avoids her sometimes.

_____

6. Anabel a une compétition de danse. – Anabel has a dancing competition.

_____

Réponses – Answers

Exercice 1

1. Marisol était écrivain.

2. Marisol est responsable du travail d'autres écrivains, elle doit s'assurer que chacun écrit un nombre minimum d'articles par semaine et que ces articles soient parfaits.

3. Tout le monde la traite avec respect et ne remet pas en question son autorité.

4. Parce qu'on lui a dit qu'elle serait la première femme éditrice du magazine, elle imaginait donc qu'ils ne respecteraient peut-être pas son autorité ou qu'ils lui manqueraient de respect parce qu'elle est une femme.

5. Elle a parfois l'impression de sacrifier le temps de qualité avec ses enfants pour pouvoir atteindre ses autres objectifs.

6. Parce qu'elle sait que c'est très important pour sa fille et que si elle manque cet événement, il se peut que sa fille ne lui pardonne jamais.

Exercice 2

1. Faux

2. Vrai

3. Faux

4. Faux

5. Vrai

6. Faux

Chapter 3: La nuit – At night

"La nuit n'est jamais complète. Il y a toujours, puisque je le dis, puisque je l'affirme, au bout du chagrin, une fenêtre ouverte, une fenêtre éclairée."

- Victor Hugo

Cela faisait dix ans que Tomás n'avait pas rendu visite à sa famille à la campagne. Son dernier souvenir dans la grande maison avait été immortalisé sur une photo : cousins, oncles, frères, grand-mère, tous enlacés, souriant. Même les chiens apparaissaient sur la photo. Mais depuis que la grand-mère de Tomás était décédée, il ne trouvait plus de raison d'aller à la campagne. Cette fois-ci, il n'y serait peut-être pas allé non plus, si ce n'était pour sa mère qui l'avait essentiellement fait culpabiliser de ne pas rendre visite à ses cousins, qui, selon elle, lui manquaient beaucoup. Elle ne voulait pas qu'il oublie sa famille.

À la campagne, les choses avaient un peu changé : la plupart de leurs animaux étaient morts, et par manque d'argent, ils avaient dû vendre une partie de leur terrain. Une des maisons appartenait à un homme appelé Alberto, un monsieur bien éduqué et quelque peu aimable. Lorsque Tomás lui demanda s'il était son oncle, l'homme rit, lui répondit que non et lui expliqua la situation.

Tomás avait toujours bien aimé ses petits cousins, surtout maintenant qu'ils le voyaient comme le grand cousin cool. Ils lui posaient des questions sur sa carrière et sur ce que c'était d'étudier à l'université. Il leur montra des photos et des vidéos du tournage d'un court-métrage et ils l'admiraient comme s'il était un dieu. Depuis son enfance, Tomás avait toujours été l'enfant différent, celui que tout le monde embêtait, celui qui ne trouvait sa place nulle part. Ça faisait du bien qu'on le traite différemment maintenant.

Un soir, Tomás regardait un film dans le salon avec ses cousins. Le film était lent et ennuyeux, et il était sur le point de s'endormir. Un de ses cousins lui demanda s'il voulait faire quelque chose d'intéressant. Il lui demanda s'il voulait sortir. Tomás y réfléchit un peu. Sa tante n'aimait pas qu'ils sortent la nuit. Elle ne voulait pas qu'ils se perdent ou tombent dans le noir. De plus, il y avait probablement des serpents ou d'autres types d'animaux dangereux dehors. Son cousin lui parla d'un fantôme qui, soi-disant, apparaissait la nuit près des écuries.

Avant que Tomás puisse prendre une décision, ses petits cousins mirent leurs chaussures et sortirent. Tomás les suivit. Il ne voulait pas qu'ils aient des ennuis avec leurs parents, ou qu'ils lui en causent avec ses oncles et tantes. Il faisait très sombre. À l'horizon, il n'y avait que des arbres. Ils suivirent un chemin de terre jusqu'aux écuries : totalement vides à l'exception d'un cheval. Tomás se souvenait qu'enfant, il y avait des animaux partout. Maintenant, ils pouvaient à peine nourrir quelques-uns. Le cheval s'appelait Prince, sa plus jeune cousine lui avait donné ce nom. C'était un cheval brun, plein d'énergie. Il était un peu maigre. Les enfants caressaient le cheval depuis la porte, car Tomás était un peu nerveux à l'idée qu'ils s'en approchent trop.

Ils entendirent un bruit. Une des petites filles cria. Le cheval s'effraya, commença à hennir et frappa la porte avec ses sabots. Tomás dit aux enfants de s'éloigner et l'un d'eux courut vers l'autre côté de l'écurie, là où il faisait plus sombre.

Tomás attrapa sa cousine de onze ans par les épaules.

- Tu es l'aînée, alors tu es responsable de tes frères et sœurs. Ramène-les à la maison pendant que je cherche Cristián, d'accord? — dit Tomás.

Sa cousine acquiesça avec sérieux, comme si elle était dans l'armée et avait reçu un ordre direct de son capitaine.

Tomás utilisa son téléphone comme lampe de poche et se dirigea dans la direction où Cristián avait couru. En passant une vieille porte en bois, Tomás vit le garçon assis par terre, les mains sur les yeux.

- Ça va?

Son cousin ne pouvait pas parler. Il tremblait. Il bougea la main, pointa du doigt devant lui. À quelques mètres, il vit la femme appuyée contre l'arbre. Elle portait une robe blanche et bien qu'il ne pût voir son visage, il sentait ses yeux qui les regardaient. Tomás ne la quitta pas des yeux une seconde. Malgré la peur qu'il ressentait, il porta son cousin sur ses épaules et fit demi-tour. Après avoir refermé la porte en bois, il se retourna une fois de plus. La femme n'était plus là.

Le lendemain, Cristián et Tomás racontèrent à tout le monde ce qu'ils avaient vu, mais personne ne les crut. C'était plutôt frustrant. Au moins, ils étaient sûrs de ce qu'ils avaient vu.

Résumé

Après plusieurs années sans rendre visite à sa famille à la campagne, Tomás décide de traverser le pays pour passer quelques jours avec eux. Il se souvient à quel point les choses étaient différentes lorsqu'il était enfant. Tout semble avoir changé pour le pire. Un soir, Tomás regarde un film ennuyeux avec ses cousins, et ils décident de sortir, bien que sa mère n'aime pas qu'ils sortent la nuit. Il fait très sombre et ils pourraient rencontrer des animaux dangereux. Dans les écuries vides, Tomás et son cousin Cristián voient quelque chose de difficile à croire, quelque chose qui pourrait changer leurs vies pour toujours.

Summary

After several years without visiting his family in the countryside, Tomás decides to travel to the other side of the country to spend some days with them. He remembers how different things were when he was a kid. Things seem to have changed for the worse. One night, Tomás is watching a boring movie with his cousins and they decide to go outside, even though their mother doesn't like them going out at night. Everything's dark, and they can run into dangerous animals. In the empty stables, Tomás and his cousin, Cristián, see something difficult to believe, something that could change their lives forever.

Glossaire – Glossary

- **Il y a dix ans que Tomás n'avait pas rendu visite à sa famille:** It's been ten years since Tomás last visited his family.

- **Cela a été immortalisé sur une photo:** It was immortalized in a picture.

- **Même les chiens apparaissaient:** Even the dogs appeared.

- **Depuis que la grand-mère de Tomás est décédée:** Since Tomás' grandma passed away.

- **Il ne trouvait pas de raison pour:** He couldn't find a reason to.

- **Cette fois, il n'y serait peut-être pas allé non plus:** This time he might not have gone either.

- **Si ce n'avait été pour sa mère:** If it hadn't been for his mother.

- **Elle l'a fait se sentir coupable de ne pas rendre visite à ses cousins:** She made him feel guilty for not visiting his cousins.

- **Qui, selon elle, lui manquaient beaucoup:** That according to her, they missed him a lot.

- **Elle ne voulait pas qu'il oublie:** She didn't want him to forget about.

- **Les choses avaient changé:** Things had changed.

- **La plupart de leurs animaux étaient morts:** Most of their animals had died.

- **Par manque d'argent:** Because they needed money.

- **Ils avaient été contraints de vendre une partie de leur terrain:** They found themselves having to sell part of their land.

- **Cela appartenait à:** It belonged to.

- **Un peu aimable:** A bit kind.

- Quand Tomás lui a demandé s'il était son oncle: When Tomás asked him if he was his uncle.

- **Il a ri:** He laughed.

- **Il a toujours bien aimé ses petits cousins:** He always liked his little cousins.

- **Surtout maintenant qu'ils le voyaient comme le grand cousin cool:** Especially now that they saw him as the cool older cousin.

- **Ils lui posaient des questions sur sa carrière:** They were asking him questions about his career.

- **Du tournage d'un court-métrage:** Of the making of a short film.

- **Ils l'admiraient comme s'il était un dieu:** They admired him like he was a god.

- **Celui que tout le monde embêtait:** The one everyone bullied.

- **Celui qui ne trouvait sa place nulle part:** The one who didn't fit anywhere.

- **Il se sentait bien d'être traité différemment maintenant:** He felt great to be treated differently now.

- **Il regardait:** He was watching.

- **C'est pourquoi il était sur le point de s'endormir:** Which is why he was about to fall asleep.

- **S'il voulait faire quelque chose d'intéressant:** If he wanted to do something interesting.

- **S'il voulait sortir:** If he wanted to go outside.

- **Sa tante n'aimait pas qu'ils sortent la nuit:** His aunt didn't like it when they went outside at night.

- **Elle ne voulait pas qu'ils se perdent ou tombent:** She didn't want them to get lost or fall.

- **Il y avait sûrement des serpents ou d'autres types d'animaux dangereux:** Surely there were snakes or other kind of dangerous animals.

- **Il lui a parlé d'un fantôme qui apparaissait soi-disant:** He told him about a ghost that supposedly appeared.

- **Avant que Tomás ne puisse prendre une décision:** Before Tomás could make a choice.

- **Ils ont mis leurs chaussures et sont sortis:** They put on their shoes and went out.

- **Il les a suivis:** He followed them.

- **Il ne voulait pas qu'ils aient des ennuis:** He didn't want them to get into trouble.

- **Ou qu'ils lui causent des ennuis avec ses oncles et tantes:** Or that they got him into trouble with his aunt and uncle.

- **Il n'y avait que des arbres à l'horizon:** There was nothing but trees on the horizon.

- **Un chemin de terre vers les écuries:** A dirt path to the stables.

- **Il y avait des animaux partout:** There were animals everywhere.

- **Ils pouvaient à peine en nourrir quelques-uns:** They could barely feed a few.

- **Elle lui avait donné ce nom:** She had given it that name.

- **Ils caressaient le cheval:** They were caressing the horse.

- **Cela rendait Tomás un peu nerveux qu'ils s'approchent trop:** It made Tomás a bit nervous for them to get too close.

- **Elle a crié:** She screamed.

- **Le cheval s'est effrayé et a commencé à hennir:** The horse got scared and started neighing.

- **Il a donné un coup:** It kicked.

- **Il a dit aux enfants de s'éloigner:** He told the kids to get away.

- **Il a couru de l'autre côté:** He went running to the other side.

- **Il a pris sa cousine de onze ans par les épaules:** He took his eleven-year-old cousin by the shoulders.

- **Tu es l'aînée, donc tu es responsable:** You're the oldest one, so you're in charge.

- **Ramène-les à la maison:** Take them to the house.

- **Elle a hoché la tête:** She nodded her head yes.

- **Comme si elle était dans l'armée et avait reçu un ordre direct de son capitaine:** As if she was in the army and she had received a direct order from her captain.

- **Il a utilisé son téléphone comme lampe de poche:** He used his phone as a flashlight.

- **Il avait couru:** He had run.

- **En passant la vieille porte en bois:** As he passed the old wooden door.

- **Les mains sur les yeux:** His hands over his eyes.

- **Il ne pouvait pas parler:** He couldn't talk.

- **Il tremblait:** He was shaking.

- **Il a pointé du doigt:** He pointed with his finger.

- **Appuyée contre l'arbre:** Leaning against the tree.

- **Il ne pouvait pas voir son visage:** He couldn't see her face.

- **Il sentait ses yeux:** He could feel her eyes.

- **Les regardant:** Watching them.

- **Il ne la quitta pas des yeux une seconde:** He didn't lose sight of her for a second.

- **Malgré la peur qu'il avait:** Despite the fear he was feeling.

- **Il a porté son cousin sur ses épaules et s'est retourné:** He carried his cousin on his shoulder and turned around.

- **La femme n'était plus là:** The woman was no longer there.

- **Personne ne les a crus:** No one believed them.

- **Ils étaient sûrs de ce qu'ils avaient vu:** They knew what they had seen.

Exercice 1

Répondez aux questions suivantes – Answer the following questions

1- Quand a-t-il voyagé pour la dernière fois à la campagne? - When was the last time he traveled to the countryside?

_____

2- Pourquoi va-t-il rendre visite à sa famille maintenant? - Why is he visiting his family now?

_____

3- Pourquoi aime-t-il ses cousins maintenant? - Why does he like his cousins now?

_____

4-Pourquoi était-il en train de s'endormir? - Why was he falling asleep?

_____

5- Pourquoi sa tante n'aimait-elle pas qu'ils sortent la nuit? - Why didn't his aunt want them to go outside at night?

_____

6- Combien de chevaux y avait-il dans les écuries? - How many horses were there in the stables?

_____

Exercice 2

Choisissez entre vrai ou faux (*Choose "true" or "false"*)

1-La grand-mère de Tomás est décédée. - Tomás' grandma passed away.

_____

2- Ils ont moins d'animaux maintenant. - They have fewer animals now.

_____

3- Ils ont plus de terrains maintenant. - They have more land now.

_____

4- Alberto est l'oncle de Tomás. - Alberto is Tomás' uncle.

_____

5- Tomás déteste ses cousins. - Tomás hates his cousins.

_____

6- Ses cousins sont sortis sans permission. - His cousins went out without permission.

_____

Réponses – Answers

Exercice 1

1. La dernière fois que Tomás est allé à la campagne, c'était il y a dix ans.

2. Tomás va rendre visite à sa famille maintenant parce que sa mère l'a convaincu en le faisant se sentir coupable, et en disant que ses petits cousins lui manquaient beaucoup.

3. Tomás aime bien ses cousins maintenant parce qu'ils le voient comme le grand cousin cool, l'admirent et le traitent différemment.

4. Tomás était en train de s'endormir parce que le film qu'il regardait était lent et ennuyeux.

5. Sa tante n'aimait pas qu'ils sortent la nuit parce qu'il faisait très sombre, et ils pouvaient rencontrer des animaux dangereux.

6. Il n'y avait qu'un seul cheval dans les écuries.

Exercice 2

1. Vrai

2. Vrai

3. Faux

4. Faux

5. Faux

6. Vrai

Chapter 4: Le dernier rendez-vous – The last date

"On ne voit bien qu'avec le cœur. L'essentiel est invisible pour les yeux."

- Antoine de Saint-Exupéry

Daniela est rentrée à la maison après avoir vu David. Raquel l'attendait avec une bouteille de vin pour qu'elle lui raconte les détails. C'était leur quatrième rendez-vous. Ils étaient allés voir une pièce intitulée "Tous sommes fous," une comédie très drôle. Ensuite, ils étaient allés manger des hamburgers et avaient passé la nuit chez David.

Daniela ne voulait pas précipiter les choses. Cela ne faisait que quelques mois qu'elle connaissait David, mais jusqu'à présent, il semblait être une bonne personne. Il avait un grand sens de l'humour, savait cuisiner, était très attentionné, et embrassait bien. Mais tout n'était pas parfait. Ils avaient eu quelques disputes, ils avaient des opinions différentes sur certaines choses, et ils faisaient des choses qui agaçaient l'autre, mais ils pouvaient régler leurs différences en parlant. Tous deux faisaient des efforts dans la relation, alors qu'ils n'étaient même pas encore en couple.

Raquel était très heureuse pour elle. Elle lui disait qu'elle méritait d'être avec quelqu'un qui la rendait heureuse. Elle se sentait très fière que, grâce à elle, ils se soient rencontrés. Elle lui disait que s'ils se mariaient, elle serait la marraine.

Le lendemain, Daniela reçut un message de Théo, un Français qu'elle avait rencontré l'année dernière. Son cœur fit un bond. Il lui disait qu'il était à Buenos Aires et qu'il avait envie de la voir. Daniela réfléchit un moment avant de lui répondre. Elle voulait en parler à Raquel mais ne savait pas si c'était une bonne idée, après tout, David était son ami, et même s'ils n'étaient pas en couple, pour Raquel, ils étaient pratiquement mariés. Elle ne voulait pas la décevoir. Mais la réalité était qu'elle était jeune. Elle n'était pas mariée. Elle pouvait faire ce qu'elle voulait.

Elle mit une robe d'été. Colorée. Aucun des deux n'aimait vraiment sortir beaucoup, alors ils choisirent quelque chose de plus tranquille. Un bar dans le quartier de Belgrano. Elle arriva à huit heures précises. Heureusement, il n'y avait pas beaucoup de monde. Elle s'assit à une table au troisième étage, d'où elle avait une belle vue sur la ville. C'était presque l'été, alors le soleil ne s'était pas encore complètement couché. Théo lui fit une forte accolade en arrivant. Il avait un parfum sucré, très agréable. Ils parlèrent un moment de leurs vies, de ce qu'ils faisaient, de leurs plans pour le reste de l'année. Il parla surtout lui. Elle avait oublié qu'il parlait beaucoup. Maintenant, il utilisait plus d'argot argentin comme "piola," "cheto," et "pibe."

Il lui dit qu'il passerait les fêtes avec sa famille en France, mais qu'il pourrait revenir à Buenos Aires en janvier ou février de l'année prochaine pour visiter ses amis.

Pendant qu'elle parlait, il la regardait, lui caressait la main. Elle devenait rouge comme une tomate. Entre les conversations et les cocktails, il y eut un baiser. Un peu plus tard, il l'embrassa de nouveau, et ensuite, ils ne voulaient plus se séparer. Elle voulait rester avec lui cette nuit-là, la suivante, et celle d'après. Mais elle trouva aussi triste de savoir que sa vie était en France et la sienne ici. Qu'ils n'auraient que des moments comme celui-ci. Sporadiques. Qui passeraient en un clin d'œil. Qu'elle ne pourrait jamais construire un avenir avec lui. Qu'ils n'avaient que le présent. Elle n'avait plus qu'à jeter l'éponge.

Daniela essaya de lui expliquer tout cela quand il l'invita chez lui. Elle lui dit que, dans ces conditions, ça n'avait pas de sens.

-   Et si je restais? – dit Théo.

-   Quelques jours de plus?

-   Non, pour toujours.

Daniela pensa qu'il plaisantait, mais il lui assura qu'il était sérieux, que pour elle, il serait prêt à le faire.

Daniela lui dit que non, que c'était de la folie, qu'il avait sa vie là-bas, et sa famille là-bas. Elle lui dit qu'il ne la connaissait pas assez, qu'ils ne se connaissaient pas assez pour prendre une telle décision. Elle lui donna un baiser de bonne nuit et prit un taxi pour rentrer chez elle.

Quand elle raconta ce qui s'était passé à Raquel, celle-ci lui demanda pourquoi elle avait pris cette décision. Elle était d'accord, mais elle était juste curieuse. Daniela ne savait pas exactement ce qui lui avait ouvert les yeux. À un moment donné, quand Théo lui avait dit toutes ces choses, tout ce qu'elle voulait entendre, elle se rendit compte que ce n'était pas réel. Qu'ils ne se connaissaient pas. Que les relations se construisent. Cette attraction qu'ils ressentaient l'un pour l'autre ne durerait pas éternellement, et parier là-dessus serait une grave erreur.

Ce dimanche-là, elle prenait un café avec David. Le soleil entrait par le balcon. Les oiseaux chantaient. L'odeur des toasts envahissait l'appartement. Un baiser sur les lèvres. Paix. Là, elle se rendit compte qu'elle avait pris la bonne décision.

Résumé

Daniela reçoit un message inattendu d'un garçon avec qui elle est sortie il y a plus d'un an. Elle se sent nerveuse en se rappelant à quel point elle l'aimait à l'époque, et le fait de le revoir la fait aussi remettre en question sa relation avec David, avec qui elle sort récemment. À la fin, elle devra tout mettre dans la balance et choisir l'un des deux, en espérant ne pas regretter sa décision à l'avenir.

Summary

Daniela gets an unexpected message from a guy she went out with over a year ago. She feels nervous remembering how much she used to like him back then, and meeting him again also makes her question her relationship with David, who she began seeing recently. In the end, she'll have to weigh the pros and cons and bet on one of the two guys, hoping she won't regret her choice in the future.

Glossaire – Glossary

- **Elle l'attendait avec une bouteille de vin pour qu'elle lui raconte tous les détails:** She was waiting for her with a bottle of wine to hear all the details.

- **Ça avait été:** That had been.

- **Ils étaient allés voir une pièce:** They had gone to see a play.

- **Ils ont passé la nuit:** They spent the night.

- **Elle ne voulait pas précipiter les choses:** She didn't want to rush things.

- **Elle ne connaissait David que depuis quelques mois:** She had known David for just a few months.

- **Il semblait être:** He seemed to be.

- **Il avait un grand sens de l'humour:** He had a great sense of humor.

- **Il embrassait bien:** He was a good kisser.

- **Ils avaient eu quelques disputes:** They had had some arguments.

- **Ils faisaient des choses qui rendaient l'autre fou:** They would do things that made the other lose it.

- **Ils pouvaient régler leurs différences en parlant:** They could fix things by talking.

- **Ils mettaient tous les deux des efforts dans la relation:** They both put effort in the relationship.

- **Ils n'étaient pas encore ensemble:** They weren't together yet.

- **Elle méritait d'être avec quelqu'un qui la rendait heureuse:** She deserved to be with someone that made her happy.

- **Ils s'étaient rencontrés grâce à elle:** They had met thanks to her.

- **S'ils se mariaient, elle serait la marraine d'honneur:** If they got together, she would be the maid of honor.

- **Elle avait rencontré l'année dernière:** She had met last year.

- **Son cœur fit un bond:** Her heart skipped a beat.

- **Il avait envie de la voir:** He wanted to see her.

- **Elle ne savait pas si c'était une bonne idée:** She didn't know if it was a good idea.

- **Après tout:** After all.

- **Pour Raquel, ils étaient pratiquement mariés:** For Raquel they were practically married.

- **La vérité était:** The truth was.

- **Elle pouvait faire ce qu'elle voulait:** She could do whatever she wanted.

- **Une robe d'été:** A summer dress.

- **Colorée:** Colorful.

- **Aucun des deux n'aimait beaucoup faire la fête:** Neither of them liked to party much.

- **Heure pile:** O'clock.

- **Le soleil ne s'était pas encore complètement couché:** The sun hadn't gone down entirely.

- **Il portait un parfum sucré:** He was wearing a sweet cologne.

- **Ce qu'ils faisaient:** What they were doing.

- **Quels étaient leurs plans pour le reste de l'année:** What were their plans for what was left of the year.

- **Il a surtout parlé:** He spoke, mostly.

- **Elle avait oublié qu'il parlait tout le temps:** She had forgotten he was a chatterbox.

- **Il utilisait plus de slang argentin:** He was using more Argentine slang.

- **Cool:** Cool.

- **Bourgeois:** Posh.

- **Mec:** Dude.

- **Il passerait les fêtes:** He would spend the holidays.

- **Il reviendrait peut-être:** He might come back.

- **Il caressait sa main:** He was caressing her hand.

- **Elle devenait rouge comme une tomate:** She was blushing profusely.

- **Il y a eu un baiser:** There was a kiss.

- **Ils ne voulaient pas se séparer l'un de l'autre:** They didn't want to be apart.

- **Et celle qui suivait:** And the one that came after.

- **Elle trouvait triste que:** She found it sad that.

- **Ils n'auraient que des moments comme celui-ci:** They would only have moments like this.

- **Sporadique:** Sporadic.

- **En un clin d'œil:** In the blink of an eye.

- **Elle ne pourrait jamais construire un avenir:** She could never be able to build a future.

- **Il ne lui restait plus qu'à jeter l'éponge:** She had no other option but to give up.

- **Elle a essayé de lui expliquer tout cela:** She tried to explain all of that to him.

- **Les choses n'avaient pas de sens:** Things didn't make sense.

- **Et si je restais?:** What if I stay?

- **Elle pensait qu'il plaisantait:** She thought he was kidding.

- **Il lui a assuré qu'il était sérieux:** He assured her he was being serious.

- **Pour elle, il serait prêt à le faire:** For her, he was willing to do it.

- **C'était de la folie:** It was crazy.

- **Il ne la connaissait pas assez:** He didn't know her enough.

- **Elle lui a donné un baiser de bonne nuit:** She gave him a goodnight kiss.

- **Elle lui a demandé pourquoi elle avait pris cette décision:** She asked her why she had made that choice.

- **Elle était d'accord:** She agreed.

- **Elle était juste curieuse:** She was just curious.

- **Qu'est-ce qui lui avait ouvert les yeux:** What had opened her eyes.

- **Elle s'est rendu compte que ce n'était pas réel:** She realized it was not real.

- **Les relations se construisent:** Relationships are built.

- **Cela ne durerait pas pour toujours:** It wouldn't last forever.

- **Parier sur ça serait une grave erreur:** Betting on that would be a big mistake.

- **Le soleil entrait par le balcon:** The sun was coming in through the balcony.

- **L'odeur des toasts envahissait:** The smell of toasts invaded.

Exercice 1

Répondez aux questions suivantes – Answer the following questions

1- Combien de fois Daniela est-elle sortie avec David? -How many times has Daniela been out with David?

_____

2- Que s'est-il passé lors de son dernier rendez-vous avec David? - What happened on her last date with David?

_____

3- Pourquoi Raquel était-elle heureuse? - Why was Raquel happy?

_____

4- Pourquoi a-t-elle décidé de sortir avec Théo? - Why did she decide to go out with Théo?

_____

5- Où est-elle allée avec Théo? - Where did she go with Théo?

_____

6- Quels étaient les plans de Théo pour les fêtes? - What were Théo's plans for the holidays?

_____

Exercice 2

Choisissez entre vrai ou faux _(Choose "true" or "false")_

1- Daniela ne veut pas précipiter les choses avec David. - Daniela doesn't want to rush things with David.

_____

2- David semblait être une bonne personne. - David seemed to be a good person.

_____

3- Elle ne se disputait jamais avec David. - She never argued with David.

_____

4- Raquel aimait David plus que comme un ami. - Raquel liked David as more than a friend.

_____

5- Elle et Théo sont allés dans un bar à Palermo. - She and Théo went to a bar in Palermo.

_____

6- Théo parlait beaucoup. - Théo talked a lot.

_____

Réponses – Answers

Exercice 1

1. Daniela est déjà sortie quatre fois avec David.

2. Elle et David sont allés voir une pièce appelée "Tous sommes fous." Ensuite, ils ont mangé des hamburgers et ont passé la nuit chez David.

3. Raquel était heureuse parce qu'elle savait que David rendait Daniela heureuse. Elle se sentait très fière qu'ils se soient rencontrés grâce à elle.

4. Après y avoir réfléchi un moment, Daniela a pensé qu'elle était une femme jeune, et qu'elle n'était pas mariée, donc elle pouvait faire ce qu'elle voulait.

5. Ils sont allés dans un bar situé dans le quartier de Belgrano.

6. Théo passerait les fêtes avec sa famille en France.

Exercice 2

1. Vrai

2. Vrai

3. Faux

4. Faux

5. Faux

6. Vrai

Conclusion

Congratulations on reaching the end of this book! Time really does fly when you're enjoying yourself. By reading all the stories and completing all the exercises in Learn French with Short Stories for Adults, the final chapter in this 7-in-1 book, you've reached a greater level of French fluency. Now, you can take your skills out into the world and enjoy more meaningful conversations in French.

Be proud of everything you've achieved! Until next time!